THE PENGUIN BOOK OF LIEDER

Siegbert Prawer was born at Cologne in 1925; he came to England
in 1939 and was educated at King Henry VIII School, Coventry,
and at Jesus and Christ's Colleges, Cambridge, where he read
English and Modern Languages. He is now Taylor Professor of
German Language and Literature at the University of Oxford, where
he is a Fellow of Queen's College. He was Professor of German in
the University of London from 1964 until 1969 and before that he
was Senior Lecturer in German in the University of Birmingham; he has
also taught in America, notably at the City University, New York,
and the University of Chicago. His publications include *German
Lyric Poetry*, *Mörike und seine Leser*, *Heine's Buch der Leider*, *Heine:
the Tragic Satirist*, *Comparative Literary Studies: an Introduction*,
Karl Marx and World Literature, and many articles on various aspects
of German poetry. In 1973 he was awarded the Goethe Medal and
in 1977 the Isaac Deutscher Memorial Prize.

THE PENGUIN BOOK OF Lieder

EDITED AND TRANSLATED BY S. S. PRAWER

PENGUIN BOOKS

Penguin Books Ltd, Harmondsworth, Middlesex, England
Penguin Books, 40 West 23rd Street, New York, New York 10010, U.S.A.
Penguin Books Australia Ltd, Ringwood, Victoria, Australia
Penguin Books Canada Ltd, 2801 John Street, Markham, Ontario Canada L3R 1B4
Penguin Books (N.Z.) Ltd, 182–190 Wairau Road, Auckland 10, New Zealand

First published in Penguin Reference Books 1964
Reprinted 1965, 1968, 1977, 1979, 1984

Made and printed in Great Britain by
Richard Clay (The Chaucer Press) Ltd, Bungay, Suffolk
Set in Monotype Fournier

For My Mother

CONTENTS

ACKNOWLEDGEMENTS

THE texts here reprinted follow, in most cases, the *Lied* rather than the original poem. Composers sometimes set earlier versions of familiar poems, omitted stanzas, or made alterations in the interest of musical form. The translations follow such texts as closely as possible – they make no claim to literary merit of their own. I have occasionally been able to improve my versions by consulting Professor Roy Pascal or comparing them with existing translations: notably those in the *Penguin Book of German Verse* (Professor L. W. Forster), *The Songs of Hugo Wolf* (Eric Sams), and the useful booklets with which the more enlightened gramophone companies enhance the value of their recital records. I am also grateful to Professor Wilfrid Mellers, Mr Paul Morby, the librarians of the Österreichische National-bibliothek, Vienna, and the staff of Universal Edition (Alfred A. Kalmus, Ltd, London), who helped me to collect my texts.

For permission to reprint copyright texts, I am indebted to the following: J. G. Cotta'sche Buchhandlung Nachf. G.m.b.H., Stuttgart (Paul Heyse and Emanuel Geibel, *Spanisches Liederbuch*; Paul Heyse, *Italienisches Liederbuch*); Insel Verlag, Wiesbaden and Frankfurt-am-Main (Rilke, *Das Marienleben*, in *Sämtliche Werke*, Vol. 1; texts of Mahler's *Das Lied von der Erde* and Webern's 'Die geheimnisvolle Flöte' in Hans Bethge, *Die chinesische Flöte*; Otto Julius Bierbaum, *Irrgarten der Liebe*); Kösel Verlag, Munich (Alfred Mombert, *Der Glühende*, in *Sämtliche Dichtungen*, to be published in the near future, in *Gesammelte Werke*, Vol. 1); Verlag Helmut Küpper (formerly Georg Bondi) Düsseldorf and Munich (Stefan George, *Das Buch der hängenden Gärten*, *Der siebente Ring*, and translations from Baudelaire in *Werke in zwei Bänden*); Otto Müller Verlag, Salzburg (Georg Trakl, *Die junge Magd*); Suhrkamp Verlag, Berlin and Frankfurt-am-Main (poems by Hermann Hesse in *Gesammelte Dichtungen*, Vol. 5); Frau Vera Tügel–Dehmel, Hamburg (poems by Richard Dehmel); Universal Edition (Alfred A. Kalmus Ltd, London) for texts by Hildegard Jone (Webern, Op. 25) and Peter Altenberg (Berg, Op. 4); Josef Weinberger Ltd, London (text of Mahler's *Lieder eines fahrenden Gesellen*).

INTRODUCTION

Nû al - rêst leb'ich mir wer - de / sît mîn sün - dic oug' er-
siht / daz lie - be lant und ouch die er - de / dem man vil der
ê - ren giht. / Nû ist ge - sche - hen als ich ie bat / ich bin
ko - men an die stat / dâ got men - nisch - lî - chen trat.

Now at last I live joyfully, since my sinful eyes behold the dear Holy Land, the earth which men hold in such high honour. What I always prayed for, has now come to pass: I have come to the place where God himself, in human form, set foot.

EVEN readers well versed in German may find the text of this song difficult to make out without the help of the translation; but few, surely, will find its musical idiom unfamiliar. A grave and beautiful melody, with one joyous rise to the seventh (in consonance with the words 'What I always prayed for, has now come to pass'); a pellucid tripartite structure (two parallel *pedes* or *Stollen* of eight bars each, followed by a longer *coda* or *Abgesang* which ends with part of the *Stollen* melody); reminiscences of folk-song and ecclesiastical modes – it might almost be the vocal line of a song by Robert Franz, and no very skilful hand or extensive surgery would be needed to adapt it to the style of Schubert or or Brahms. It was in fact written – or adapted – by one of Germany's greatest lyric poets, Walther von der Vogelweide, in the early years of the thirteenth century; and though it lacks its instrumental accompaniment (of which no notation has been preserved) it demonstrates forcibly that the history of the German *Lied* does not begin with Schubert, or the 'Berlin school', or even the invention of the thoroughbass in the sixteenth century, but goes back to the oldest music recorded in German-speaking lands. In view of the dominant part which Austrian composers played in the history of the *Lied* it is not without interest to hear Walther himself confess, in a well known poem, that he learnt the arts of music and poetry in Austria.

Walther von der Vogelweide, like almost all the lyric poets of the Middle Ages and like some folk-singers even today, was poet and composer in one. This is rare in modern times, though the example of Wagner tempted some composers, including Mahler and Peter Cornelius, to try their hand at writing their own texts. As a rule, however, the modern *Lied* is a collaboration of two different personalities working in different media and often even in two different generations. The musical and poetic ideas do not arise together; the poem is there first, and inspires in a composer a corresponding – or supplementary – musical conception. Richard Strauss has described the subsequent process as follows:

Two bars of music come to me spontaneously; and now I continue spinning this thread, placing brick upon brick until I arrive at my definitive version. This sometimes takes a very long time. A melody that seems born in a moment is almost invariably the result of hard work. . . . Work is a matter of talent too!

In this way a text written to be spoken, or even to be read with the eyes alone, is transformed into a vocal melody which often varies from stanza to stanza; and this melody in its turn is made to enter many harmonic or contrapuntal relations with a pianoforte or orchestral part which in Schumann, Wolf, Mahler, and Strauss assumes such importance that it can hardly be called a mere 'accompaniment'. It is this complex organism which is nowadays called a *Lied* – the word itself simply means 'song' and was in use long before Mozart in 'Das Veilchen' and more especially Schubert in 'Gretchen am Spinnrad' created the new type.

How the *Lied* fuses poetry and music into a new whole may be well observed in Schubert's dealings with the fine (though a little mannered) poem by Friedrich Rückert whose text appears on p. 40. Its original title was 'Come in to me' ('*Kehr ein bei mir*'); but the composer, as the opening bars of his piano part unmistakably demonstrate, found himself impressed above all by the peace, fulfilment, and contentment that seemed to be just within the grasp of the still yearning poet. He therefore discarded the poet's own title and called his *Lied* by the poem's opening line: *Du bist die Ruh*. Schubert then found himself constrained, in the interest of musical form, to alter the shape – the very structure – of Rückert's poem. Rückert's five brief stanzas were reorganized into three musical strophes – and this made it necessary for the last stanza to be set twice. (Poets are not always too pleased with this kind of procedure: 'Why', Tennyson is reported to have growled on one occasion, 'do these damned musicians make me say a thing twice when I said it only once?') Each of the resulting three strophes Schubert built up on the same *Stollen–Stollen–Abgesang* plan that we already observed in the song by Walther von der Vogelweide; and by making the first two strophes musically identical while varying the third (with its slow ascent to A♭, its repeated bar of silence, its richer piano part), he brilliantly reflected in the shape of the *whole song* the shape of its parts.

With his unforgettable *legato* melody, a piano accompaniment that speaks of peace while at the same time suggesting the tensions and obstacles still to be overcome, and a musical organization that has a power and simplicity which can only be called classical, Schubert has transformed Rückert's fine poem into a great *Lied*. He has made of it something better than it was before. This happens not infrequently. When we hear works like Brahms's 'Immer leiser wird mein Schlummer' or Strauss's

'Traum durch die Dämmerung', we respond to a poem indifferent or even poor when taken by itself, but capable of suggesting a scene or an emotion from which the composer's musical imagination soared into regions inaccessible to his poet.

Many composers – including such diverse figures as Weber and Max Reger – have declared their preference for a minor poem, for a poem which has not, as Weber once said, 'too much music to start with'. Elsa Reger, Max Reger's widow, in her book on the composer, *Regers Schaffensintentionen*, gives an amusing instance of this attitude:

When Reger felt the urge to write *Lieder*, he would turn to me and say: 'Find me some texts, dear!' Then I would go and fetch my Goethe. If I then read a poem to him or put it on his desk, he would say: 'Wonderful – but this tells us everything already, what can I possibly add in my composition? . . . I find Goethe's poems so perfect that nothing more can be said about them.' But often, when Reger read a little poem that others thought insignificant, a melody would suddenly come to him and he would write it down, making out of the union of the little poem and his music a perfect work of art.

Others, however – Schumann and Wolf are the examples that spring most readily to mind – felt drawn almost exclusively to poetry which they thought great in its own right. 'There can be nothing more beautiful', Schumann declared, 'than to adorn with music the brow of a true poet. But why trouble to waste music on a common, an everyday face?'; and Heinrich Werner reports a conversation with Hugo Wolf, in the course of which Wolf declared: 'Today it is no longer possible to set to music a bad text. Schubert could still do this. He made something beautiful out of a "cheese-label". However trivial it was, Schubert made something important out of it. But today one must stick to the poet. This is the crux of the matter.' Yet if we look at the texts such composers chose to set, it becomes obvious at once that not all great poetry lends itself equally well to composition. Words and thoughts, it would seem, have to be comparatively simple, so that an audience can follow them even when sung; and 'bold, intense, or closely wrought images' (as C. Day Lewis has rightly said) 'tend to destroy the balance between the word-pattern and the melodic line'. The poem must be terse, to prevent the song from going on too long – even the genius of a Fischer-Dieskau cannot make Schubert's setting of Schiller's 'Der Taucher' anything but wearisome. The poet, lastly, must not say all; much must be left to the music, according to the principle so well laid down by Paul Hindemith: 'We have tried to express that which was *not* said in one constructional element [the text] in the other [the music] – and vice versa.'

It was Hegel who faced this problem most fully, in his *Aesthetics*, a series of lectures delivered at Berlin University in the eighteen-twenties. 'It is . . . a harmful prejudice', Hegel declared, 'to think the nature of the text of no importance to the composition. . . . Nothing musically deep and worth-while can be coaxed from a text that is in itself flat, trivial, bald, and absurd.' But neither, he went on to say, must the poem be 'too burdened with thought, too philosophical and deep'. The most suitable material for music he found (and the practice of composers since his day has borne him out) in a 'middle kind of poetry': 'lyrically true, of the utmost simplicity, suggesting situations and feelings with few words; when dramatic, it is clear and vivid but without elaborate development'. In such poetry, Hegel thought, composers would find what they needed: 'a basis on which to erect their own constructions, inventing, developing all motifs, moving unencumbered to all sides. For since music must connect itself to the words, these must not go into too great detail – otherwise musical declamation becomes petty, diffused, drawn to too many sides; then unity will be lost and the total effect weakened.' In lyric poetry, he concludes, it is the simple, terse, deeply felt poem which most stimulates the composer's imagination: 'either poems which express, tersely and feelingly, some mood or situation of the heart; or else poems which are light and gay.' These words of Hegel's describe exactly the poems to be found in this book.

Most of the best *Lieder* represent – as Hegel suggested – a meeting of affinities. Mozart's one creative encounter with Goethe (in 'Das Veilchen' – see p. 20) is a case in point: poet and composer have here given us, each in his own way, the very essence of the pastoral Rococo at the threshold of the Age of Sensibility. The music follows the action and sentiment of the poem at every point – through rhythmic variation (beginning in 4/8 time, it quickens to 2/4 at the shepherdess's approach), through alternations between major and minor (the violet expresses its love-longing and dies in the minor key), and through meaningful piano interludes like that after the words '*und sang*' (which gives us the shepherdess's song); yet it never sacrifices one iota of its own inner formal logic. Other composers have met contemporary poets in a fundamentally similar way: we need think only of Schumann and Heine, Brahms and Klaus Groth, Schoenberg and Stefan George, Hindemith and Rilke, Webern and Hildegard Jone. Some, however, have preferred to look for beloved dead in the 'great morgue' of the past – Hugo Wolf for instance, of all the great composers the most sensitive to poetic values, never set any living poets at all.

It may happen, on occasions, that a composer feels drawn to a poet with whom he has no clear affinity, who represents his aspiration rather than his reality; and then there will result a work of art in which two different – even opposite – personalities blend and fuse. This happens, notably, in Gustav Mahler's settings of folk poems from the collection known as *Des Knaben Wunderhorn*. Mahler, a complicated man of the twentieth century who spent most of his life in great cities, felt ever attracted to simple poetry and simple tunes, to the very things that were most alien to his nervous, over-cultivated nature. This tension is clearly reflected in the *Wunderhorn* settings. 'Der Tamboursg'sell', for instance (p. 145), begins with a simple march-rhythm and melody which remain with us throughout three stanzas. The accompaniment, however, with its subtle orchestral coloration (two oboes changing to cor anglais, two clarinets, bass clarinet, two bassoons, double bassoon, four horns, timpani, muted side-drum, bass drum, gong, cellos, and double basses) and its poisoned harmonies, belies this simplicity; and between the third and fourth stanzas the voice falls silent and the orchestra takes over altogether in an incontrovertibly modern, complex, Mahlerian interlude which is clearly related to a similar, and very unfolk-like, interlude in the last section of *Das Lied von der Erde*. 'Der Tamboursg'sell' thus constitutes a strange but hauntingly successful blend of folk-song, post-Wagnerian harmony, and the feelings of a complex man of our own time.

Writers on the German *Lied* have made much of occasional conflicts between the demands of the speech-rhythm and metre of the poem, and those of musical time. The champions of Hugo Wolf especially, led by the late Ernest Newman, have pointed out how careless of proper speech-accentuation Schumann and Brahms (and even Schubert) could be at times, and how much superior Wolf was to all his great predecessors and contemporaries in this respect. There is some truth in these observations. The first line of one of Brahms's most famous songs, for instance (text and translation on p. 95), would naturally be stressed as follows:

Wie bist du, meine Königin . . .

Brahms's musical accents fall in every case on the wrong syllable:

Wie bist du, meine Königin . . .

It would, however, be absurd and pedantic to stress such divergences in face of so lovely a song, in which the spirit of the poetry and that of the music are so perfectly in harmony. One of the finest performers of Brahms's songs, Harry Plunket Greene, has rightly reminded us that a skilful singer can easily minimize the conflict of poetic and musical accent: 'Why should two crotchets, *written* of even value, be sung with even values? [One] does not *speak* them with even values. [A singer] may give them . . . equal *time* values, but surely there is no necessity for equal *pressure* values.' This distinction between 'time values' and 'pressure values' in singing is in fact observed by all the great *Lieder* singers of the recorded repertoire, from Erb, Hüsch, and Elena Gerhardt to Fischer-Dieskau, Hotter, and Elisabeth Schwarzkopf, and it helps us to forget that a melody appropriate in spirit may occasionally prove a bed of Procrustes to the accentuation of its text. I cannot, however, agree with Michael Tippett when he roundly declares: 'The music of a song destroys the verbal music of a poem utterly.' When listening to German *Lieder*, or Mr Tippett's own 'The Heart's Assurance', I am as aware of the sound of the poetry as I am of the sound and shape of the music – and in this, surely, I am not alone. The Countess in Richard Strauss's *Capriccio*, for one, finds her appreciation of Olivier's poem actually enhanced by Flamand's music, and speaks of their combination in terms that echo the feelings of many lovers of the *Lied*:

Sind es die Worte, die mein Herz bewegen, oder sind es die Töne, die stärker sprechen? . . . Vergebliches Müh'n, die beiden zu trennen. In eins verschmolzen sind Worte und Töne – zu einem Neuen verbunden. . . . (Is it the words that move my heart, or is it the music? . . . It is vain to try to separate these two: words and music have melted into one, fused into a new whole.)

Most of the *Lieder* represented in this book belong to the period of Romanticism in literature and music. They range between the two characteristic extremes of Romantic music: on the one hand a gentle lyric murmuring, using the finest tones of human voice and pianoforte, exploiting the subtlest key-relationships (e.g. Schumann's 'Liederkreis', Op. 39); on the other, large gestures made with all the resources of a modern symphony orchestra (the first section of Mahler's *Lied von der Erde*, which makes use of such startling effects as the 'flutter-tongue' treatment of wind instruments). For the *Lied*, it would seem, satisfied in its small compass one of the deepest desires of the German Romantic movement: the desire for a fusion of the arts, for a *Gesamtkunstwerk* that would demonstrate the underlying unity of all the manifestations of art and life. 'Through all the tones in earth's colourful dream,' said Friedrich Schlegel, in a poem which Schumann used as epigraph for one of his piano pieces, 'there sounds a single soft note for him who listens secretly':

> Durch alle Töne tönt, im bunten Erdentraume,
> *Ein* leiser Ton für den, der heimlich lauschet.

The Romantic and post-Romantic *Lied* thus resolves itself into an attempt to put Humpty-Dumpty together again: to reunite two arts – poetry and music – that were inseparable in the work of men like Walther von der Vogelweide, but had drifted apart in the modern world.

In his authoritative book on Schubert's songs, Richard Capell has shown that the rise of the *Lied* is connected, not only with the advent of Goethe and a new lyric poetry, but also with the eclipse of the harpsichord by the pianoforte. This new instrument proved from the first an ideally expressive partner of the human voice, and *Lied* came to mean above all a song for voice and piano accompaniment. The balance between these two elements has varied from composer to composer. Men like Reichardt used the piano part principally as harmonic support for the all-important vocal line; Schubert, in his greatest works, achieved a unique balance, making the piano set the scene, establish a mood, and supplement what the voice has to say; while in Schumann the piano part often becomes more memorable and important than the vocal – some of Schumann's happiest inventions, in fact, come in the preludes, postludes, and intermezzi of his songs and song-cycles. Brahms (who once claimed that Schumann taught him nothing except how to play chess) reverses this direction, giving primacy to the vocal line, with the piano as a subtle but definitely subordinate partner; but with Hugo Wolf the piano parts become so vital to the total effect of his songs that one can hardly speak of 'accompaniments' at all. More and more, however, as the nineteenth century went on, the colouristic possibilities of the piano seemed inadequate. Many of Loewe's songs, and some of Schubert's, seem to strain after effects possible only in orchestral music – and works like Wolf's *Prometheus*, originally conceived for voice and piano, so clearly demanded an orchestral setting that the composer found himself compelled to re-score them. With Mahler and Strauss, the orchestral song becomes the rule rather than the exception. Mahler soon realized, however, that the full orchestra (especially that of the post-Wagnerian era) might overwhelm the frail lyric on which a *Lied* is founded. He therefore experimented with small chamber groups of instruments that partnered the singer's voice more successfully than the full symphony orchestra. The possibilities of such chamber groups were explored, with notable effect, by Mahler in his Rückert settings, by Schoenberg in *Pierrot Lunaire*, by Anton Webern in his *Geistliche Lieder* of 1923, and by Alban Berg in the orchestration of some early impressionistic songs – *Sieben frühe Lieder* – published in 1928.

A successful *Lied* – as H. C. Colles and others have recognized – marries the principles of recitative and aria. In an oratorio, the narrative and the emotions it arouses tend to be presented alternately; in a *Lied* they go together. Like an aria, a *Lied* can bear a certain amount of word-repetition, in the service of musical form and expressiveness; but a *Lied* is less static than an aria, taking into itself the continuity, the forward thrust, of recitative. This is true, not only of dramatic ballads like Loewe's *Edward*, but also of lyric statements of feeling like Schumann's 'Mondnacht'. In some earlier songs – Beethoven's *Adelaide* springs at once to mind – the aria or cantata element clearly predominates; while in more recent times the recitative element has acquired new prominence through the use of 'speech-song' (*Sprechgesang*) in such works as Schoenberg's *Gurrelieder*. A great deal, however, of the power of every successful *Lied* lies precisely in its delicate balance of aria and recitative, of static and dynamic qualities.

The German *Lied* grew out of German folk-song; and right up to Mahler and Strauss it preserves (though in more and more tenuous ways) its link with folk-song and domestic music-making. However subtle its variations and its accompaniment, its central melody can usually be sung without difficulty by any music-lover who has heard two or three performances of it or who reads the score. This changes with atonic and dodecaphonic music, which has few suggestions of folk-song and whose vocal line is often so angular and difficult as to preclude its use as *Hausmusik*. Yet I believe it is true to say that the most distinguished contributions to the German *Lied* in recent times have been made by composers who wrote in an atonic or dodecaphonic idiom; and that those who tried to carry on the traditional line of the *Lied* – as have, in their different ways, Othmar Schoeck, Armin Knab, and Hermann Reutter – produced nothing as memorable as Schoenberg's *Buch der hängenden Gärten*, Berg's Altenberg songs, or Webern's settings of poems by Hildegard Jone. The one exception is Hindemith's later version of *Das Marienleben*; and even this, it can be argued, is musically less interesting than the version it is meant to supersede, a version which presented such formidable difficulties to its singer.[1]

At the moment, the *Lied* seems to be having a difficult time. Composers seem to shy away from it, preferring – like Carl Orff, Hans Werner Henze, Werner Egk, and Ernst Krenek – to woo opera and choral music rather than solo song; and it is hard to resist the feeling that in their own field of the *Lied* German composers of recent years have little to set against the splendid Hölderlin songs of Benjamin Britten. Yet there have been crises before; there are even those who think that the whole of the nineteenth century represents a crisis, pointing to such things as the misinterpretation of poems by composers from Schubert onwards, the disregard of the rhythm of great lyrics even by Hugo Wolf, the lavishing of great music on inferior poems and the liberties taken by Schumann, for example, with his literary texts.[2] He would be bold indeed who would assert that the *Lied* is dead. I prefer to think of it as a Sleeping Beauty who awaits her prince.

1. cf. Rudolf Stephan: 'Hindemith's *Marienleben* (1922–48). An Assessment of its Two Versions', *The Music Review*, xv, 1954.

2. For a spirited statement of the case for the prosecution, see Jack M. Stein: 'Was Goethe wrong about the Nineteenth Century Lied? An Examination of the Relation of Poem and Music', *Publications of the Modern Language Association*, LXXVII, 1962.

FRANZ JOSEPH HAYDN

Born at Rohrau, an Austrian village near the Hungarian border, on 31 March 1732. Became a chorister of St Stephen's, Vienna, at the age of eight; from 1749 onwards he made his living at first by teaching and playing in various orchestras, then by acting as director of music in various noble houses (notably those of the princes Esterházy at Eisenstadt and by the Neusiedler lake). He made his home in Vienna from 1790 onwards. Haydn paid two visits to England (in 1790 and 1749) – a fact which had great influence on his vocal compositions. He died in Vienna on 31 May 1809. His works include over one hundred symphonies, some eighty string quartets and thirty string trios, about twenty-four works for the stage, fourteen masses, and the oratorios *The Creation* (1798) and *The Seasons* (1801).

Haydn's solo songs have not lately been popular in the concert hall, though British listeners have always retained an interest in his settings of English texts (one of which is reprinted below) and of Scottish, Irish, and Welsh airs, and though his Austrian national hymn – later fitted to different words to become the German national anthem – must be one of the most frequently sung tunes in the world. The reason for this neglect is partly that Haydn often set wretched texts chosen for him by others, partly that his songs tend to be monotonously strophic; but mainly because they have been overshadowed by his many other great works. Haydn was one of the first composers to write out the music of his songs in three staves instead of two, thus preparing the way for the greater elaboration of the piano accompaniment characteristic of the nineteenth-century *Lied*.

I NO. 21 [JOHANN WILHELM LUDWIG GLEIM]

Das Leben ist ein Traum

Das Leben ist ein Traum!
Wir schlüpfen in die Welt und schweben
Mit jungem Zahn und frischem Gaum
Auf ihrem Wahn und ihrem Schaum
Bis wir nicht mehr an Erde kleben.
Und dann, was ist's? Was ist das Leben?
Das Leben ist ein Traum.

Das Leben ist ein Traum!
Wir lieben, unsre Herzen schlagen,
Und Herz an Herz gefüget kaum,
Wird Lieb und Scherz ein leerer Schaum,
Ist hingeschwunden, weggetragen.
Was ist das Leben? hör ich fragen.
Das Leben ist ein Traum.

Das Leben ist ein Traum!
Wir denken, zweifeln, werden weise,
Wir teilen ein in Ort und Raum,
In Licht und Schein, in Kraut und Baum,
Sind Euler und gewinnen Preise;
Doch noch im Grabe sagen Weise:
Das Leben ist ein Traum.

Life is a Dream

Life is a dream!
We slip into the world,
and with unspoilt teeth and unjaded palate
we float on the bubbles of its illusions
until we can cling to earth no more.
And then – what is this life?
Life is a dream.

Life is a dream!
We love, our hearts beat,
and hardly has heart joined heart
when love and jest turn to empty bubbles,
vanish, are borne away.
I hear the question: 'What is life?'
Life is a dream.

Life is a dream!
We think, doubt, grow wise,
distinguish 'place' from 'space',
clear light from delusion, herb from tree,
potter about and win prizes;
but at grave's edge the wise still say:
Life is a dream.

2 NO. 22 [GOTTHOLD EPHRAIM LESSING]

Lob der Faulheit	*Praise of Indolence*

Faulheit, endlich muß ich dir
Auch ein kleines Loblied bringen!
O!... Wie... sauer... wird es mir
Dich nach Würde zu besingen!
Doch ich will mein Bestes tun:
Nach der Arbeit ist gut ruhn.

Höchstes Gut, wer dich nur hat,
Dessen ungestörtes Leben ...
Ach!... ich gähn!... ich ... werde matt.
Nun, so magst du mir's vergeben,
Daß ich dich nicht singen kann:
Du verhinderst mich ja dran.

Indolence, at last I must sing
a short paean to you!
Oh ... I ... find it ... so hard
to celebrate you as you deserve.
But I will do my best:
after labour, rest is sweet.

Highest boon, whoever has you,
will lead his undisturbed life ...
Ah!... How I yawn!... I... am growing tired.
Well, you must forgive me then
if I cannot sing your praises:
for you yourself are preventing me.

3 NO. 37 [ANNE HUNTER]

O Tuneful Voice

O tuneful voice I still deplore,
Thy accents, which I hear no more,
Still vibrate on my heart.

In Echo's cave I long to dwell
And still to hear that sad farewell
When we were forced to part.

Bright eyes! O that the task were mine
To guard the liquid fires that shine
And round your orbits play,

To watch them with a vestal's care,
To feed with smiles a light so fair
That it may ne'er decay.

WOLFGANG AMADEUS MOZART

Born at Salzburg on 27 January 1756. Mozart was an infant prodigy who astonished first his – very musical – family, and then the society and courts of Europe, as a composer and pianist. Concert tours through Germany, Austria, the Netherlands, France, and England (1763–6) were followed by similar tours through Italy (1769–73). At Salzburg Mozart served as court organist and director of music to the local archbishop – a hated service from which he escaped when, after his marriage to Constanze Weber in 1782, he settled in Vienna. There his operas were at first enthusiastically received, but he was later neglected in favour of other, more immediately pleasing composers, so that he died (5 December 1791) in comparative poverty. Posterity came to recognize in him 'the greatest musical miracle the world has ever seen' (Max Reger). There are many excellent biographies and critical studies of Mozart, but nowhere has the essence of his genius and its relation to his time been as perfectly conveyed as in Eduard Mörike's *Mozart on the Journey to Prague* (1856). His works include nineteen operas, seventeen masses, over fifty symphonies, twenty-five string quartets, some thirty piano concertos, concertos for horn, flute, clarinet, and bassoon, and an unfinished Requiem.

Mozart's finest songs may be found in his operas: Osmin's 'Wer ein Liebchen hat gefunden' in *The Seraglio* (1782), Cherubino's 'Voi che sapete' in *The Marriage of Figaro* (1786), the Serenade in *Don Giovanni* (1787), and Papageno's 'birdcatcher' song in *The Magic Flute* (1791). Of his thirty-six solo songs with piano accompaniment, many are unpretentiously strophic (like 'Die Alte', to a text by Hagedorn); some are declamatory concert-pieces ('Als Luise die Briefe ihres ungetreuen Liebhabers verbrannte'); some are mood-pictures ('Abendempfindung'), such as Schubert was later to perfect; while the best of them – 'Das Veilchen' – is a drama in miniature which yet has the economy and thematic unity of the true *Lied*.

I K476 [JOHANN WOLFGANG VON GOETHE]

Das Veilchen

Ein Veilchen auf der Wiese stand,
Gebückt in sich und unbekannt;
Es war ein herzigs Veilchen.
Da kam eine junge Schäferin
Mit leichtem Schritt und muntrem Sinn
Daher, daher,
Die Wiese her, und sang.

Ach! denkt das Veilchen, wär ich nur
Die schönste Blume der Natur,
Ach, nur ein kleines Weilchen,
Bis mich das Liebchen abgepflückt
Und an dem Busen mattgedrückt!
Ach nur, ach nur
Ein Viertelstündchen lang!

Ach! aber ach! das Mädchen kam
Und nicht in acht das Veilchen nahm,
Ertrat das arme Veilchen.

The Violet

A violet stood in the meadow,
cowering, withdrawn, and obscure;
it was a dear little violet.
Then a young shepherdess came
(light of step and gay of spirit)
along the meadow and sang.

'If only,' the violet thinks, 'if only I were
the loveliest flower in all nature,
just for a little while,
until this dear girl has gathered me
and pressed me against her bosom –
just for
a quarter of an hour!'

But alas! the girl came,
paid no attention to the violet
and trod the poor violet underfoot.

Es sank und starb und freut' sich noch:
Und sterb ich denn, so sterb ich doch
Durch sie, durch sie,
Zu ihren Füßen doch.

[Das arme Veilchen!
Es war ein herzigs Veilchen.]

As it sank and died it yet was glad:
'For if I die, at least I die
through her,
at her feet.'

[The poor violet!
It was a dear little violet.]

2 K523 [JOACHIM HEINRICH CAMPE]

Abendempfindung

Abend ist's, die Sonne ist verschwunden,
Und der Mond strahlt Silberglanz;
So entfliehn des Lebens schönste Stunden,
Fliehn vorüber wie im Tanz.

Bald entflieht des Lebens bunte Szene,
Und der Vorhang rollt herab;
Aus ist unser Spiel, des Freundes Träne
Fließet schon auf unser Grab.

Bald vielleicht (mir weht, wie Westwind leise,
Eine stille Ahnung zu),
Schließ ich dieses Lebens Pilgerreise,
Fliege in das Land der Ruh.

Werdet ihr dann an meinem Grabe weinen,
Trauernd meine Asche sehn,
Dann, o Freunde, will ich euch erscheinen
Und will himmelauf euch wehn.

Schenk auch du ein Tränchen mir
Und pflücke mir ein Veilchen auf mein Grab,
Und mit deinem seelenvollen Blicke
Sieh dann sanft auf mich herab.

Weih mir eine Träne, und ach!
Schäm dich nur nicht, sie mir zu weihn;
Oh, sie wird in meinem Diademe
Dann die schönste Perle sein!

Feelings at Evening

It is evening, the sun has vanished,
and the moon sheds its silvery light;
so the loveliest hours of life speed away,
they fly past us as in a dance.

Soon the motley scene of life escapes us
and the curtain falls;
our play is over, our friends' tears
already flow on our grave.

Soon, perhaps (like the west wind
a still foreboding is gently borne towards me)
I will end this life's pilgrimage
and fly to a land of rest.

If you will then weep by my grave
and look sadly on my ashes,
then, O friends, I will appear to you
and bear you towards heaven.

Pay me then the tribute of a tear
and gather a violet for my grave,
and with your affectionate eye
look softly down upon me.

Dedicate a tear to me,
and be not ashamed to do so;
for in my diadem
it will be the finest pearl!

3 K596 [CHRISTIAN ADOLF OVERBECK]

Sehnsucht nach dem Frühling(e)

Komm, lieber Mai, und mache
Die Bäume wieder grün,
Und laß mir an dem Bache
Die kleinen Veilchen blühn!

Longing for Spring

Come, dear May, and turn
the trees green again,
and make the little violets
flower for me by the brook!

Wie möcht ich doch so gerne
Ein Veilchen wieder sehn,
Ach, lieber Mai, wie gerne
Einmal spazieren gehn!

Zwar Wintertage haben
Wohl auch der Freuden viel;
Man kann im Schnee eins traben
Und treibt manch Abendspiel,

Baut Häuschen von Karten,
Spielt Blindekuh und Pfand;
Auch gibt's wohl Schlittenfahrten
Auf's liebe freie Land.

Doch wenn die Vöglein singen
Und wir dann froh und flink
Auf grünen Rasen springen,
Das ist ein ander Ding!

Jetzt muß mein Steckenpferdchen
Dort in dem Winkel stehn;
Denn draußen in dem Gärtchen
Kann man vor Kot nicht gehn.

Am meisten aber dauert
Mich Lottchens Herzeleid;
Das arme Mädchen lauert
Recht auf die Blumenzeit;

Umsonst hol ich ihr Spielchen
Zum Zeitvertreib herbei,
Sie sitzt in ihrem Stühlchen
Wie's Hühnchen auf dem Ei.

Ach, wenn's doch erst gelinder
Und grüner draußen wär!
Komm, lieber Mai, wir Kinder,
Wir bitten dich gar sehr!

O komm und bring vor allen
Uns viele Veilchen mit,
Bring auch viel Nachtigallen
Und schöne Kuckucks mit!

How I long to see
a violet again;
how much, dear May, I would like
to take a walk!

The winter, it is true,
also brings many pleasures:
you can jog through the snow
and play games in the evening –

You can build houses of cards,
play blind-man's-buff and forfeits;
and you can ride in a sleigh
into the open country.

But when the birds sing,
and we run quickly, gaily,
on the green lawn –
that's a much greater pleasure!

Now my hobby-horse
must stay in its corner there;
for in the garden
you cannot walk for mud.

Most of all I am sorry
for Lottchen, who is so sad;
the poor girl waits all the time
for the flowers to bloom again.

It is vain for me to bring her games
to while away the time;
she sits on her little chair
like a hen on its egg.

If only the weather turned mild,
and the world grew green again!
Come, dear May, we children
beg you to come!

O come, and let us, before anyone else,
have many violets,
bring nightingales too,
and beautiful cuckoos!

LUDWIG VAN BEETHOVEN

Born at Bonn on 16 December 1770, the son of a court musician. Became a pianist and organist at Bonn, and played in various theatre and opera orchestras. In 1792 he moved to Vienna (where he numbered Haydn and Salieri among his teachers) and soon made a name for himself as a pianist and composer. Vienna now became his permanent home. In 1801 Beethoven began to be hard of hearing – a condition disastrously worsened by a serious illness in 1812. From 1819 until his death (26 March 1827) he was almost totally deaf. His works, which fuse Romantic Titanism with classical form, include nine symphonies, five piano concertos, a violin concerto, thirty-two piano sonatas, sixteen string quartets and a *Great Fugue* for string quartet, the opera *Fidelio* (1805), two masses, six concert overtures, and incidental music for Goethe's *Egmont*.

Among Beethoven's solo songs it was chiefly the cantata *Adelaide* which delighted his contemporaries; most of the others have never had the attention they deserve. One must not come to these songs with the wrong expectations, for Beethoven's style is here that of the eighteenth rather than that of the nineteenth century: he delights, for instance, in word-repetitions such as are associated with aria and cantata rather than with the *Lied*. He experimented with many forms and tried – in his settings of Goethe's 'Neue Liebe, neues Leben' and 'Mit einem gemalten Band' – to build up *Lieder* in the sonata form he had perfected elsewhere. Some of his Goethe songs (notably Mignon's 'Kennst du das Land?' and the strangely haunting nonsense-song 'Marmotte') have never been surpassed in their power of embodying musically a spiritual situation: a power exemplified also in his greatest declamatory song 'Resignation' and the song-cycle *An die ferne Geliebte*.

1 OP. 64 [FRIEDRICH VON MATTHISSOHN]

Adelaide

Einsam wandelt dein Freund im Frühlings-
    garten,
Mild vom lieblichen Zauberlicht umflossen,
Das durch wankende Blütenzweige zittert,
Adelaide!

In der spiegelnden Flut, im Schnee der
    Alpen,
In des sinkenden Tages Goldgewölken,
Im Gefilde der Sterne strahlt dein Bildnis,
Adelaide!

Abendlüfte im zarten Laube flüstern,
Silberglöckchen des Mais im Grase säuseln,
Wellen rauschen und Nachtigallen flöten:
Adelaide!

Adelaide

Your friend wanders, lonely, in the spring-
    time garden,
mildly encompassed by the magic light
that trembles through swaying, blossoming
    branches,
Adelaide!

In the mirroring flood, in the snow of the
    Alps,
in the golden clouds of departing day,
in starry fields your image shines forth,
Adelaide!

Evening breezes whisper in the gentle leaves,
silver bells of May sound in the grass,
waves murmur and nightingales call:
Adelaide!

Einst, o Wunder! entblüht auf meinem
  Grabe
Eine Blume der Asche meines Herzens;
Deutlich schimmert auf jedem Purpur-
  blättchen:
Adelaide!

One day – O wonder! – on my grave
a flower will spring from the ashes of my
  heart;
and clearly on every red leaf will shine the
  name
Adelaide!

2 OP. 48 [CHRISTIAN FÜRCHTEGOTT GELLERT]

Die Ehre Gottes aus der Natur

God's Glory Divined in Nature

Die Himmel rühmen des Ewigen Ehre;
Ihr Schall pflanzt seinen Namen fort.
Ihn rühmt der Erdkreis, ihn preisen die
  Meere;
Vernimm, o Mensch, ihr göttlich Wort!

Wer trägt der Himmel unzählbare Sterne?
Wer führt die Sonn aus ihrem Zelt?
Sie kommt und leuchtet und lacht uns von
  ferne
Und läuft den Weg gleich als ein Held.

The heavens proclaim the glory of the Lord;
their sound perpetuates His name.
This earthly sphere magnifies Him, the seas
  praise Him;
hear, O Man, their divine words!

Who bears the heavens' unnumbered stars?
Who leads the sun from its tent?
The sun appears, shines, smiles to us from
  afar,
and runs its course like a hero.

3 OP. 75 [GOETHE]

Aus Goethes Faust

'Song of the Flea', from Faust

Es war einmal ein König,
Der hatt einen großen Floh,
Den liebt er gar nicht wenig,
Als wie seinen eignen Sohn.
Da rief er seinen Schneider,
Der Schneider kam heran:
'Da, miß dem Junker Kleider
Und miß ihm Hosen an!'

In Sammet und in Seide
War er nun angetan,
Hatte Bänder auf dem Kleide,
Hatt auch ein Kreuz daran,
Und war sogleich Minister,
Und hatt einen großen Stern.
Da wurden seine Geschwister
Bei Hof auch große Herrn.

Und Herrn und Fraun am Hofe,
Die waren sehr geplagt,
Die Königin und die Zofe
Gestochen und genagt,

There once was a king,
who had a large flea;
he loved this flea as dearly
as his own son.
He called his tailor,
the tailor came:
'Here – make robes for this knight,
and a pair of trousers!'

Now the flea was clothed
in silk and satins,
with ribands on its coat
and a cross for distinguished service.
Straight away he became a minister
and wore a large star.
His brothers and sisters too
could now lord it at court.

And the gentlemen and ladies of the court
were greatly plagued,
queen and waiting-woman
were pricked and nibbled.

Und durften sie nicht knicken,
Und weg sie jucken nicht.
Wir knicken und ersticken
Doch gleich, wenn einer sticht.

Yet they dared not crack them
or scratch them away.
We crack them and we choke them
as soon as we feel a bite!

4 OP. 83 [GOETHE]

Wonne der Wehmut

Trocknet nicht, trocknet nicht,
Tränen der ewigen Liebe!
Ach, nur dem halbgetrockneten Auge
Wie öde, wie tot die Welt ihm erscheint!
Trocknet nicht, trocknet nicht,
Tränen unglücklicher Liebe!

Delight in Melancholy

Do not run dry, do not run dry,
tears of eternal love!
Even to the half-dried eye
the world appears so dull and dead!
Do not run dry, do not run dry,
tears of unhappy love!

5 G252 [PAUL GRAF VON HAUGWITZ]

Resignation

Lisch aus, mein Licht! Was dir gebricht,
Das ist nun fort, an diesem Ort
Kannst du's nicht wieder finden!
Du mußt nun los dich binden.

Sonst hast du lustig aufgebrannt,
Nun hat man dir die Luft entwandt;
Wenn diese fort gewehet, die Flamme irre-
    gehet,
Sucht, findet nicht; lisch aus, mein Licht!

Resignation

Go out, my light! What you need
is gone, in this place
you will not find it again.
You must learn to do without it.

You used to burn so brightly;
now you have been deprived of air.
When air is gone, the flame wavers,
searches, finds nothing. Go out, my light!

6 OP. 98 [ALOIS JEITTELES]

An die ferne Geliebte

(1)
Auf dem Hügel sitz ich spähend
In das blaue Nebelland,
Nach den fernen Triften sehend,
Wo ich dich, Geliebte, fand.

Weit bin ich von dir geschieden,
Trennend liegen Berg und Tal
Zwischen uns und unserm Frieden,
Unserm Glück und unsrer Qual.

Ach, den Blick kannst du nicht sehen,
Der zu dir so glühend eilt,
Und die Seufzer, sie verwehen
In dem Raume, der uns teilt.

To the Distant Beloved

(1)
I sit on the hill-top and gaze
into the misty blue land,
looking towards those meadows far away
where I first found you, my love.

Now I am far from you,
mountain and valley separate us
from each other, from our peace,
from our happiness, from our sorrow.

Alas, you cannot see the fiery gaze
directed towards you,
and my sighs are lost
in the space that divides us.

Will denn nichts mehr zu dir dringen,
Nichts der Liebe Bote sein?
Singen will ich, Lieder singen,
Die dir klagen meine Pein!

Denn vor Liebesklang entweichet
Jeder Raum und jede Zeit,
Und ein liebend Herz erreichet
Was ein liebend Herz geweiht!

(2)
Wo die Berge so blau
Aus dem nebligen Grau
Schauen herein,
Wo die Sonne verglüht,
Wo die Wolke umzieht,
Möchte ich sein!

Dort im ruhigen Tal
Schweigen Schmerzen und Qual.
Wo im Gestein
Still die Primel dort sinnt,
Weht so leise der Wind,
Möchte ich sein!

Hin zum sinnigen Wald
Drängt mich Liebesgewalt,
Innere Pein.
Ach, mich zög's nicht von hier,
Könnt ich, Traute, bei dir
Ewiglich sein!

(3)
Leichte Segler in den Höhen,
Und du, Bächlein klein und schmal,
Könnt mein Liebchen ihr erspähen,
Grüßt sie mir viel tausendmal.

Seht ihr, Wolken, sie dann gehen
Sinnend in dem stillen Tal,
Laßt mein Bild vor ihr entstehen
In dem luft'gen Himmelssaal.

Wird sie an den Büschen stehen,
Die nun herbstlich falb und kahl,
Klagt ihr, wie mir ist geschehen,
Klagt ihr, Vöglein, meine Qual.

Stille Weste, bringt im Wehen
Hin zu meiner Herzenswahl
Meine Seufzer, die vergehen
Wie der Sonne letzter Strahl.

Will nothing reach you,
will nothing be a messenger of love?
I will sing, then, I will sing songs
that speak to you of my anguish.

For sounds of love can put to flight
all space and all time;
and a loving heart may be reached
by what a loving heart has hallowed.

(2)
Where the blue mountains
look towards me
out of the grey mists,
where the sun sheds its last rays
and the clouds roll by –
there I would like to be!

There, in the silent valley,
pain and anguish cease.
There, where among the rocks
the primrose meditates silently,
where the wind blows so softly –
there I would like to be!

I am driven to the pensive wood
by the power of love
and the anguish within.
Nothing would draw me from here,
if only, my love,
I could be ever with you.

(3)
You light clouds sailing on high,
and you, narrow little brook:
if you can spy out my love,
bring her a thousand greetings from me.

If, O clouds, you then see her walk
deep in thought in the quiet valley –
conjure up my image before her
in the airy dome of the sky.

If she stands by the bushes
that are now autumnally pale and bare –
then, O birds, lament my fate
and tell her of my anguish.

Soft west winds, waft my sighs
towards her my heart has chosen –
sighs that vanish
like the sun's last ray.

Flüstr' ihr zu mein Liebesflehen,
Laß sie, Bächlein klein und schmal,
Treu in deinen Wogen sehen
Meine Tränen ohne Zahl!

(4)
Diese Wolken in den Höhen,
Dieser Vöglein muntrer Zug,
Werden dich, o Huldin, sehen.
Nehmt mich mit im leichten Flug!

Diese Weste werden spielen
Scherzend dir um Wang' und Brust,
In den seidnen Locken wühlen.
Teilt ich mit euch diese Lust!

Hin zu dir von jenen Hügeln
Emsig dieses Bächlein eilt.
Wird ihr Bild sich in dir spiegeln,
Fließ zurück dann unverweilt!

(5)
Es kehret der Maien, es blühet die Au,
Die Lüfte, sie wehen so milde, so lau,
Geschwätzig die Bäche nun rinnen.

Die Schwalbe, die kehret zum wirtlichen
      Dach,
Sie baut sich so emsig ihr bräutlich Gemach,
Die Liebe soll wohnen da drinnen.

Sie bringt sich geschäftig von kreuz und von
      quer
Manch weicheres Stück zu dem Brautbett
      hieher,
Manch wärmendes Stück für die Kleinen.

Nun wohnen die Gatten beisammen so treu,
Was Winter geschieden, verband nun der
      Mai,
Was liebet, das weiß er zu einen.

Es kehret der Maien, es blühet die Au.
Die Lüfte, sie wehen so milde, so lau.
Nur ich kann nicht ziehen von hinnen.

Wenn alles, was liebet, der Frühling vereint,
Nur unserer Liebe kein Frühling erscheint,
Und Tränen sind all ihr Gewinnen.

(6)
Nimm sie hin denn, diese Lieder,
Die ich dir, Geliebte, sang,
Singe sie dann abends wieder
Zu der Laute süßem Klang.

Whisper my loving supplication to her,
narrow little brook!
in your ripples show her faithfully
my numberless tears.

(4)
These clouds on high,
this gay flock of birds –
they will see you, gracious one.
O take me with you in your effortless flight!

These west winds will merrily play
about your cheek and bosom,
they will agitate your silken tresses.
If I could only share in your delight!

This brooklet hastens
eagerly towards you from those hills,
If you find her image mirrored in your
      waters,
flow back without delay!

(5)
May is returning, the meadow is in flower,
the winds blow mild and warm,
the brooks flow chattering on.

The swallow, returning to the hospitable
      roof,
eagerly builds her bridal chamber –
love shall dwell within.

Busily she brings from every direction
soft scraps for her bridal bed,
warm scraps for her little ones.

Now the pair lives faithfully together;
What winter parted, May has joined.
May knows how to bring lovers together.

May is returning, the meadow is in flower,
the winds blow mild and warm;
only I cannot go where I would.

When springtime unites all lovers
our love alone knows no spring,
and gains nothing but tears.

(6)
Take these songs now
Which I sang to you, my love,
sing them over to yourself in the evening
to the sweet sound of the lute.

Wenn das Dämmrungsrot dann ziehet
Nach dem stillen blauen See,
Und sein letzter Strahl verglühet
Hinter jener Bergeshöh;

Und du singst, was ich gesungen,
Was mir aus der vollen Brust
ohne Kunstgepräng erklungen,
Nur der Sehnsucht sich bewußt:

Dann vor diesen Liedern weichet
Was geschieden uns so weit,
Und ein liebend Herz erreichet
Was ein liebend Herz geweiht.

When the red glow of evening then passes
to the still blue lake,
and the last ray flashes to its end
behind those mountain heights;

And you sing what I sang,
what issued from my overflowing heart
without an artist's ostentation
(I was conscious only of my longing):

Then the distance that parted us
is surmounted by these songs,
and a loving heart is reached
by what a loving heart has hallowed.

JOHANN CARL GOTTFRIED LOEWE

Born at Löbejün near Halle on 30 November 1796, the youngest son of a poor schoolmaster who died early, leaving his numerous family to make their way as best they could. The gifted boy obtained various scholarships and became cantor and organist at Stettin in 1820. In 1821 he was made municipal *Musikdirektor* of Stettin, a post he retained until his retirement in 1866. Loewe taught music, sang his own compositions in recitals at home and abroad (including one before Queen Victoria in 1847), guided various choirs, and directed the Pomeranian music festivals. He died at Kiel on 20 April 1869. His works include five operas, sixteen oratorios, and a number of orchestral and instrumental works – but only his songs are alive today.

Loewe's greatest songs are ballad settings. He had a special flair for the uncanny and demonic ('Erlkönig', 'Ritter Olaf', 'Odins Meeresritt', 'Walpurgisnacht'); he knew how to characterize persons and events with a simple melodic and rhythmic motif which he would then vary throughout the song ('Edward', for instance, is built almost entirely on three such motifs); his works are generally 'through-composed', yet the strophic nature of the ballad is unmistakably preserved; his melismatic piano accompaniments ('Der Nöck') often use the same musical material as that of the vocal line. His soldier songs take a worthy place beside the 'uncanny' ballads – notably 'Prinz Eugen', with its strangely concealed tune which only at the end is heard in its full form; but when he leaves his own field he can be unbearably philistine and coy. The once popular 'Die Uhr', for instance, is now nothing more than a quaint invitation to parody, and even the perennial 'Tom der Reimer' can hardly be sung without embarrassment by a modern singer.

I OP. 1 [SCOTTISH BALLAD, TRANSLATED BY HERDER]

Edward

Dein Schwert, wie ist's von Blut so rot?
Edward, Edward!
Dein Schwert, wie ist's von Blut so rot?
Und gehst so traurig da? O!

Ich hab geschlagen meinen Geier tot,
Mutter, Mutter!
Ich hab geschlagen meinen Geier tot,
Und das, das geht mir nah. O!

Deines Geiers Blut ist nicht so rot,
Edward, Edward!
Deines Geier Blut ist nicht so rot,
Mein Sohn, bekenn mir frei. O!

Ich hab geschlagen mein Rotroß tot,
Mutter, Mutter!
Ich hab geschlagen mein Rotroß tot,
Und's war so stolz und treu. O!

Edward

Why does your sword so drop with blood,
Edward, Edward,
why does your sword so drop with blood,
and why do you walk so sadly?

I have killed my hawk,
mother, mother,
I have killed my hawk,
and I grieve for that.

Your hawk's blood is not so red,
Edward, Edward,
your hawk's blood is not so red –
confess the truth to me, my son.

I have killed my red roan steed,
mother, mother,
I have killed my red roan steed,
which was so proud and so faithful.

Dein Roß war alt und hast's nicht not,
Edward, Edward!
Dein Roß war alt und hast's nicht not,
Dich drückt ein andrer Schmerz. O!

Ich hab geschlagen meinen Vater tot!
Mutter, Mutter!
Ich hab geschlagen meinen Vater tot,
Und das, das quält mein Herz! O!

Und was wirst du nun an dir tun,
Edward, Edward?
Und was wirst du nun an dir tun?
Mein Sohn, das sage mir! O!

Auf Erden soll mein Fuß nicht ruhn!
Mutter, Mutter!
Auf Erden soll mein Fuß nicht ruhn!
Will wandern übers Meer! O!

Und was soll werden dein Hof und Hall,
Edward, Edward?
Und was soll werden dein Hof und Hall,
So herrlich sonst, so schön? O!

Ach immer steh's und sink und fall!
Mutter, Mutter!
Ach immer steh's und sink und fall,
Ich werd es nimmer sehn! O!

Und was soll werden aus Weib und Kind,
Edward, Edward?
Und was soll werden aus Weib und Kind,
Wann du gehst über's Meer? O!

Die Welt ist groß, laß sie betteln drin,
Mutter, Mutter!
Die Welt ist groß, laß sie betteln drin,
Ich seh sie nimmermehr! O!

Und was soll deine Mutter tun,
Edward, Edward?
Und was soll deine Mutter tun,
Mein Sohn, das sage mir? O!

Your steed was old, and you do not need it,
Edward, Edward,
your steed was old, and you do not need it,
some other sorrow weighs you down.

I have killed my father,
mother, mother,
I have killed my father,
and that torments my heart.

What penance will you do for that,
Edward, Edward?
What penance will you do for that?
Tell me, my son!

My feet shall not rest on this earth,
mother, mother,
my feet shall not rest on this earth.
I will wander beyond the sea.

And what will become of your house and
     hall,
Edward, Edward,
and what will become of your house and
     hall,
so glorious, so fair?

I'll let them stand till they fall down,
mother, mother,
I'll let them stand till they fall down;
I shall never see them again.

And what will become of your wife and your
     child,
Edward, Edward,
and what will become of your wife and your
     child,
when you go over the sea?

The world is wide – let them beg through
     life,
mother, mother,
the world is wide, let them beg through
     life –
I shall never see them again.

And what is your mother to do,
Edward, Edward,
and what is your mother to do –
tell me, my son!

Der Fluch der Hölle soll auf euch ruhn,
Mutter, Mutter!
Der Fluch der Hölle soll auf euch ruhn,
Denn ihr, ihr rietet's mir! O!

The curse of hell shall fall upon you,
mother, mother,
the curse of hell shall fall upon you –
for it was you who counselled me!

2 OP. 92 [FERDINAND FREILIGRATH]

Prinz Eugen, der edle Ritter

Prince Eugene, The Noble Knight

Zelte, Posten, Werdarufer!
Lust'ge Nacht am Donauufer!
Pferde stehn im Kreis umher
Angebunden an den Pflöcken;
An den engen Sattelböcken
Hangen Karabiner schwer.

Tents, sentries, men calling: 'Who goes
there?'
It is a merry night by the banks of the
Danube.
Horses stand in a circle,
tethered to pegs.
Heavy carbines hang
from narrow saddles.

Um das Feuer auf der Erde,
Vor den Hufen seiner Pferde
Liegt das östreichsche Piket.
Auf dem Mantel liegt ein jeder;
Von den Tschackos weht die Feder,
Leutnant würfelt und Kornet.

Round the fire,
before their horses' hooves,
men of the Austrian picket lie on the ground.
Each one lies on his cloak;
feathers wave from helmets;
lieutenants and cornets play at dice.

Neben seinem müden Schecken
Ruht auf einer wollnen Decken
Der Trompeter ganz allein:
'Laßt die Knöchel, laßt die Karten!
Kaiserliche Feldstandarten
Wird ein Reiterlied erfreun!

Beside his weary dapple-grey,
on a woollen blanket,
the trumpeter rests all by himself.
'Leave your dice, leave your cards!
The Imperial army in the field
will now be treated to a cavalry song!

'Vor acht Tagen die Affaire
Hab ich, zu Nutz dem ganzen Heere,
In gehör'gen Reim gebracht;
Selber auch gesetzt die Noten;
Drum, ihr Weißen und ihr Roten!
Merket auf und gebet Acht!'

'That battle we fought eight days ago –
for the benefit of the whole army I have now
put it into rhyme.
I have also written the music to it.
You in your white and red uniforms –
now listen and attend!'

Und er singt die neue Weise
Einmal, zweimal, dreimal leise
Denen Reitersleuten vor;
Und wie er zum letzten Male
Endet, bricht mit einem Male
Los der volle, kräft'ge Chor:

And softly he sings the new song over –
once, twice, three times –
to the cavalrymen.
And when, for the last time,
he comes to the end, the men all at once
join lustily in the chorus:

'Prinz Eugen, der edle Ritter!'
Hei, das klang wie Ungewitter
Weit in's Türkenlager hin.
Der Trompeter tät den Schnurrbart streichen
Und sich auf die Seite schleichen
Zu der Marketenderin.

'Prince Eugene, the noble knight!'
That song roared like thunder
far into the Turkish camp.
The trumpeter stroked his whiskers
and stole away
to join the *vivandière*.

3 OP. 135 [SCOTTISH BALLAD]

Tom der Reimer   *Thomas the Rhymer*

Der Reimer Thomas lag am Bach,
Am Kieselbach bei Huntly Schloß.
Da sah er eine blonde Frau,
Die saß auf einem weißen Roß.

Sie saß auf einem weißen Roß,
Die Mähne war geflochten fein,
Und hell an jeder Flechte hing
Ein silberblankes Glöckelein.

Und Tom der Reimer zog den Hut
Und fiel auf's Knie, er grüßt und spricht:
Du bist die Himmelskönigin!
Du bist von dieser Erde nicht!

Die blonde Frau hält an ihr Roß:
'Ich will dir sagen, wer ich bin;
Ich bin die Himmelsjungfrau nicht,
Ich bin die Elfenkönigin!

'Nimm deine Harf und spiel und sing
Und laß dein bestes Lied erschalln,
Doch wenn du meine Lippe küßt,
Bist du mir sieben Jahr verfalln!'

'Wohl! sieben Jahr, o Königin,
Zu dienen dir, es schreckt mich kaum!'
Er küßte sie, sie küßte ihn,
Ein Vogel sang im Eschenbaum.

'Nun bist du mein, nun zieh mit mir,
Nun bist du mein auf sieben Jahr.'
Sie ritten durch den grünen Wald
Wie glücklich da der Reimer war!

Sie ritten durch den grünen Wald
Bei Vogelsang und Sonnenschein,
Und wenn sie leicht am Zügel zog,
So klangen hell die Glöckelein.

Thomas the Rhymer lay
by the pebbly brook near Huntly castle.
He saw a fair lady
riding a white horse.

She sat on a white horse,
whose mane was finely braided;
and from every braid hung down
a little silver bell.

Tom doffed his hat,
dropped on one knee, and greeted her:
'You must be the Queen of Heaven –
you cannot belong to this earth.'

The fair lady curbed her steed:
'I will tell you who I am;
I am not the Queen of Heaven,
I am queen of the elves!

'Take up your harp and play and sing,
and let me hear your finest song;
but if you kiss my lips
you are my thrall for seven years.'

'To serve you, O queen, for seven years
holds little terror for me!'
He kissed her, she kissed him,
a little bird sang in the ash tree.

'Now you are mine, now go with me,
now you are mine for seven years.'
They rode through the green woods –
how happy the Rhymer was then!

They rode through the green woods
while the birds sang and the sun shone
     down;
and when she lightly pulled the bridle
the little bells tinkled merrily.

FRANZ PETER SCHUBERT

Born at Lichtenthal near Vienna on 31 January 1797, the son of an elementary school-master. Like Haydn, Schubert received early musical training as a chorister of St Stephen's, Vienna. He was soon drawn to composition – his settings of ballads and lyrics were influenced mainly by Zumsteeg, until he surpassed all predecessors with 'Gretchen am Spinnrad', a song written when Schubert was only seventeen. After an unhappy interlude as a schoolmaster (1813–17), Schubert settled in Vienna, where he tried, henceforth, to make his living as a composer. He was helped by many friends (often themselves poor) who shared lodgings and food with him and with whom he arranged musical and literary evenings (*Schubertiads*). He died on 19 November 1828, poor but with a growing reputation outside his own circle. His works include a number of operas and *Singspiele*, seven masses, eight symphonies, an octet, a piano quintet, and sixteen string quartets as well as many impromptus, *moments musicaux*, and dances.

Schubert is the greatest master of the *Lied*. He wrote over 600 songs, developing and anticipating every form; the purely strophic, the strophic variation, the 'through-composed', the declamatory, the tiny lyric, the extended *scena*, the song-cycle. Melodies poured out of him, and he exhibited an unsurpassed power of developing and moulding them into a musically significant whole. He could transform all the world into music – natural phenomena (a rippling brook, a crow), man-made objects (a creaking weather-vane, a wheezy hurdy-gurdy), human types (a deserted lover, a wandering poet, a smug Philistine), and human emotions and gestures – but he never allowed this gift to tempt him to facile imitation and 'programme music'. His literary taste has been much maligned: he chose with sure tact, among the poems produced by his own contemporaries, those that would lend themselves to musical composition without being in themselves mawkish and insignificant. Brahms rightly said of him: 'There is not a song of Schubert's from which one cannot learn something.'

I D118 [GOETHE]

Gretchen am Spinnrad(e)

'Margaret at the Spinning-Wheel' from Faust

Meine Ruh ist hin,
Mein Herz ist schwer
Ich finde sie nimmer
Und nimmermehr.

My peace is gone,
my heart is heavy;
never, never again
will I find rest.

Wo ich ihn nicht hab
Ist mir das Grab,
Die ganze Welt
Ist mir vergällt.

Where I am not with him
I am in my grave,
the whole world
turns to bitter gall.

Mein armer Kopf
Ist mir verrückt,
Mein armer Sinn
Ist mir zerstückt.

My poor head
is in a whirl,
my poor thoughts
are all distracted.

Meine Ruh ist hin,
Mein Herz ist schwer,
Ich finde sie nimmer
Und nimmermehr.

Nach ihm nur schau ich
Zum Fenster hinaus,
Nach ihm nur geh ich
Aus dem Haus.

Sein hoher Gang,
Sein' edle Gestalt,
Seines Mundes Lächeln,
Seiner Augen Gewalt,

Und seiner Rede
Zauberfluß,
Sein Händedruck,
Und ach, sein Kuß!

Meine Ruh ist hin,
Mein Herz ist schwer,
Ich finde sie nimmer
Und nimmermehr.

Mein Busen drängt
Sich nach ihm hin.
Ach dürft ich fassen
Und halten ihn,

Und küssen ihn,
So wie ich wollt,
An seinen Küssen
Vergehen sollt!

[Meine Ruh ist hin,
Mein Herz ist schwer . . .]

My peace is gone,
my heart is heavy;
never, never again
will I find rest.

I seek only him when I look
out of the window,
I seek only him when I leave
the house.

His noble gait,
his fine stature,
the smile of his lips,
the power of his eyes,

and the magic flow
of his speech,
the pressure of his hand,
and his kiss!

My peace is gone,
my heart is heavy;
never, never again
will I find rest.

My bosom yearns
towards him.
If only I could seize him
and hold him

and kiss him
to my heart's content –
under his kisses
I should die!

[My peace is gone,
my heart is heavy . . .]

2 D328 [GOETHE]

Erlkönig

Wer reitet so spät durch Nacht und Wind?
Es ist der Vater mit seinem Kind;
Er hat den Knaben wohl in dem Arm,
Er faßt ihn sicher, er hält ihn warm.

'Mein Sohn, was birgst du so bang dein
    Gesicht?'
'Siehst, Vater, du den Erlkönig nicht?
Den Erlenkönig mit Kron und Schweif?'
'Mein Sohn, es ist ein Nebelstreif.'

The Erl-King

Who rides so late through the night and the
    wind?
It is the father with his child.
He holds the boy in his arm,
grasps him securely, keeps him warm.

'My son, why do you hide your face so
    anxiously?'
'Father, do you not see the Erl-King?
The Erl-King with his crown and tail?'
'My son, it is only a streak of mist.'

'Du liebes Kind, komm, geh mit mir!
Gar schöne Spiele spiel ich mit dir;
Manch bunte Blumen sind an dem Strand,
Meine Mutter hat manch gülden Gewand.'

'Darling child, come away with me!
I will play fine games with you.
Many gay flowers grow by the shore;
my mother has many golden robes.'

'Mein Vater, mein Vater, und hörest du
    nicht,
Was Erlenkönig mir leise verspricht?'
'Sei ruhig, bleibe ruhig, mein Kind:
In dürren Blättern säuselt der Wind.'

'Father, father, do you not hear
what the Erl-King softly promises me?'
'Be calm, dear child, be calm –
the wind is rustling in the dry leaves.'

'Willst, feiner Knabe, du mit mir gehn?
Meine Töchter sollen dich warten schön;
Meine Töchter führen den nächtlichen Reihn
Und wiegen und tanzen und singen dich ein.'

'You beautiful boy, will you come with me?
My daughters will wait upon you.
My daughters lead the nightly round,
they will rock you, dance to you, sing you to
    sleep!'

'Mein Vater, mein Vater, und siehst du nicht
    dort
Erlkönigs Töchter am düstern Ort?'
'Mein Sohn, mein Sohn, ich seh es genau:
Es scheinen die alten Weiden so grau.'

'Father, father, do you not see
the Erl-King's daughters there, in that dark
    place?'
'My son, my son, I see it clearly:
it is the grey gleam of the old willow-trees.'

'Ich liebe dich, mich reizt deine schöne
    Gestalt;
Und bist du nicht willig, so brauch ich
    Gewalt.'
'Mein Vater, mein Vater, jetzt faßt er mich
    an!
Erlkönig hat mir ein Leid's getan!' –

'I love you, your beauty allures me,
and if you do not come willingly, I shall use
    force.'
'Father, father, now he is seizing me!
The Erl-King has hurt me!'

Dem Vater grauset's, er reitet geschwind
Er hält in den Armen das ächzende Kind,
Erreicht den Hof mit Müh und Not;
In seinen Armen das Kind war tot.

Fear grips the father, he rides swiftly,
holding the moaning child in his arms;
with effort and toil he reaches the house –
the child in his arms was dead.

3 D257 [GOETHE]

Heidenröslein

Meadow Rose

Sah ein Knab ein Röslein stehn
Röslein auf der Heiden,
War so jung und morgenschön,
Lief er schnell, es nah zu sehn,
Sah's mit vielen Freuden.
Röslein, Röslein, Röslein rot,
Röslein auf der Heiden.

A boy saw a rose
growing in a meadow.
It was young and fair as the morning.
Quickly he ran to look at it more closely;
he saw it with great joy.
Rose, rose, little red rose,
rose in the meadow.

Knabe sprach: Ich breche dich,
Röslein auf der Heiden!
Röslein sprach: Ich steche dich,
Dass du ewig denkst an mich,

The boy said: 'I will pick you,
rose in the meadow!'
The rose said: 'I will prick you
so that you will always remember me.

Und ich will's nicht leiden.
Röslein, Röslein, Röslein rot,
Röslein auf der Heiden.

Und der wilde Knabe brach
's Röslein auf der Heiden;
Röslein wehrte sich und stach,
Half ihm doch kein Weh und Ach,
Mußt es eben leiden.
Röslein, Röslein, Röslein rot,
Röslein auf der Heiden.

I will not suffer it.'
Rose, rose, little red rose,
rose in the meadow.

The wild boy picked
the rose in the meadow;
the rose defended itself and pricked him.
But its laments were of no avail —
it had to suffer.
Rose, rose, little red rose,
rose in the meadow.

4 D367 [GOETHE]

Der König in Thule

Es war ein König in Thule,
Gar treu bis an das Grab,
Dem sterbend seine Buhle
Einen goldnen Becher gab.

Es ging ihm nichts darüber,
Er leert' ihn jeden Schmaus;
Die Augen gingen ihm über,
So oft er trank daraus.

Und als er kam zu sterben,
Zählt' er seine Städt' im Reich,
Gönnt' alles seinen Erben,
Den Becher nicht zugleich.

Er saß beim Königsmahle,
Die Ritter um ihn her,—
Auf hohem Vätersaale,
Dort auf dem Schloß am Meer.

Dort stand der alte Zecher,
Trank letzte Lebensglut,
Und warf den heil'gen Becher
Hinunter in die Flut.

Er sah ihn stürzen, trinken
Und sinken tief ins Meer.
Die Augen täten ihm sinken
Trank nie einen Tropfen mehr.

The King of Thule

There was a king in Thule,
faithful to the grave,
to whom his love, on her death-bed,
gave a golden goblet.

He valued it beyond all his possessions,
he drained it at every repast;
tears came to his eyes
whenever he drank from it.

And when he felt himself near to death
he counted the cities in his realm,
was content to leave all to his heirs —
but not the goblet.

He sat at the royal banquet,
surrounded by his knights,
in the lofty hall of his ancestors
in the castle by the sea.

There stood that old lover of wine
and drank the last fire of life,
and cast the sacred goblet
into the waters below.

He saw it fall, fill with water
and sink deep into the sea.
His eyes grew weary
and he never drank again.

5 D463 [SCHMIDT VON LÜBECK]

Der Wanderer

Ich komme vom Gebirge her,
Es dampft das Tal, es braust das Meer.

The Wanderer

I come from the mountains;
the valley steams, the sea roars.

Ich wandle still, bin wenig froh,
Und immer fragt der Seufzer, wo?

Die Sonne dünkt mich hier so kalt,
Die Blüte welk, das Leben alt,
Und was sie reden leerer Schall;
Ich bin ein Fremdling überall.

Wo bist du, mein geliebtes Land?
Gesucht, geahnt, und nie gekannt!
Das Land, das Land so hoffnungsgrün,
Das Land, wo meine Rosen blühn.

Wo meine Freunde wandelnd gehn,
Wo meine Toten auferstehn,
Das Land, das meine Sprache spricht,
O Land, wo bist du? . . .

Ich wandle still, bin wenig froh,
Und immer fragt der Seufzer, wo?
Im Geisterhauch tönt's mir zurück:
'Dort, wo du nicht bist, dort ist das Glück.'

I wander in silence, with little joy,
and my sighs constantly ask: 'Where?'

The sun seems so cold here,
the flowers seem faded, life old,
what people say, nothing but empty sound.
Everywhere I am a stranger.

Where are you, land that I love?
Land sought, land dreamed of, but never
    found?
Land so green with hope,
Land where my roses bloom?

Land where my friends roam,
where my dead come to life,
where my language is spoken –
where are you?

I wander in silence, with little joy,
and my sighs constantly ask: 'Where?'
A ghostly whisper returns the answer:
'Where you are *not* – there is happiness.'

6 D547 [FRANZ VON SCHOBER]

An die Musik

Du holde Kunst, in wieviel grauen Stunden,
Wo mich des Lebens wilder Kreis umstrickt
Hast du mein Herz zu warmer Lieb ent-
    zunden,
Hast mich in eine bessre Welt entrückt!

Oft hat ein Seufzer, deiner Harf entflossen,
Ein süßer, heiliger Akkord von dir
Den Himmel bessrer Zeiten mir erschlossen,
Du holde Kunst, ich danke dir dafür!

To Music

O art that I hold dear – how often, in hours of
    gloom,
when life had caught me in its savage toils,
you have kindled warm love in my heart
and have borne me to a better world!

Often a sigh from your harp,
a sweet sacred chord from you,
gave me heavenly visions of happier times.
O dearest art – for all this I thank you.

7 D550 [C.F.D. SCHUBART]

Die Forelle

In einem Bächlein helle,
Da schoß in froher Eil
Die launische Forelle
Vorüber wie ein Pfeil.
Ich stand an dem Gestade
Und sah in süßer Ruh
Des muntern Fischleins Bade
Im klaren Bächlein zu.

The Trout

In a bright little stream,
in joyous haste,
a playful trout
flashed past me like an arrow.
I stood by the shore
and in sweet contentment I watched
the little fish bathing
in the clear stream.

Ein Fischer mit der Rute
Wohl an dem Ufer stand,
Und sah's mit kaltem Blute,
Wie sich das Fischlein wand.
So lang dem Wasser Helle,
So dacht ich, nicht gebricht,
So fängt er die Forelle
Mit seiner Angel nicht.

Doch endlich ward dem Diebe
Die Zeit zu lang. Er macht'
Das Bächlein tückisch trübe,
Und eh ich es gedacht,
So zuckte seine Rute,
Das Fischlein zappelt' dran,
Und ich mit regem Blute
Sah die Betrogne an.

A fisherman with his rod
stood on the bank
and coldly watched
the trout's windings.
So long as the water
– I thought – remains clear,
he will not catch the trout
with his line.

But at last the thief
grew impatient. He
treacherously dulled the clear stream,
and before I could think it
his rod quivered
and the fish was struggling on his hook.
I felt the blood stir within me
as I looked at the cheated trout

8 D583 [FRIEDRICH VON SCHILLER]

Gruppe aus dem Tartarus

Horch – wie Murmeln des empörten Meeres,
Wie durch hohler Felsen Becken weint ein
   Bach,
Stöhnt dort dumpfigtief ein schweres, leeres
Qualerpresstes Ach!

Schmerz verzerret
Ihr Gesicht, Verzweiflung sperret
Ihren Rachen fluchend auf.
Hohl sind ihre Augen, ihre Blicke
Spähen bang nach des Cocytus Brücke,
Folgen tränend seinem Trauerlauf.

Fragen sich einander ängstlich leise,
Ob noch nicht Vollendung sei!
Ewigkeit schwingt über ihnen Kreise,
Bricht die Sense des Saturns entzwei.

A Group in Tartarus

Listen – like the angry murmuring of the sea,
like a brook weeping through gullies of
   hollow rocks,
sounds the deep, hollow, heavy, toneless
groan forced from those in torment.

Pain distorts
their faces, despair opens
their cursing mouths.
Their eyes are hollow, they peer
Anxiously at the bridge over Cocytus
and follow its mournful course with tears.

In fear they softly ask one another
if the end has not yet come.
Eternity circles over them,
Saturn's scythe breaks in two.

9 D531 [MATTHIAS CLAUDIUS]

Der Tod und das Mädchen

'Vorüber! ach, vorüber
Geh, wilder Knochenmann!
Ich bin noch jung, geh, Lieber!
Und rühre mich nicht an.'

Death and the Girl

'Pass me by, pass me by,
Go away, wild skeleton!
I am still young – go, dear Death,
and do not touch me.'

'Gib deine Hand, du schön und zart Gebild,
Bin Freund und komme nicht zu strafen.
Sei gutes Muts! Ich bin nicht wild,
Sollst sanft in meinen Armen schlafen.'

'Give me your hand, you lovely and tender
    creature;
I am your friend and do not come to punish.
Be comforted! I am not wild.
You will sleep gently in my arms.'

10 D752 [JOHANN MAYRHOFER]

Nachtviolen

Nachtviolen, Nachtviolen!
Dunkle Augen, seelenvolle,
Selig ist es, sich versenken
In dem samtnen Blau.

Grüne Blätter streben freudig
Euch zu helfen, euch zu schmücken;
Doch ihr blicket ernst und schweigend
In die laue Frühlingsluft.

Mit erhabnen Wehmutsstrahlen
Trafet ihr mein treues Herz,
Und nun blüht in stummen Nächten
Fort die heilige Verbindung.

Dame's Violets

Violets of the night!
Dark, soulful eyes!
It is sweet to sink oneself
into your velvet blue.

Green leaves strive joyfully
to set you off and adorn you;
but you gaze, solemn and still,
into the mild spring air.

With rays of noble sadness
you struck my faithful heart,
and now in silent nights
this sacred union blossoms.

11 D764 [GOETHE]

Der Musensohn

Durch Feld und Wald zu schweifen
Mein Liedchen wegzupfeifen,
So geht's von Ort zu Ort!
Und nach dem Takte reget,
Und nach dem Maß beweget
Sich alles an mir fort.

Ich kann sie kaum erwarten,
Die erste Blum im Garten,
Die erste Blüt am Baum.
Sie grüßen meine Lieder,
Und kommt der Winter wieder,
Sing ich noch jenen Traum.

Ich sing ihn in der Weite,
Auf Eises Läng und Breite
Da blüht der Winter schön!
Auch diese Blüte schwindet,
Und neue Freude findet
Sich auf bebauten Höhn.

Son of the Muses

Rambling through woods and fields,
whistling my song –
so I go from place to place.
In time to my song
and in its measure
everything about me moves.

I can scarcely wait for
the first flower in the garden
and the first blossom on the tree.
They greet my songs,
and when winter returns
I still sing of my dream.

I sing it in the wide world,
along the length and breadth of the ice –
that makes the winter blossom!
But these blooms vanish too,
and new joys are to be found
on the tilled uplands.

Denn wie ich bei der Linde
Das junge Völkchen finde,
Sogleich erreg ich sie.
Der stumpfe Bursch bläht sich.
Das steife Mädchen dreht sich
Nach meiner Melodie.

Ihr gebt den Sohlen Flügel,
Und treibt durch Tal und Hügel
Den Liebling weit von Haus.
Ihr lieben, holden Musen,
Wann ruh ich ihr am Busen
Auch endlich wieder aus?

For as soon as I see
young people by the lime-tree
I stir their blood.
Dull fellows preen themselves,
Gawky girls turn,
to my tune.

You give my feet wings
and drive your favourite over hills and dales
far from his home.
Dear, gracious muses –
when may I rest again
on the bosom of my love?

12 D774 [FRIEDRICH VON STOLBERG]

Auf dem Wasser zu singen

To be sung on the water

Mitten im Schimmer der spiegelnden Wellen
Gleitet, wie Schwäne, der wankende Kahn;
Auch, auf der Freude sanftschimmernden
   Wellen
Gleitet die Seele dahin wie der Kahn,
Denn von dem Himmel herab auf die Wellen
Tanzet das Abendrot rund um den Kahn.

In the midst of the shimmering, mirroring
   waves
the rocking boat glides like a swan;
on the softly shimmering waves of joy
the soul glides like a boat;
for from the sky the last rays of the sun
shine on the waves and dance about the boat.

Über den Wipfeln des westlichen Haines
Winket uns freundlich der rötliche Schein;
Unter den Zweigen des östlichen Haines
Säuselt der Kalmus im rötlichen Schein;
Freude des Himmels und Ruhe des Haines
Atmet die Seel' im errötenden Schein.

Over the tree-tops of the westerly woods
the red glow pleasantly beckons to us;
under the branches of the wood in the east
reeds rustle in the red glow;
the soul breathes the joy of heaven and calm
   of the woods
in the reddening glow.

Ach, es entschwindet mit tauigem Flügel
Mir auf den wiegenden Wellen die Zeit;
Morgen entschwinde mit schimmernden
   Flügel
Wieder wie gestern und heute die Zeit,
Bis ich auf höherem strahlenden Flügel
Selber entschwinde der wechselnden Zeit.

Alas – on dewy wings
time escapes me amidst the rippling waves.
On shimmering wings let time fly tomorrow
as it did yesterday and today –
until I myself – on greater, brighter wings –
escape from time and its changes.

13 D776 [FRIEDRICH RÜCKERT]

Du bist die Ruh

You are Rest and Peace

Du bist die Ruh,
Der Friede mild,
Die Sehnsucht du,
Und was sie stillt.

You are rest
and gentle peace;
you are longing
and what stills it.

Ich weihe dir
Voll Lust und Schmerz
Zur Wohnung hier
Mein Aug und Herz.

To you I consecrate –
full of joy and of grief –
my eyes and my heart
as a dwelling-place.

Kehr ein bei mir
Und schließe du
Still hinter dir
Die Pforte zu.

Come in to me,
and silently close
the gate
behind you.

Treib andern Schmerz
Aus dieser Brust!
Voll sei dies Herz
Von deiner Lust.

Drive other griefs
out of my breast.
Let my heart be full
of your joy.

Dies Augenzelt,
Von deinem Glanz
Allein erhellt,
O füll es ganz!

This tent of my eyes,
lit solely
by your brightness –
O fill it wholly!

14 D828 [CRAIGHER DE JACHELUTTA]

Die junge Nonne

The Young Nun

Wie braust durch die Wipfel der heulende
    Sturm!
Es klirren die Balken, es zittert das Haus!
Es rollet der Donner, es leuchtet der Blitz,
Und finster die Nacht, wie das Grab!

How the howling storm rages through the
    tree-tops!
The rafters creak, the whole house trembles!
Thunder rolls, lightning flashes,
and the night is as dark as the grave.

Immerhin, immerhin, so tobt' es auch jüngst
    noch in mir!
Es brauste das Leben, wie jetzo der Sturm,
Es bebten die Glieder, wie jetzo das Haus,
Es flammte die Liebe, wie jetzo der Blitz,
Und finster die Brust, wie das Grab.

Let the storm rage – so it raged in me but a
    short while ago.
Life roared as the storm does now;
my limbs trembled, as the house now
    trembles;
love flared as the lightning now flares;
and my heart was as dark as the grave.

Nun tobe, du wilder gewalt'ger Sturm,
Im Herzen ist Friede, im Herzen ist Ruh,
Des Bräutigams harret die liebende Braut,
Gereinigt in prüfender Glut,
Der ewigen Liebe getraut.

Rage on, wild and mighty storm,
In my heart there is peace and repose.
The loving bride awaits the bridegroom –
she is purified in the testing fire
and betrothed to eternal love.

Ich harre, mein Heiland! mit sehnendem
    Blick!
Komm, himmlischer Bräutigam, hole die
    Braut,
Erlöse die Seele von irdischer Haft.

I await you with longing, my Saviour!
Come, heavenly bridegroom, to claim your
    bride,
deliver my soul from its earthly bonds.

Horch, friedlich ertönet das Glöcklein vom
  Turm!
Es lockt mich das süße Getön
Allmächtig zu ewigen Höhn.
Alleluja!

Listen – how peacefully the bell sounds from
  the tower!
Its sweet sound calls me
powerfully to the eternal heights.
Hallelujah!

15 D827 [MATTHAUS VON COLLIN]

Nacht und Träume

Night and Dreams

Heil'ge Nacht, du sinkest nieder,
Nieder wallen auch die Träume,
Wie dein Mondlicht durch die Räume,
Durch der Menschen stille Brust.
Die belauschen sie mit Lust;
Rufen, wenn der Tag erwacht:
Kehre wieder, holde Nacht!
Holde Träume, kehret wieder!

Sacred night, you sink down upon us;
dreams too descend
(as your moonlight descends through space)
into the stilled hearts of men.
Men joyfully listen to these dreams
and call, when day breaks:
'Return, sweet night!
Return, O you sweet dreams!'

16 D795 [WILHELM MÜLLER]

Die schöne Müllerin

The Fair Maid of the Mill

(1) Das Wandern

(1) Wandering

Das Wandern ist des Müllers Lust,
Das Wandern!
Das muß ein schlechter Müller sein,
Dem niemals fiel das Wandern ein,
Das Wandern.

Wandering is what the miller enjoys,
Wandering!
He must be a poor miller
who never thought of
wandering.

Vom Wasser haben wir's gelernt,
Vom Wasser!
Das hat nicht Rast bei Tag und Nacht,
Ist stets auf Wanderschaft bedacht,
Das Wasser.

We have learnt it of the water,
the water!
It never rests, by day or night,
but always thinks of wandering,
the water.

Das sehn wir auch den Rädern ab,
Den Rädern!
Die gar nicht gerne stille stehn,
Die sich mein Tag nicht müde drehn,
Die Räder.

We have learnt it, too, by looking at
the mill-wheels!
They do not like to stand still
and never tire of turning –
the mill-wheels.

Die Steine selbst, so schwer sie sind,
Die Steine!
Sie tanzen mit den muntern Reihn
Und wollen gar noch schneller sein,
Die Steine.

The very mill-stones, heavy as they are,
the mill-stones!
They join in the merry round
and long to move even faster –
the mill-stones.

O Wandern, Wandern, meine Lust,
O Wandern!
Herr Meister und Frau Meisterin
Laßt mich in Frieden weiterziehn
Und wandern.

Wandering is my delight,
wandering!
Master and mistress,
let me go my way in peace,
and wander.

(2) Wohin?

Ich hört ein Bächlein rauschen
Wohl aus dem Felsenquell.
Hinab zum Tale rauschen
So frisch und wunderhell.

Ich weiß nicht, wie mir wurde,
Nicht, wer den Rat mir gab,
Ich mußte auch hinunter
Mit meinem Wanderstab.

Hinunter und immer weiter,
Und immer dem Bache nach,
Und immer frischer rauschte
Und immer heller der Bach.

Ist das denn meine Straße?
O Bächlein, sprich, wohin?
Du hast mit deinem Rauschen
Mir ganz berauscht den Sinn.

Was sag ich denn vom Rauschen?
Das kann kein Rauschen sein:
Es singen wohl die Nixen
Tief unten ihren Reihn.

Laß singen, Gesell, laß rauschen,
Und wandre fröhlich nach!
Es gehn ja Mühlenräder
In jedem klaren Bach.

(2) Where To?

I heard a little stream rushing
from its source among the rocks,
bubbling down to the valley
so clear, so strangely bright.

I do not know what came over me,
nor who counselled me:
but I too had to go down
with my staff in my hand.

Down and ever onwards,
ever following the stream,
and, ever more clear and ever more bright,
the stream babbled on.

Is this the road I am to go?
Where will it lead, O stream?
Your murmuring
has quite bemused my senses.

Why do I speak of murmuring?
That is not what I hear.
The water nymphs are singing
as they dance their round below.

Let them sing, let the stream murmur,
and follow it gaily!
Mill-wheels turn
In every clear stream.

(3) Halt

Eine Mühle seh ich blinken
Aus den Erlen heraus,
Durch Rauschen und Singen
Bricht Rädergebraus.

Ei willkommen, ei willkommen,
Süßer Mühlengesang!
Und das Haus, wie so traulich!
Und die Fenster, wie blank!

(3) Halt

I see a mill gleaming
through the alders;
the rushing of mill-wheels
breaks through murmuring and singing.

Welcome, welcome,
sweet song of the mill!
How inviting that house looks,
how bright its windows!

Und die Sonne, wie helle
Vom Himmel sie scheint!
Ei, Bächlein, liebes Bächlein,
War es also gemeint?

And how brightly the sun
shines down from the sky!
You dear little mill-stream –
is *that* what you meant?

(4) *Danksagung an den Bach*

War es also gemeint,
Mein rauschender Freund?
Dein Singen, dein Klingen,
War es also gemeint?

Zur Müllerin hin!
So lautet der Sinn.
Gelt, hab ich's verstanden?
Zur Müllerin hin!

Hat sie dich geschickt?
Oder hast du mich berückt?
Das möcht ich noch wissen,
Ob sie dich geschickt.

Nun, wie's auch mag sein,
Ich gebe mich drein;
Was ich such, ist gefunden,
Wie's immer mag sein.

Nach Arbeit ich frug.
Nun hab ich genug;
Für die Hände, für's Herze
Vollauf genug!

(4) *A Grateful Address to the Mill-Stream*

Is this what you meant,
my murmuring friend?
Your singing, your rippling –
did they mean this?

'To the maid of the mill!'
That is what you wanted to say.
Have I understood you now?
'To the maid of the mill!'

Did she send you?
Or have you enchanted me?
I would dearly like to know
whether she sent you.

Be that as it may –
I accept my fate.
What I sought is found.
I do not ask how it came about.

I asked for work:
now I have enough
for my hands and my heart –
enough and to spare!

(5) *Am Feierabend*

Hätt ich tausend
Arme zu rühren!
Könnt ich brausend
Die Räder führen!
Könnt ich wehen
Durch alle Haine!
Könnt ich drehen
Alle Steine!
Daß die schöne Müllerin
Merkte meinen treuen Sinn!

Ach, wie ist mein Arm so schwach!
Was ich hebe, was ich trage,
was ich schneide, was ich schlage,
Jeder Knappe tut mir's nach.
Und da sitz ich in der großen Runde,
In der stillen kühlen Feierstunde,

(5) *After the Day's Work*

If only I had a thousand
arms to work with!
If I could only guide
the rushing mill-wheels!
If I could ride like the wind
through every wood!
If I could turn
every millstone!
Then the lovely maid of the mill might see
how faithfully I seek to serve her.

But my arm, alas, is so weak!
All this lifting, carrying,
cutting and hammering
any apprentice could do as well as I.
And there I sit in a circle with all the others
in the still cool time when the work is done,

Und der Meister spricht zu allen:
Euer Werk hat mir gefallen;
Und das liebe Mädchen sagt
Allen eine gute Nacht.

and the master says to us all:
'I was pleased with your work today';
and the dear girl bids
everyone good night.

(6) Der Neugierige

Ich frage keine Blume,
Ich frage keinen Stern;
Sie können mir alle nicht sagen,
Was ich erführ so gern.

Ich bin ja auch kein Gärtner,
Die Sterne stehn zu hoch;
Mein Bächlein will ich fragen,
Ob mich mein Herz belog.

O Bächlein meiner Liebe,
Wie bist du heut so stumm!
Will ja nur eines wissen,
Ein Wörtchen um und um.

'Ja' heißt das eine Wörtchen,
Das andre heißet 'nein',
Die beiden Wörtchen schließen
Die ganze Welt mir ein.

O Bächlein meiner Liebe,
Was bist du wunderlich!
Will's ja nicht weiter sagen,
Sag, Bächlein, liebt sie mich?

(6) Curiosity

I do not question the flowers,
I do not question the stars;
they all cannot tell me
what I would so dearly like to know.

I am not a gardener,
and I cannot reach the stars;
I will ask the mill-stream
if my heart deceived me.

Brook of my love,
how silent you are today!
I only ask one thing,
a single word one way or the other.

One word is 'yes',
the other 'no';
These two words include
the whole world for me.

O brook of my love,
how strange you are!
I will tell no one else:
tell me, does she love me?

(7) Ungeduld

Ich schnitt' es gern in alle Rinden ein,
Ich grüb es gern in jeden Kieselstein,
Ich möcht es sä'n auf jedes frische Beet
Mit Kressensamen, der es schnell verrät,
Auf jeden weißen Zettel möcht ich's schrei-
        ben:
Dein ist mein Herz, und soll es ewig bleiben.

Ich möcht mir ziehen einen jungen Star,
Bis daß er spräch die Worte rein und klar,
Bis er sie spräch mit meines Mundes Klang,
Mit meines Herzens vollem, heißem Drang;
Dann säng er hell durch ihre Fensterscheiben:
Dein ist mein Herz, und soll es ewig bleiben.

(7) Impatience

I would like to carve it on every tree-trunk,
engrave it on every pebble,
sow it on every newly turned plot
with cress-seed that will soon betray it,
write it on every scrap of white paper:
My heart is yours, and will ever remain yours.

I would like to train a young starling
to speak the words loud and clear,
to speak them with my own voice,
out of the fullness of my own heart;
then he would brightly sing at her window:
My heart is yours, and will ever remain yours.

Den Morgenwinden möcht ich's hauchen ein,
Ich möcht es säuseln durch den regen Hain;
Oh, leuchtet' es aus jedem Blumenstern!
Trüg es der Duft zu ihr von nah und fern!
Ihr Wogen, könnt ihr nichts als Räder
    treiben?
Dein ist mein Herz, und soll es ewig bleiben.

Ich meint, es müßt in meinen Augen stehn,
Auf meinen Wangen müßt man's brennen
    sehn,
Zu lesen wär's auf meinem stummen Mund,
Ein jeder Atemzug gäb's laut ihr kund,
Uns sie merkt nichts von all dem bangen
    Treiben:
Dein ist mein Herz, und soll es ewig bleiben!

I would like to whisper it into the morning
    breeze,
to breathe it through the waving woods.
If it could but shine from every starry flower!
If the flowers' scent could bear it to her from
    near and far!
Waves – can you move nothing but mill-
    wheels?
My heart is yours, and will ever remain yours.

I should have thought it shone from my
    eyes,
it blazed on my cheeks,
it could be read on my silent lips,
every breath proclaimed it to her –
yet she notices nothing of all this anxious
    yearning:
My heart is yours, and will ever remain
    yours.

(8) *Morgengruß*

Guten Morgen, schöne Müllerin!
Wo steckst du gleich das Köpfchen hin,
Als wär das was geschehen?
Verdrießt dich denn mein Gruß so schwer?
Verstört dich denn mein Blick so sehr?
So muß ich wieder gehen.

O laß mich nur von ferne stehn,
Nach deinem lieben Fenster sehn,
Von ferne, ganz von ferne!
Du blondes Köpfchen, komm hervor!
Hervor aus eurem runden Tor,
Ihr blauen Morgensterne!

Ihr schlummertrunknen Äugelein,
Ihr taubetrübten Blümelein,
Was scheuet ihr die Sonne?
Hat es die Nacht so gut gemeint,
Daß ihr euch schließt und bückt und weint
Nach ihrer stillen Wonne?

Nun schüttelt ab der Träume Flor,
Und hebt euch frisch und frei empor
In Gottes hellen Morgen!
Die Lerche wirbelt in der Luft,
Und aus dem tiefen Herzen ruft
Die Liebe Leid und Sorgen.

(8) *Morning Greeting*

Good morning, lovely maid of the mill!
Why do you turn your face away
as though something were troubling you?
Does my greeting so displease you?
Does my glance so disturb you?
Then I must go my ways.

O let me but stand far off
and gaze up at your dear window
from the distance!
Fair little head, appear!
Come from your round gates,
you blue morning-stars!

Eyes still heavy with sleep,
flowers still dimmed with dew –
why do you shrink from the sunlight?
Was night so good to you
that you close, bow down, and weep
for night's silent delight?

Shake off the veil of dreams,
and look up gladly and freely
to God's bright morning!
The lark trills high in the air,
and love charms care and sorrow
from the depths of the heart.

(9) *Des Müllers Blumen*

Am Bach viel kleine Blumen stehn,
Aus hellen blauen Augen sehn;
Der Bach, der ist des Müllers Freund,
Und hellblau Liebchens Auge scheint,
Drum sind es meine Blumen.

Dicht unter ihrem Fensterlein,
Da will ich pflanzen die Blumen ein;
Da ruft ihr zu, wenn alles schweigt,
Wenn sich ihr Haupt zum Schlummer neigt,
Ihr wißt ja, was ich meine.

Und wenn sie tät die Äuglein zu
Und schläft in süßer, süßer Ruh,
Dann lispelt als ein Traumgesicht
Ihr zu: Vergiß, vergiß mein nicht!
Das ist es, was ich meine.

Und schließt sie früh die Laden auf,
Dann schaut mit Liebesblick hinauf;
Der Tau in euern Äugelein,
Das sollen meine Tränen sein,
Die will ich auf euch weinen.

(10) *Tränenregen*

Wir saßen so traulich beisammen
Im kühlen Erlendach,
Wir schauten so traulich zusammen
Hinab in den rieselnden Bach.

Der Mond war auch gekommen,
Die Sternlein hintendrein,
Und schauten so traulich zusammen
In den silbernen Spiegel hinein.

Ich sah nach keinem Monde,
Nach keinem Sternenschein,
Ich schaute nach ihrem Bilde,
Nach ihren Augen allein.

Und sahe sie nicken und blicken
Herauf aus dem seligen Bach,
Die Blümlein am Ufer, die blauen
Sie nickten und blickten ihr nach.

Und in den Bach versunken
Der ganze Himmel schien
Und wollte mich mit hinunter
In seine Tiefe ziehn.

(9) *The Miller's Flowers*

Many tiny flowers grow by the stream,
peeping from clear blue eyes;
the mill-stream is the miller's friend,
and my love's eyes are a bright azure blue –
therefore these are my flowers.

Right under her window
I will plant the flowers;
there, flowers, you shall call to her, when all
   is silent
you know what I want to say.

And when she closes her eyes
and slumbers in sweet repose,
then whisper into her dreams:
'Forget-me-not!'
That is what I would say.

And when, in the morning, she opens her
   shutters,
you must gaze up with glances of love.
The dew in your eyes
shall be the tears
that I will weep on you.

(10) *Rain of Tears*

Cosily we sat together
under the cool roof of the alders,
and gazed together
into the rippling stream.

The moon had come out too,
followed by the stars –
they looked down together
into the silvery, mirroring water.

I did not look at the moon,
I did not look at the stars,
I looked only at her reflection
and her eyes.

I saw them nodding and glancing
from the happy stream,
the little blue flowers on the bank
nodded and glanced at her.

And the whole sky seemed
sunk into the stream
and wanted to drag me down
into its depths.

Und über den Wolken und Sternen,
Da rieselte munter der Bach
Und rief mit Singen und Klingen:
'Geselle, Geselle, mir nach!'

Da gingen die Augen mir über,
Da ward es im Spiegel so kraus;
Sie sprach: 'Es kommt ein Regen,
Ade, ich geh nach Haus.'

(11) *Mein*

Bächlein, laß dein Rauschen sein!
Räder, stellt eu'r Brausen ein!
All ihr muntern Waldvögelein,
Groß und klein,
Endet eure Melodein!

Durch den Hain
Aus und ein
Schalle heut ein Reim allein:
Die geliebte Müllerin ist mein!
Mein!

Frühling, sind das alle dein Blümelein?
Sonne, hast du keinen hellern Schein?
Ach, so muß ich ganz allein
Mit dem seligen Worte mein
Unverstanden in der weiten Schöpfung sein!

(12) *Pause*

Meine Laute hab ich gehängt an die Wand,
Hab sie umschlungen mit einem grünen
    Band –
Ich kann nicht mehr singen, mein Herz ist
    zu voll,
Weiß nicht, wie ich's in Reime zwingen soll.
Meiner Sehnsucht allerheißesten Schmerz
Durft ich aushauchen in Liederscherz,
Und wie ich klagte so süß und fein,
Glaubt ich doch, mein Leiden wär nicht klein.
Ei, wie groß ist wohl meines Glückes Last,
Daß kein Klang auf Erden es in sich faßt?

Nun, liebe Laute, ruh an dem Nagel hier!
Und weht ein Lüftchen über die Saiten dir,
Und streift eine Biene mit ihren Flügeln dich,
Da wird mir so bange und es durchschauert
    mich.

And over the clouds and the stars
the stream rippled merrily
and called to me with its music:
'Come – follow me!'

The tears welled up in my eyes
and the watery mirror was blurred.
She said: 'We shall have rain.
Good-bye – I am going home.'

(11) 'Mine'

Mill-stream, cease your babbling!
Mill-wheels, cease your rumbling!
All you gay wood-birds
great and small
cease your singing!

Through the woods,
in and out,
one rhyme alone shall sound today:
The one I love, the maid of the mill, is mine!
Mine!

Spring, are these all the flowers you have?
Sun, cannot you shine more brightly?
Then I must be all alone
with that happy word of mine –
and no one in all creation understands me!

(12) Pause

I have hung my lute on the wall
and have twined a green ribbon around it –
I cannot sing any more, my heart is too full,
I do not know how to force it into rhyme.
Even the most searing pain of my longing
I could breathe into playful song,
and as I lamented gently and sweetly
I still thought my sorrows heavy enough.
How great the load of my happiness must be
that no earthly harmony can contain it!

Well, dear lute, rest on this nail.
And when a breeze strays over your strings
or a bee brushes you with its wings
I feel sudden fear, and shudder.

Warum ließ ich das Band auch hängen so
    lang?
Oft fliegt's um die Saiten mit seufzendem
    Klang.
Ist es der Nachklang meiner Liebespein?
Soll es das Vorspiel neuer Lieder sein?

Why did I let the riband hang down so low?

Often it trails round the strings with a sigh-
    ing sound.
Is this the echo of my love's sorrow
or the prelude of new songs?

(13) *Mit dem grünen Lautenbande*

'Schad um das schöne grüne Band,
Daß es verbleicht hier an der Wand,
Ich hab das Grün so gern!'
So sprachst du, Liebchen, heut zur mir;
Gleich knüpf ich's ab und send es dir:
Nun hab das Grüne gern!

Ist auch dein ganzer Liebster weiß,
Soll Grün doch haben seinen Preis,
Und ich auch hab es gern.
Weil unsre Lieb ist immergrün,
Weil Grün der Hoffnung Fernen blühn,
Drum haben wir es gern.

Nun schlinge in die Locken dein
Das grüne Band gefällig ein,
Du hast ja's Grün so gern.
Dann weiß ich, wo die Hoffnung wohnt,
Dann weiß ich, wo die Liebe thront,
Dann hab ich's Grün erst gern.

(13) *Lines with the Lute's Green Ribbon*

'What a pity to let the beautiful green
    ribbon
fade here on the wall –
I am so fond of green!'
That is what you said to me today, my love,
and straightaway I untie it and send it to you.
Be ever fond of green!

Even though your lover is dressed all in white,
green deserves praise,
and I too am fond of it.
For our love is evergreen,
and the far reaches of hope are green –
that is why we are fond of it.

Now twine the green ribbon
charmingly into your hair –
for you are so fond of green.
Then I know where hope dwells
and where love is enthroned:
then I will really love green.

(14) *Der Jäger*

Was sucht denn der Jäger am Mühlbach
    hier?
Bleib, trotziger Jäger, in deinem Revier!
Hier gibt es kein Wild zu jagen für dich,
Hier wohnt nur ein Rehlein, ein zahmes, für
    mich.
Und willst du das zärtliche Rehlein sehn,
So laß deine Büchsen im Walde stehn,
Und laß deine klaffenden Hunde zu Haus,
Und laß auf dem Horne den Saus und Braus,
Und schere vom Kinne das struppige Haar;
Sonst scheut sich im Garten das Rehlein
    fürwahr.

(14) *The Huntsman*

What is the huntsman doing by the mill-
    stream here?
Stay in your preserve, bold hunter!
Here is no game for you to track down,
only my own tame doe.
And if you would see that gentle doe,
then leave your guns in the forest
and your yapping hounds at home,
stop blowing your horn
and shave the rough beard from your chin;
or my doe in her garden will take fright.

Doch besser, du bliebest im Walde dazu,
Und ließest die Mühlen und Müller in Ruh.
Was taugen die Fischlein im grünen Ge-
zweig?
Was will denn das Eichhorn im bläulichen
Teich?
Drum bleibe, du trotziger Jäger, im Hain,
Und laß mich mit meinen drei Rädern allein;
Und willst meinem Schätzchen dich machen
beliebt,
So wisse, mein Freund, was ihr Herzchen
betrübt:
Die Eber, die kommen zu Nacht aus dem
Hain
Und brechen in ihren Kohlgarten ein,
Und treten und wühlen herum in dem Feld;
Die Eber, die schieße, du Jägerheld!

But it would be better if you stayed in the
forest
and left mills and millers alone.
What should fishes do among the green
branches
or squirrels in the blue pond?
Then stay in your wood, bold hunter,
and leave me alone with my three mill-wheels.
And if you want to win my love's favour
then you must know what troubles her:
wild boars come out of the forest at night,
break into her cabbage patch,
trample her field and root about in the earth:
shoot those boars, you brave huntsman!

(15) *Eifersucht und Stolz*

Wohin so schnell, so kraus und wild, mein
lieber Bach?
Eilst du voll Zorn dem frechen Bruder Jäger
nach?
Kehr um, kehr um, und schilt erst deine
Müllerin
Für ihren leichten, losen, kleinen Flattersinn.
Sahst du sie gestern Abend nicht am Tore
stehn,
Mit langem Halse nach der großen Straße
sehn?

Wenn von dem Fang der Jäger lustig zieht
nach Haus,
Da steckt kein sittsam Kind den Kopf zum
Fenster 'naus.
Geh, Bächlein, hin und sag ihr das; doch sag
ihr nicht,
Hörst du, kein Wort von meinem traurigen
Gesicht;
Sag ihr: Er schnitzt' bei mir sich eine Pfeif'
aus Rohr
Und bläst den Kindern schöne Tänz' und
Lieder vor.

(15) *Jealousy and Pride*

Whither so fast, so ruffled and wild, my dear
stream?
Are you hurrying angrily after that impu-
dent huntsman?
Return, return and scold your maid of the
mill
for her inconstancy of mind.
Did you not see her stand at the gate last
night,
craning her neck to watch the big road?

When the huntsman gaily returns from the
kill
a well brought up girl does not peer from
her window.
Go, mill-stream, go tell her this; but do not –
do you hear? – say a word about my sad face.
Say rather: he cut himself a reed-pipe by my
banks
and is piping lovely dance-tunes and songs
to the children.

(16) *Die liebe Farbe*

In Grün will ich mich kleiden,
In grüne Tränenweiden:
Mein Schatz hat's Grün so gern.

(16) *The Beloved Colour*

I will dress in green,
the colour of weeping willows:
my love is so fond of green.

Will suchen einen Zypressenhain,
Eine Heide voll grünen Rosmarein:
Mein Schatz hat's Grün so gern.

Wohlauf zum fröhlichen Jagen!
Wohlauf durch Heid und Hagen!
Mein Schatz hat's Jagen so gern.
Das Wild, das ich jage, das ist der Tod;
Die Heide, die heiß ich die Liebesnot:
Mein Schatz hat's Jagen so gern.

Grabt mir ein Grab im Wasen,
Deckt mich mit grünen Rasen:
Mein Schatz hat's Grün so gern.
Kein Kreuzlein schwarz, kein Blümlein bunt,
Grün, alles grün so rings und rund:
Mein Schatz hat's Grün so gern.

(17) *Die böse Farbe*

Ich möchte ziehn in die Welt hinaus,
Hinaus in die weite Welt;
Wenn's nur so grün, so grün nicht wär,
Da draußen in Wald und Feld!

Ich möchte die grünen Blätter all
Pflücken von jedem Zweig,
Ich möchte die grünen Gräser all
Weinen ganz totenbleich.

Ach Grün, du böse Farbe du,
Was siehst mich immer an
So stolz, so keck, so schadenfroh,
Mich armen weißen Mann?

Ich möchte liegen vor ihrer Tür,
In Sturm und Regen und Schnee,
Und singen ganz leise bei Tag und Nacht
Das eine Wörtchen Ade!

Horch, wenn im Wald ein Jagdhorn ruft,
Da klingt ihr Fensterlein!
Und schaut sie auch nach mir nicht aus,
Darf ich doch schauen hinein.

O binde von der Stirn dir ab
Das grüne, grüne Band;
Ade, ade! und reiche mir
Zum Abschied deine Hand.

I will seek a cypress grove,
a field full of green rosemary:
my love is so fond of green.

The gay hunt is up!
Halloo through field and thicket!
My love is so fond of hunting.
The game I hunt is Death,
the field I call 'Love's Anguish':
my love is so fond of hunting.

Dig me a grave in the swards,
cover me with green turf:
my love is so fond of green.
No black cross, no gay flowers –
let all around be green:
my love is so fond of green.

(17) *The Hateful Colour*

I would like to go out into the world,
the wide world –
If only everything were not so green
out there in the fields and woods!

I would like to pluck the green leaves
from every branch,
I would like to turn the green grass as pale
    as death
with my tears.

O green, you hateful colour,
why do you look at me everywhere
so proudly, boldly, mockingly?
I am but a poor white miller.

I would like to lie before her door,
in storm, in rain, in snow;
day and night I would softly sing
the one word: 'Farewell!'

When a hunting-horn peals in the wood,
her window is heard to open,
and though it is not for me she looks out
yet I can look in at her.

O untie the green ribbon
from your forehead,
and give me your hand
in token of farewell!

(18) *Trockne Blumen*

Ihr Blümlein alle, die sie mir gab,
Euch soll man legen mit mir ins Grab.

Wie seht ihr alle mich an so weh,
Als ob ihr wüßtet, wie mir gescheh?

Ihr Blümlein alle, wie welk, wie blaß?
Ihr Blümlein alle, wovon so naß?

Ach, Tränen machen nicht maiengrün,
Machen tote Liebe nicht wieder blühn.

Und Lenz wird kommen, und Winter wird
   gehn,
Und Blümlein werden im Grase stehn.

Und Blümlein liegen in meinen Grab,
Die Blümlein alle, die sie mir gab.

Und wenn sie wandelt am Hügel vorbei
Und denkt im Herzen: der meint' es treu!

Dann, Blümlein alle, heraus, heraus!
Der Mai ist kommen, der Winter ist aus.

(19) *Der Müller und der Bach*

Wo ein treues Herze in Liebe vergeht,
Da welken die Lilien auf jedem Beet;
Da muß in die Wolken der Vollmond gehn,
Damit seine Tränen die Menschen nicht
   sehn;
Da halten die Englein die Augen sich zu
Und schluchzen und singen die Seele zur
   Ruh.

Der Bach:
Und wenn sich die Liebe dem Schmerz
   entringt,
Ein Sternlein, ein neues, am Himmel erblinkt;
Da springen drei Rosen, halb rot, halb weiß,
Die welken nicht wieder aus Dornenreis.
Und die Engelein schneiden die Flügel sich ab
Und gehn alle Morgen zur Erde hinab.

(18) *Dry Flowers*

You flowers all, which she gave me:
you shall be laid into the grave with me.

How sadly you all gaze at me,
as though you knew what was happening
   to me!

How withered you all are, how pale!
and how come you to be so wet?

Tears, alas, do not bring back the green of
   May,
nor can they make a dead love bloom again.

Spring will come, winter will go,
flowers will spring up in the grass.

Flowers will lie in my grave –
all the flowers which she gave me.

And when she walks past my mound
and thinks in her heart: 'He was faithful to
   me!'

Then, all you flowers, spring up, spring up!
Then May has come and winter has gone.

(19) *The Miller and the Mill-Stream*

Where a true heart dies of love,
there lilies fade on their beds,
there the full moon hides behind clouds,
so that mortals should not see her tears,
there angels cover their eyes
and, sobbing, sing the soul to rest.

The mill-stream speaks:
And when love struggles free of its sorrow
a new star twinkles in the sky;
three roses – half red and half white –
spring from a thorny branch and fade no
   more;
and the angels cut off their wings
and come down to earth every morning.

Der Müller:
Ach Bächlein, liebes Bächlein, du meinst es
    so gut;
Ach Bächlein, aber weißt du, wie Liebe tut?
Ach unten, da unten die kühle Ruh!
Ach Bächlein, liebes Bächlein, so singe nur
    zu.

The miller speaks:
O stream, dear mill-stream, you mean so
    well;
but do you know how love can feel?
Down there, down there, is cool repose –
sing on, sing on, dear stream.

(20) *Des Baches Wiegenlied*

Gute Ruh, gute Ruh!
Tu die Augen zu!
Wandrer, du müder, du bist zu Haus.
Die Treu ist hier,
Sollst liegen bei mir,
Bis das Meer will trinken die Bächlein aus.

Will betten dich kühl
Auf weichem Pfühl
In dem blauen kristallenen Kämmerlein.
Heran, heran,
Was wiegen kann,
Woget und wieget den Knaben mir ein!

Wenn ein Jagdhorn schallt
Aus dem grünen Wald,
Will ich sausen und brausen wohl um dich
    her.
Blickt nicht herein,
Blaue Blümelein!
Ihr macht meinem Schläfer die Träume so
    schwer.

Hinweg, hinweg
Von dem Mühlensteg,
Böses Mägdelein, daß ihn dein Schatten nicht
    weckt!
Wirf mir herein
Dein Tüchlein fein,
Daß ich die Augen ihm halte bedeckt.

Gute Nacht, gute Nacht!
Bis alles wacht,
Schlaf aus deine Freude, schlaf aus dein
    Leid!
Der Vollmond steigt,
Der Nebel weicht,
Und der Himmel da oben, wie ist er so weit!

(20) *The Mill-Stream's Lullaby*

Rest, rest!
Close your eyes!
You tired wanderer, now you are at home.
Here all is true,
you shall lie with me
Until the sea drinks up all the streams.

I will bed you down
on a cool, soft pillow
in my blue crystal chamber.
Approach –
all you that can rock him to rest!
Flow about him and rock my boy to sleep.

When a hunting-horn sounds
from the green woods
I will rush and roar about you.
Do not look in,
little blue flowers!
You bring such bad dreams to this sleeper.

Off with you,
away from the mill-path,
wicked girl – let not your shadow wake him!
Throw in
your little kerchief
that I may cover his eyes.

Good night, good night;
until all the world wakes
rest from your joy, rest from your sorrow.
The full moon is rising,
the mists are parting,
and the heavens up there – how far they
    are, and how spacious!

17 D911 [WILHELM MÜLLER]

Die Winterreise	Journey in Winter

(1) *Gute Nacht*

(1) *Good Night*

Fremd bin ich eingezogen,
Fremd zieh ich wieder aus.
Der Mai war mir gewogen
Mit manchem Blumenstrauß.

Das Mädchen sprach von Liebe,
Die Mutter gar von Eh',
Nun ist die Welt so trübe,
Der Weg gehüllt in Schnee.

Ich kann zu meiner Reisen
Nicht wählen mit der Zeit,
Muß selbst den Weg mir weisen
In dieser Dunkelheit.

Es zieht ein Mondenschatten
Als mein Gefährte mit,
Und auf den weißen Matten
Such ich des Wildes Tritt.

Was soll ich länger weilen,
Daß man mich trieb hinaus?
Laß irre Hunde heulen
Vor ihres Herren Haus!

Die Liebe liebt das Wandern
Gott hat sie so gemacht
Von einem zu dem andern
Fein Liebchen, gute Nacht!

Will dich im Traum nicht stören,
Wär schad um deine Ruh.
Sollst meinen Tritt nicht hören
Sacht, sacht die Türe zu!

Schreib im Vorübergehen
Ans Tor dir: gute Nacht,
Damit du mögest sehen,
An dich hab ich gedacht.

A stranger I came,
a stranger I depart.
The month of May favoured me
with many a nosegay of flowers.

The girl spoke of love,
her mother even of marriage;
now the world is dreary,
the path covered with snow.

I cannot choose the time
for my journey,
I must find my own way
in this darkness.

My shadow, cast by the moon,
accompanies me,
and on the white fields
I seek the tracks of deer.

Why should I stay longer,
until I am driven away?
Let straying dogs howl
before their master's house.

Love likes to wander
(for God has made it so)
from one to another.
Good night, my sweetheart!

I will not disturb your dreams;
why should I spoil your rest?
You shall not hear my footsteps.
I close the door softly.

As I pass, I write
'Good night' on your gate,
so that you should see
I thought of you.

(2) *Die Wetterfahne*

(2) *The Weather-Vane*

Der Wind spielt mit der Wetterfahne
Auf meines schönen Liebchens Haus.
Da dacht ich schon in meinem Wahne,
Sie pfiff den armen Flüchtling aus.

The wind plays with the weather-vane
on my sweetheart's house.
In my distress I thought
it mocked the poor fugitive.

Er hätt es eher bemerken sollen,
Des Hauses aufgestecktes Schild,
So hätt er nimmer suchen wollen
Im Haus ein treues Frauenbild.

Der Wind spielt drinnen mit den Herzen
Wie auf dem Dach, nur nicht so laut.
Was fragen sie nach meinen Schmerzen?
Ihr Kind ist eine reiche Braut.

(3) *Gefrorne Tränen*

Gefrorne Tropfen fallen
Von meinen Wangen ab;
Ob es mir denn entgangen,
Daß ich geweinet hab?

Ei Tränen, meine Tränen,
Und seid ihr gar so lau,
Daß ihr erstarrt zu Eise,
Wie kühler Morgentau?

Und dringt doch aus der Quelle
Der Brust so glühend heiß,
Als wolltet ihr zerschmelzen
Des ganzen Winters Eis!

(4) *Erstarrung*

Ich such im Schnee vergebens
Nach ihrer Tritte Spur,
Wo sie an meinem Arme
Durchstrich die grüne Flur.

Ich will den Boden küssen,
Durchdringen Eis und Schnee
Mit meinen heißen Tränen ,
Bis ich die Erde seh.

Wo find ich eine Blüte,
Wo find ich grünes Gras?
Die Blumen sind erstorben,
Der Rasen sieht so blaß.

Soll denn kein Angedenken
Ich nehmen mit von hier?
Wenn meine Schmerzen schweigen,
Wer sagt mir dann von ihr?

Mein Herz ist wie erstorben,
Kalt starrt ihr Bild darin;
Schmilzt je das Herz mir wieder,
Fließt auch ihr Bild dahin.

He should have noticed
this token on the house before:
then he would never have sought
a faithful woman within.

Inside the house the wind plays with hearts,
though it is less loud than on the roof.
What do they care for my grief?
Their child is a wealthy bride.

(3) *Frozen Tears*

Frozen drops fall
from my cheeks:
have I been weeping, then,
without noticing it?

Tears, my tears,
how tepid you must be
that you can turn to ice
like the cool dew of morning!

And yet you spring from my heart
with as fierce a heat
as if you would melt
all the winter's ice.

(4) *Frozen Rigidity*

In vain I seek her footprints
in the snow,
where she walked, arm in arm with me,
over the green fields.

I will kiss the ground
and pierce ice and snow
with my scalding tears
until I see the earth beneath.

Where shall I find a blossom,
where shall I find green grass?
The flowers have withered,
the turf looks wan.

Is there no keepsake, then,
that I may take from here?
When my grief is silent,
who will speak to me of her?

My heart seems dead;
within it, her image stands rigid and cold;
if ever my heart should thaw
her image will melt away.

(5) *Der Lindenbaum*

Am Brunnen vor dem Tore
Da steht ein Lindenbaum;
Ich träumt in seinem Schatten
So manchen süßen Traum.

Ich schnitt in seine Rinde
So manches liebe Wort;
Es zog in Freud und Leide
Zu ihm mich immer fort.

Ich mußt auch heute wandern
Vorbei in tiefer Nacht,
Da hab ich noch im Dunkel
Die Augen zugemacht.

Und seine Zweige rauschten,
Als riefen sie mir zu:
'Komm her zu mir, Geselle,
Hier findst du deine Ruh!'

Die kalten Winde bliesen
Mir grad in's Angesicht,
Der Hut flog mir vom Kopfe,
Ich wendete mich nicht.

Nun bin ich manche Stunde
Entfernt von jenem Ort,
Und immer hör ich's rauschen:
Du fändest Ruhe dort!

(6) *Wasserflut*

Manche Trän aus meinen Augen
Ist gefallen in den Schnee;
Seine kalten Flocken saugen
Durstig ein das heiße Weh.

Wenn die Gräser sprossen wollen,
Weht daher ein lauer Wind,
Und das Eis zerspringt in Schollen
Und der weiche Schnee zerrinnt.

Schnee, du weißt von meinem Sehnen,
Sag, wohin doch geht dein Lauf?
Folge nach nur meinen Tränen,
Nimmt dich bald das Bächlein auf.

Wirst mit ihm die Stadt durchziehen,
Muntre Straßen ein und aus;
Fühlst du meine Tränen glühen,
Da ist meiner Liebsten Haus.

(5) *The Lime-Tree*

By the well before the gate
there stands a lime-tree;
in its shade I dreamt
many a sweet dream.

In its bark I carved
many a word of love;
in joy as in sorrow
I felt ever drawn to it.

Today I had to wander
past it at dead of night,
and even in the darkness
I closed my eyes.

And its branches rustled
as if they were calling to me
'Friend, come here to me –
Here you will find rest.'

The cold winds blew
straight into my face,
my hat flew from my head –
but I did not turn round.

Now I am many hours' journey
away from that place;
but I always hear the rustling:
'There you would find rest!'

(6) *Flood*

Many a tear has fallen
from my eyes into the snow,
its cold flakes greedily drink in
my burning anguish.

When the grass is ready to grow
a warm wind blows,
the ice breaks into fragments,
and the soft snow melts.

Snow, you know of my longing –
tell me where you go!
You have only to follow my tears
And you will soon flow into the brook.

With the brook you will flow through the
    town,
in and out of merry streets;
where you feel the glow of my tears
there is my love's house.

(7) *Auf dem Flusse*

Der du so lustig rauschtest,
Du heller, wilder Fluß,
Wie still bist du geworden,
Gibst keinen Scheidegruß!

Mit harter, starrer Rinde
Hast du dich überdeckt,
Liegst kalt und unbeweglich
Im Sande ausgestreckt.

In deine Decke grab ich
Mit einem spitzen Stein
Den Namen meiner Liebsten
Und Stund und Tag hinein:

Den Tag des ersten Grußes,
Den Tag, an dem ich ging:
Um Nam' und Zahlen windet
Sich ein zerbrochner Ring.

Mein Herz, in diesem Bache
Erkennst du nun dein Bild?
Ob's unter seiner Rinde
Wohl auch so reißend schwillt?

(8) *Rückblick*

Es brennt mir unter beiden Sohlen,
Tret ich auch schon auf Eis und Schnee,
Ich möcht nicht wieder Atem holen,
Bis ich nicht mehr die Türme seh.

Hab mich an jeden Stein gestoßen,
So eilt ich zu der Stadt hinaus;
Die Krähen warfen Bäll' und Schloßen
Auf meinen Hut von jedem Haus.

Wie anders hast du mich empfangen,
Du Stadt der Unbeständigkeit!
An deinen blanken Fenstern sangen
Die Lerch' und Nachtigall im Streit.

Die runden Lindenbäume blühten,
Die klaren Rinnen rauschten hell,
Und ach, zwei Mädchenaugen glühten!
Da war's geschehn um dich, Gesell!

Kommt mir der Tag in die Gedanken,
Möcht ich noch einmal rückwärts sehn,
Möcht ich zurücke wieder wanken,
Vor ihrem Hause stille stehn.

(7) *On the River*

You clear wild stream
that once rippled so gaily –
How silent you have become!
You do not bid me farewell.

With a hard, stiff crust
you have covered yourself,
and you lie cold and motionless
stretched out in the sand.

On to your surface I carve
(with a sharp stone)
the name of my love,
and the hour and day:

The day of our first greeting,
and the day I went away:
a broken ring twines
round name and figures.

My heart, do you now see
your own likeness in this stream?
Is there a raging torrent
beneath *its* surface too?

(8) *A Backward Glance*

The soles of my feet are burning,
though I tread on ice and snow.
I do not want to draw breath again
until the turrets are out of sight.

I bruised myself on every stone
in my hurry to leave the town;
the crows threw snow and hailstones
on to my hat from all the house-tops.

How differently you once received me,
fickle town!
Before your bright windows
lark and nightingale vied in song.

The round lime-trees were in flower,
the fountains played limpid and clear,
and two fair eyes flashed fire –
and then, friend, you lost your heart.

When I think of that day
I long to look back,
I long to stumble back
and stand before her house.

(9) *Irrlicht*

In die tiefsten Felsengründe
Lockte mich ein Irrlicht hin:
Wie ich einen Ausgang finde,
Liegt nicht schwer mir in dem Sinn.

Bin gewohnt das Irregehen.
's führt ja jeder Weg zum Ziel:
Unsre Freuden, unsre Leiden,
Alles eines Irrlichts Spiel!

Durch des Bergstrom's trockne Rinnen
Wind' ich ruhig mich hinab;
Jeder Strom wird's Meer gewinnen,
Jedes Leiden auch sein Grab.

(10) *Rast*

Nun merk ich erst, wie müd ich bin,
Da ich zur Ruh mich lege;
Das Wandern hielt mich munter hin
Auf unwirtbarem Wege.

Die Füße frugen nicht nach Rast,
Es war zu kalt zum Stehen;
Der Rücken fühlte keine Last,
Der Sturm half fort mich wehen.

In eines Köhlers engem Haus
Hab Obdach ich gefunden;
Doch meine Glieder ruhn nicht aus,
So brennen ihre Wunden.

Auch du, mein Herz, in Kampf und Sturm
So wild und so verwegen,
Fühlst in der Still' erst deinen Wurm
mit heißem Stich sich regen!

(11) *Frühlingstraum*

Ich träumte von bunten Blumen,
So wie sie wohl blühen im Mai;
Ich träumte von grünen Wiesen,
Von lustigem Vogelgeschrei.

Und als die Hähne krähten,
Da ward mein Auge wach;
Da war es kalt und finster
Es schrieen die Raben vom Dach.

(9) *Will-o'-the-Wisp*

A will-o'-the-wisp lured me
deep into the mountains;
how to find my way out again
does not worry me greatly.

I am used to going astray,
every path leads to the goal.
Our joys, our sorrows
are all a will-o'-the-wisp's game.

Through the dry bed of the mountain-
stream
I calmly go on my way.
Every stream will reach the sea,
every sorrow will reach its grave.

(10) *Rest*

Only now that I lie down to rest
I notice how tired I am;
wandering kept up my spirits
on the inhospitable road.

My feet demanded no rest —
it was too cold to stand still;
my back did not feel its burden,
the storm helped to drive me on.

In a charcoal-burner's narrow hut
I found shelter;
but my limbs cannot find rest,
their wounds burn so.

You too, my heart, so wild and bold
in battle and storm —
now, in this quiet time, you feel your serpent
stir and sting.

(11) *Dream of Spring*

I dreamt of bright flowers
that blossom in May;
I dreamt of green meadows
and merry bird-calls.

And when the cocks crowed
my eyes opened;
it was cold and dark,
and the ravens croaked from the roof-top.

Doch an den Fensterscheiben,
Wer malte die Blätter da?
Ihr lacht wohl über den Träumer,
Der Blumen im Winter sah?

Ich träumte von Lieb um Liebe,
Von einer schönen Maid,
Von Herzen und von Küssen,
Von Wonne und Seligkeit.

und als die Hähne krähten,
Da ward mein Herze wach;
Nun sitz ich hier alleine
Und denke dem Traume nach.

Die Augen schließ ich wieder,
Noch schlägt das Herz so warm.
Wann grünt ihr Blätter am Fenster?
Wann halt ich mein Liebchen im Arm?

But who had painted those leaves
on the window-panes?
Do you laugh at the dreamer
who saw flowers in the winter?

I dreamt of love returned,
and of a beautiful girl,
of hugging and kissing,
of joy and delight.

And when the cocks crowed
my heart awoke;
now I sit here alone
and think of my dream.

I close my eyes again;
my heart still beats so warmly.
Leaves on my window, when will you grow
    green?
When will I hold my love in my arms?

(12) *Einsamkeit*

Wie eine trübe Wolke
Durch heitre Lüfte geht,
Wenn in der Tanne Wipfel
Ein mattes Lüftchen weht:

So zieh ich meine Straße
Dahin mit trägem Fuß,
Durch helles, frohes Leben
Einsam und ohne Gruß.

Ach! daß die Luft so ruhig!
Ach! daß die Welt so licht!
Als noch die Stürme tobten,
War ich so elend nicht.

(12) *Loneliness*

As a dismal cloud
drifts across clear skies
when a feeble breeze
blows through the fir-tops –

So I go on my way
with dragging step,
passing solitary and ungreeted
through bright, joyful life.

Alas – that the air should be so calm
and the world so bright!
When the storms still raged
I was not as wretched as this.

(13) *Die Post*

Von der Straße her ein Posthorn klingt.
Was hat es, daß es so hoch aufspringt,
mein Herz?

Die Post bringt keinen Brief für dich.
Was drängst du denn so wunderlich,
mein Herz?

Nun ja, die Post kommt aus der Stadt,
Wo ich ein liebes Liebchen hatt,
mein Herz!

(13) *The Post*

A posthorn sounds from the road.
Why do you leap so wildly,
my heart?

The post brings no letter for you.
Why then do you strain so strangely,
my heart?

I know – the post comes from the town
where I once had a sweetheart I dearly loved,
my heart!

Willst wohl einmal hinübersehn
Und fragen, wie es dort mag gehn,
mein Herz?

Do you want to look in
and ask how things are there,
my heart?

(14) *Der greise Kopf*

Der Reif hat einen weißen Schein
Mir übers Haar gestreuet;
Da glaubt ich schon ein Greis zu sein
Und hab mich sehr gefreuet.

Doch bald ist er hinweggetaut,
Hab wieder schwarze Haare,
Daß mir's vor meiner Jugend graut:
Wie weit noch bis zur Bahre!

Vom Abendrot zum Morgenlicht
Ward mancher Kopf zum Greise.
Wer glaubt's? und meiner ward es nicht
Auf dieser ganzen Reise.

(14) *The Hoary Head*

The frost has overspread my hair
with a hoary sheen;
I believed I had already grown old
and was overjoyed.

But soon it melted away,
my hair turned black again.
How I shudder at my youth –
how far off the grave still is!

Many a head has turned white
between dusk and dawn.
Who can believe it? mine has not changed
on all this long journey.

(15) *Die Krähe*

Eine Krähe war mit mir
Aus der Stadt gezogen,
Ist bis heute für und für
Um mein Haupt geflogen.

Krähe, wunderliches Tier,
Willst mich nicht verlassen?
Meinst wohl bald als Beute hier
Meinen Leib zu fassen?

Nun, es wird nicht weit mehr gehn
An dem Wanderstabe.
Krähe, laß mich endlich sehn
Treue bis zum Grabe.

(15) *The Crow*

A crow came with me
out of the town,
and has been steadily flying
above my head until today.

Crow, you strange creature,
will you not leave me?
Do you think my body will soon
fall prey to you?

Well, my journey will not
take me much farther.
Crow, let me see – at last! –
constancy unto death.

(16) *Letzte Hoffnung*

Hie und da ist an den Bäumen
Noch ein buntes Blatt zu sehn,
Und ich bleibe vor den Bäumen
Oftmals in Gedanken stehn.

Schaue nach dem einen Blatte,
Hänge meine Hoffnung dran;
Spielt der Wind mit meinem Blatte,
Zittr' ich, was ich zittern kann.

(16) *Last Hope*

Here and there on the trees
a coloured leaf may still be seen.
Often I stand in thought
before the trees.

I look at the one remaining leaf
and hang my hope upon it.
If the wind plays with my leaf
I tremble.

Ach, und fällt das Blatt zu Boden,
Fällt mit ihm die Hoffnung ab,
Fall ich selber mit zu Boden,
Wein auf meiner Hoffnung Grab.

And should the leaf fall to the ground
My hope falls with it;
I too fall on the ground
and weep on the grave of my hope.

(17) *Im Dorfe*

Es bellen die Hunde, es rasseln die Ketten;
Es schlafen die Menschen in ihren Betten,
Träumen sich manches, was sie nicht haben,
Tun sich im Guten und Argen erlaben;

Und morgen früh ist alles zerflossen.
Je nun, sie haben ihr Teil genossen,
Und hoffen, was sie noch übrig ließen,
Doch wieder zu finden auf ihren Kissen

Bellt mich nur fort, ihr wachen Hunde,
Laßt mich nicht ruhn in der Schlummer-
        stunde!
Ich bin zu Ende mit allen Träumen,
Was will ich unter den Schläfern säumen?

(17) *In the Village*

The dogs are barking and rattling their
        chains;
people are asleep in their beds,
dreaming of things they do not possess,
refreshing themselves in good ways or bad;

And in the morning all is vanished.
Well – they have enjoyed their share of life,
and hope to find in their dreams
what they have not yet tasted.

Chase me away with your barking, you
        watchful dogs,
give me no rest in these hours of sleep!
All my dreams are at an end;
why should I linger among the slumberers?

(18) *Der stürmische Morgen*

Wie hat der Sturm zerrissen
Des Himmels graues Kleid!
Die Wolkenfetzen flattern
Umher in mattem Streit,

Und rote Feuerflammen
Ziehn zwischen ihnen hin:
Das nenn ich einen Morgen
So recht nach meinem Sinn!

Mein Herz sieht an dem Himmel
Gemalt sein eignes Bild –
Es ist nichts als der Winter,
Der Winter kalt und wild!

(18) *Stormy Morning*

How the storm has torn
the grey robe of the sky!
Ragged clouds flutter
in feeble conflict,

and red flames
flash among them –
this I call a morning
after my own heart.

My heart sees its own likeness
painted on the sky;
it is nothing but winter,
cold, savage winter.

(19) *Täuschung*

Ein Licht tanzt freundlich vor mir her,
Ich folg ihm nach die Kreuz und Quer;
Ich folg ihm gern, und seh's ihm an,
Daß es verlockt den Wandersmann.

(19) *Delusion*

A friendly light dances before me,
and I follow its zigzag course.
I follow willingly and see
that it lures me off my path.

Ach! wer wie ich so elend ist,
Gibt gern sich hin der bunten List,
Die hinter Eis und Nacht und Graus
Ihm weist ein helles, warmes Haus
Und eine liebe Seele drin:
Nur Täuschung ist für mich Gewinn!

A man as wretched as I
gladly surrenders to such a brightly-hued
    guile,
which shows him – beyond ice, darkness, and
    terror –
a bright, warm house
and a dear one within.
Delusion – that is all I would win!

(20) *Der Wegweiser*

Was vermeid ich denn die Wege,
Wo die andern Wandrer gehn,
Suche mir versteckte Stege
Durch verschneite Felsenhöhn?

Habe ja doch nichts begangen,
Daß ich Menschen sollte scheun,
Welch ein törichtes Verlangen
Treibt mich in die Wüstenein?

Weiser stehen auf den Straßer,
Weisen auf die Städte zu,
Und ich wandre sonder Maßen,
Ohne Ruh, und suche Ruh.

Einen Weiser seh ich stehen
Unverrückt vor meinem Blick;
Eine Straße muß ich gehen,
Die noch keiner ging zurück.

(20) *The Signpost*

Why do I avoid the roads
used by other travellers,
and seek hidden paths
among the snow-bound rocks?

I have committed no crime –
why should I shun mankind?
What is this foolish desire
that drives me into the wilderness?

Signposts stand on the roads,
Pointing towards the towns;
and I wander ever onwards,
restless, yet seeking rest.

I see a signpost that stands
immovably before me;
I must travel a road
by which no one has ever returned.

(21) *Das Wirtshaus*

Auf einen Totenacker
Hat mich mein Weg gebracht.
Allhier will ich einkehren,
Hab ich bei mir gedacht.

Ihr grünen Totenkränze
Könnt wohl die Zeichen sein,
Die müde Wandrer laden
Ins kühle Wirtshaus ein.

Sind denn in diesem Hause
Die Kammern all besetzt?
Bin matt zum Niedersinken,
Bin tödlich schwer verletzt.

O unbarmherzige Schenke,
Doch weisest du mich ab?
Nun weiter denn, nur weiter,
Mein treuer Wanderstab!

(21) *The Inn*

My journey has led me
to a graveyard.
Here, I thought,
I will stay the night.

Green funeral wreaths –
you can be the inn-signs
that invite weary travellers
into the cool house.

Are all the rooms in this house
already taken?
I am weary and ready to sink,
I am mortally wounded.

Cruel inn,
will you yet turn me away?
On then, ever onwards,
my trusty staff!

(22) *Mut*

Fliegt der Schnee mir in's Gesicht,
Schüttl' ich ihn herunter.
Wenn mein Herz im Busen spricht,
Sing ich hell und munter;

Höre nicht, was es mir sagt,
Habe keine Ohren,
Fühle nicht, was es mir klagt,
Klagen ist für Toren.

Lustig in die Welt hinein
Gegen Wind und Wetter!
Will kein Gott auf Erden sein
Sind wir selber Götter!

(22) *Courage*

If the snow flies into my face
I shake it off.
If my heart speaks in my bosom
I sing brightly and merrily;

I have no ears
for what it tells me,
no feeling for its laments.
Let fools lament!

Gaily on into the world,
braving wind and weather!
If there is no God on earth,
we ourselves are gods!

(23) *Die Nebensonnen*

Drei Sonnen sah ich am Himmel stehn,
Hab lang und fest sie angesehn;
Und sie auch standen da so stier,
Als wollten sie nicht weg von mir.
Ach, meine Sonnen seid ihr nicht!
Schaut andern doch ins Angesicht!
Ja, neulich hatt ich auch wohl drei;
Nun sind hinab die besten zwei.
Ging nur die dritt' erst hinterdrein!
Im Dunkeln wird mir wohler sein.

(23) *Phantom Suns*

I saw three suns in the sky.
I looked at them long and fixedly
and they stood as firmly
as if they would never leave me.
You are not my suns!
Go, gaze into other faces!
Not long ago I had three suns –
now the two best have gone down.
If only the third would follow them –
I shall feel better in the dark.

(24) *Der Leiermann*

Drüben hinterm Dorfe steht ein Leiermann,
Und mit starren Fingern dreht er, was er
kann.
Barfuß auf dem Eise wankt er hin und her,
Und sein kleiner Teller bleibt ihm immer
leer.
Keiner mag ihn hören, keiner sieht ihn an,
Und die Hunde knurren um den alten Mann.
Und er läßt es gehen, alles wie es will,
Dreht, und seine Leier steht ihm nimmer still.
Wunderlicher Alter, soll ich mit dir gehn?
Willst zu meinen Liedern deine Leier
drehn?

(24) *The Hurdy-Gurdy Man*

Over there, beyond the village, a hurdy-
gurdy man stands,
grinding away with numbed fingers as best
he can.
He staggers barefoot on the ice
and his little plate remains ever empty.
No one wants to hear him, no one looks at
him
and the dogs snarl about the old man.
But he lets the world go by,
he turns the handle, and his hurdy-gurdy is
never still.
Strange old man – shall I go with you?
Will you grind your music to my songs?

18 D957 [LUDWIG RELLSTAB AND HEINRICH HEINE]

Seven Songs from Schwanengesang, op. posth.

(The first of these songs is by Rellstab; the others are by Heine.)

(1) *Ständchen*

Leise flehen meine Lieder
Durch die Nacht zu dir;
In den stillen Hain hernieder,
Liebchen, komm zu mir!

Flüsternd schlanke Wipfel rauschen
In des Mondes Licht;
Des Verräters feindlich Lauschen
Fürchte, Holde, nicht.

Hörst die Nachtigallen schlagen?
Ach! sie flehen dich,
Mit der Töne süßen Klagen
Flehen sie für mich.

Sie verstehn des Busens Sehnen,
Kennen Liebesschmerz,
Rühren mit den Silbertönen
Jedes weiche Herz.

Laß auch dir die Brust bewegen,
Liebchen, höre mich!
Bebend harr' ich dir entgegen!
Komm, beglücke mich!

(2) *Der Atlas*

Ich unglückseliger Atlas! Eine Welt,
Die ganze Welt der Schmerzen muß ich
    tragen.
Ich trage Unerträgliches, und brechen
Will mir das Herz im Leibe.

Du stolzes Herz, du hast es ja gewollt!
Du wolltest glücklich sein, unendlich
    glücklich,
Oder unendlich elend, stolzes Herz,
Und jetzo bist du elend.

(3) *Ihr Bild*

Ich stand in dunkeln Träumen
Und starrt ihr Bildnis an,
Und das geliebte Antlitz
Heimlich zu leben begann.

(1) *Serenade*   -

Softly my songs
cry to you through the night;
come down to me, my love,
into the silent grove!

Slender tree-tops rustle
and whisper in the moonlight;
you need not, my darling,
fear lurking treason.

Do you hear the nightingales sing?
They are crying to you,
with their sweet plaints
They beg favour for me.

They know the heart's yearning
and the pain of love;
with their silver tones
they touch every tender heart.

Let your heart too be moved –
hear me, my love!
Trembling I wait for you;
come: make me happy!

(2) *Atlas*

Unhappy Atlas that I am, I must bear a world,
the whole world of sorrows.
I bear what is unbearable
and my heart wants to break.

Proud heart – you have what you wished.
You wanted to be happy, infinitely happy,
or infinitely wretched – proud heart!
And now you are wretched.

(3) *Her Portrait*

I stood in dark dreams
and gazed at her portrait,
and the beloved features
took on a secret life.

Um ihre Lippen zog sich
Ein Lächeln wunderbar,
Und wie von Wehmutstränen
Erglänzte ihr Augenpaar.

Auch meine Tränen flossen
Mir von den Wangen herab.
Und ach! ich kann es nicht glauben,
Daß ich dich verloren hab!

(4) *Das Fischermädchen*

Du schönes Fischermädchen,
Treibe den Kahn ans Land;
Komm zu mir und setze dich nieder,
Wir kosen Hand in Hand.

Leg an mein Herz dein Köpfchen
Und fürchte dich nicht zu sehr;
Vertraust du dich doch sorglos
Täglich dem wilden Meer!

Mein Herz gleicht ganz dem Meere,
Hat Sturm und Ebb und Flut,
Und manche schöne Perle
In seiner Tiefe ruht.

(5) *Die Stadt*

Am fernen Horizonte
Erscheint, wie ein Nebelbild,
Die Stadt mit ihren Türmen
In Abenddämmrung gehüllt.

Ein feuchter Windzug kräuselt
Die graue Wasserbahn;
Mit traurigem Takte rudert
Der Schiffer in meinem Kahn.

Die Sonne hebt sich noch einmal
Leuchtend vom Boden empor
Und zeigt mir jene Stelle,
Wo ich das Liebste verlor.

(6) *Am Meer*

Das Meer erglänzte weit hinaus
Im letzten Abendscheine;
Wir saßen am einsamen Fischerhaus,
Wir saßen stumm und alleine.

Upon her lips played
a wondrous smile,
and what seemed melancholy tears
glistened in her eyes.

My tears too flowed
down from my cheeks –
and ah, I cannot believe
that I have lost you!

(4) *The Fisher Girl*

Lovely fisher girl,
let your boat glide to the shore;
come and sit by my side,
and hand in hand we will whisper together.

Lay your head on my heart
and be not too much afraid.
Fearlessly you entrust yourself
to the wild sea every day.

My heart is just like the sea:
it has its storms, its ebb, its flood;
and many a lovely pearl
rests in its depths.

(5) *The Town*

On the distant horizon,
like a misty image, appears
the town with its turrets,
veiled in evening twilight.

A damp gust ruffles
the grey expanse of water;
with weary strokes
the boatman rows my boat.

The sun rises once again,
radiant, from the earth,
and shows me the place
where I loved and lost.

(6) *By the Sea*

The wide sea glittered
in the last rays of evening;
we sat by the fisherman's lonely hut,
silent and alone.

Der Nebel stieg, das Wasser schwoll,
Die Möwe flog hin und wieder;
Aus deinen Augen liebevoll
Fielen die Tränen nieder.

Ich sah sie fallen auf deine Hand,
Und bin auf's Knie gesunken;
Ich habe von deiner weißen Hand
Die Tränen fortgetrunken.

Seit jener Stunde verzehrt sich mein Leib,
Die Seele stirbt vor Sehnen;
Mich hat das unglücksel'ge Weib
Vergiftet mit ihren Tränen.

The mist rose, the waters swelled,
the sea-gull flew hither and thither.
From your loving eyes
tears welled forth.

I saw them drop on to your hand –
and I sank to my knees;
from your white hand
I drank the tears.

Since that hour my body wastes away,
my soul dies of desire.
The unhappy woman
has poisoned me with her tears.

(7) *Der Doppelgänger*

Still ist die Nacht, es ruhen die Gassen,
In diesem Hause wohnte mein Schatz;
Sie hat schon längst die Stadt verlassen,
Doch steht noch das Haus auf demselben
    Platz.

Da steht auch ein Mensch und starrt in die
    Höhe,
Und ringt die Hände vor Schmerzensgewalt;
Mir graust es, wenn ich sein Antlitz sehe –
Der Mond zeigt mir meine eigne Gestalt.

Du Doppelgänger, du bleicher Geselle!
Was äffst du nach mein Liebesleid,
Das mich gequält auf dieser Stelle
So manche Nacht, in alter Zeit?

(7) *The Double*

The night is still, the streets are at rest,
my sweetheart lived in this house.
Long ago she has left the town,
but the house still stands where it always
    stood.

And there stands a man, who gazes upwards
and wrings his hands with grief and pain;
I shudder when I see his face:
the moon shows me my own features and
    form.

You ghostly double, pale companion –
why do you ape the pain of love
that tortured me, in this very place,
so many nights in times gone by?

JAKOB LUDWIG FELIX
MENDELSSOHN-BARTHOLDY

Born at Hamburg on 3 February 1809, into a wealthy, cultured, and respected family: his grandfather was Moses Mendelssohn, the philosopher and friend of Lessing. Mendelssohn's path through life was unusually smooth: he was educated by the best music-teachers available in the Berlin of his day (including Goethe's friend Zelter) and became a masterly pianist. At the age of seventeen he composed a work he was never to surpass: the overture to Shakespeare's *Midsummer Night's Dream*. He travelled abroad (visiting England ten times in all), became municipal director of music at Düsseldorf in 1833 and moved to Leipzig as director of the *Gewandhaus* concerts in 1835. As conductor and director of music he performed not only his own works, but also those of other composers – he helped, above all, to rescue the works of Johann Sebastian Bach from the neglect into which they had fallen. He died at Leipzig on 4 November 1847, at the zenith of his fame and popularity. His works include the oratorios *St Paul* and *Elijah, Walpurgisnacht* for solo voices, choir and orchestra, a number of (now forgotten) operas, incidental music to plays by Sophocles, Shakespeare, Racine, and Hugo, five symphonies, several concert overtures, seven string quartets, an octet, a violin concerto, and many pieces for solo piano (including forty-eight *Songs without Words*).

Although Brahms revered him as 'the last great master', Mendelssohn has had hardly any influence on the development of the German *Lied*. His songs, for all their melodiousness and sweetness, seem pale when compared with those of a Schubert or a Wolf; their unproblematic tunefulness recalls the eighteenth century and the Berlin school. Only occasionally – in the generous A flat major tune and fluttering accompaniment of 'Auf Flügeln des Gesanges', in the galloping fairy-music (clearly related to that of the *Midsummer Night's Dream* overture), and the hidden menace of 'Neue Liebe' – does Mendelssohn achieve in the song form anything as memorable as his 'Lieder ohne Worte'.

1 OP. 19/4 [HEINE]

Neue Liebe

In dem Mondenschein im Walde
Sah ich jüngst die Elfen reiten,
Ihre Hörner hört ich klingen,
Ihre Glöcklein hört ich läuten.

Ihre weißen Rößlein trugen
Goldne Hirschgeweih und flogen
Rasch dahin; wie wilde Schwäne
Kam es durch die Luft gezogen.

Lächelnd nickte mir die Königin,
Lächelnd im Vorüberreiten.
Galt das meiner neuen Liebe?
Oder soll es Tod bedeuten!

New Love

Not long ago I saw the elves
riding through the moonlit woods,
I heard their horns sound
and their bells tinkle.

Their little white horses bore
golden stags' antlers and flew
swiftly along; it was as if wild swans
drew through the air.

The queen nodded to me
and smiled as she rode past.
Did she mean my new love –
or am I to die?

2 OP. 34/2 [HEINE]

Auf Flügeln des Gesanges

Auf Flügeln des Gesanges,
Herzliebchen, trag ich dich fort,
Fort nach den Fluren des Ganges,
Dort weiß ich den schönsten Ort;

Dort liegt ein rotblühender Garten
Im stillen Mondenschein,
Die Lotosblumen erwarten
Ihr trautes Schwesterlein.

Die Veilchen kichern und kosen,
Und schaun nach den Sternen empor,
Heimlich erzählen die Rosen
Sich duftende Märchen ins Ohr.

Es hüpfen herbei und lauschen
Die frommen, klugen Gazelln,
Und in der Ferne rauschen
Des heilgen Stromes Welln.

Dort wollen wir niedersinken
Unter dem Palmenbaum,
Und Liebe und Ruhe trinken,
Und träumen seligen Traum.

On Wings of Song

On wings of song
I bear you away, my love –
to fields by the Ganges
where I know the most beautiful spot.

A garden full of red blossoms
lies in the soft moonlight there;
the lotus-flowers await
their dear sister.

The violets titter and whisper
and look up at the stars;
the roses secretively
tell each other fragrant tales.

The guileless, bright gazelles
leap near and listen;
and the waves of the sacred stream
Murmur in the distance.

There we will sink down
under the palm-tree,
quaffing love and peace,
and dreaming a blissful dream.

ROBERT ALEXANDER SCHUMANN

Born at Zwickau on 8 June 1810, Schumann grew up among books (his father was a book-seller and publisher) and was soon drawn with equal power to music and literature. After several semesters as a law student at the universities of Leipzig and Heidelberg, he decided to devote himself wholly to music and musical journalism. He founded the *Neue Zeitschrift für Musik* in 1834 and edited it for ten years. After a courtship as full of obstacles (and now as famous) as that of Robert Browning and Elizabeth Barrett, he married the gifted pianist Clara Wieck in 1840. In 1844 he moved from Leipzig to Dresden, where he headed a music academy, and followed in 1850 a call to Düsseldorf, where he became municipal director of music. In 1853, after a stormy and unhappy time in his new post, alarming symptoms showed that Schumann was losing his reason; he attempted, unsuccessfully, to commit suicide in 1854, and spent the rest of his life as a patient in an asylum at Endenich near Bonn. He died on 29 July 1856. His works include the opera *Genoveva*, fifteen choral works, four symphonies five concert overtures, and thirty-six opus numbers of music for solo piano, including 'Davidsbündlertänze', 'Carnaval', 'Kinderszenen', and 'Kreisleriana'. He left thirty-five opus numbers of solo songs, including several cycles and *Liederkreise*.

Schumann was a composer for the piano before he turned to the *Lied* – and it is not, there-fore, surprising to find that in many of his songs the piano 'accompaniment' is as important as (sometimes even more important than) the vocal line. In his earliest and best works the most distinguished music is often to be found in piano preludes and postludes; the piano answers the voice, or contradicts it, or develops what it leaves unspoken. He is a master at creating an atmosphere that is dream-like, delicate and yet precise: of 'Auf einer Burg', with its falling fifth and ascending third, Hans Pfitzner said: 'One *knows* it is three o'clock in the afternoon.' Two poets brought out the best in him: Eichendorff, whose romantically en-chanted world he matched (as in the peerless 'Mondnacht') with equally enchanted music; and Heine, whose blend of simplicity and sophistication, melancholy and irony, inspired 'Dichterliebe' and *Liederkreis* Op. 24.

I OP. 25/3 [JULIUS MOSEN]

Der Nußbaum

Es grünet ein Nußbaum vor dem Haus,
Duftig, luftig breitet er blättrig die Blätter aus.
Viel liebliche Blüten stehen dran;
Linde Winde kommen, sie herzlich zu umfahn.
Es flüstern je zwei zu zwei gepaart,
Neigend, beugend zierlich zum Kusse die Häuptchen zart.
Sie flüstern von einem Mägdlein,
Das dächte die Nächte und Tage lang,
Wüßte, ach! selber nicht was.
Sie flüstern – wer mag verstehn so gar leise Weis? –

The Nut Tree

In front of the house stands a green nut tree;
fragrantly, airily it spreads its leaves.
It bears many lovely blossoms;
gentle winds come to caress them.
They whisper together in pairs,
gracefully inclining their gentle heads to kiss.
They whisper of a girl
who thinks night and day of –
she herself knows not what.
They whisper (but who can understand so soft a song?)

Flüstern von Bräut'gam und nächstem Jahr.
Das Mägdlein horchet, es rauscht im Baum;
Sehnend, wähnend sinkt es lächelnd in
    Schlaf und Traum.

of a bridegroom and the year to come.
The girl listens, the tree rustles;
longing and wondering she sinks, smiling,
    into sleep and dream.

2 OP. 35/6 [JUSTINUS KERNER]

Auf das Trinkglas eines verstorbenen Freundes

A Dead Friend's Drinking Glass

Du herrlich Glas, nun stehst du leer,
Glas, das er oft mit Lust gehoben;
Die Spinne hat rings um dich her
Indes den düstren Flor gewoben.

Beautiful glass, now you stand empty;
glass he so often raised with joy;
round about you the spider
has spun its dull web.

Jetzt sollst du mir gefüllet sein
Mondhell mit Gold der deutschen Reben!
In deiner Tiefe heil'gen Schein
Schau ich hinab mit frommem Beben.

But now in the bright moonlight I fill you,
with the golden juice of German grapes!
Into your sacred, luminous depths
I gaze with a pious shudder.

Was ich erschau in deinem Grund
Ist nicht Gewöhnlichen zu nennen.
Doch wird mir klar zu dieser Stund,
Wie nichts den Freund vom Freund kann
    trennen.

What I see down there
cannot be told to common men.
But in this hour I realize
that nothing can part friend from friend.

Auf diesen Glauben, Glas so hold!
Trink ich dich aus mit hohem Mute.
Klar spiegelt sich der Sterne Gold,
Pokal, in deinem teuren Blute!

In this faith, dear glass,
I drain you with good cheer.
The precious wine within the goblet
brightly reflects the golden stars.

Still geht der Mond das Tal entlang.
Ernst tönt die mitternächt'ge Stunde.
Leer steht das Glas! Der heil'ge Klang
Tönt nach in dem kristallnen Grunde.

The moon passes silently over the valley.
The midnight hour strikes solemnly.
The glass stands empty. The sacred sound
reverberates in its crystal depths.

3 OP. 49/1 [HEINE]

Die beiden Grenadiere

The Two Grenadiers

Nach Frankreich zogen zwei Grenadier,
Die waren in Rußland gefangen.
Und als sie kamen ins deutsche Quartier,
Sie ließen die Köpfe hangen.

Two grenadiers, who had been prisoners in
    Russia,
were making their way to France;
and when they came to their quarters in
    Germany
they hung their heads in sorrow.

Da hörten sie beide die traurige Mär:
Daß Frankreich verloren gegangen,
Besiegt und geschlagen das tapfere Heer
Und der Kaiser, der Kaiser gefangen.

There they heard the sad news
that France was lost,
the brave army conquered
and the Emperor a prisoner.

Da weinten zusammen die Grenadier
Wohl ob der kläglichen Kunde.
Der eine sprach: 'Wie weh wird mir,
Wie brennt meine alte Wunde!'

Der andre sprach: 'Das Lied ist aus,
Auch ich möcht mit dir sterben,
Doch hab ich Weib und Kind zu Haus,
Die ohne mich verderben.'

'Was schert mich Weib, was schert mich
    Kind,
Ich trage weit beßres Verlangen;
Laß sie betteln gehn, wenn sie hungrig
    sind –
Mein Kaiser, mein Kaiser gefangen!

Gewähr mir, Bruder, eine Bitt:
Wenn ich jetzt sterben werde,
So nimm meine Leiche nach Frankreich mit,
Begrab mich in Frankreichs Erde.

Das Ehrenkreuz am roten Band
Sollst du aufs Herz mir legen;
Die Flinte gib mir in die Hand,
Und gürt mir um den Degen.

So will ich liegen und horchen still,
Wie eine Schildwach, im Grabe,
Bis einst ich höre Kanonengebrüll
Und wiehernder Rosse Getrabe.

Dann reitet mein Kaiser wohl über mein
    Grab,
Viel Schwerter klirren und blitzen;
Dann steig ich gewaffnet hervor aus dem
    Grab –
Den Kaiser, den Kaiser zu schützen!'

Then the grenadiers wept together
at this sad news.
One said: 'I feel such pain
and my old wound burns so!'

The other said: 'All is lost.
I would like to die with you,
but I have a wife and children at home
who will perish without me.'

'What do I care for wife and child –
I have other, better desires;
let them go beg if they are hungry –
my Emperor, my Emperor a prisoner!

Grant me one boon, dear brother:
when I now die
take my body to France with you
and bury me in French earth.

My cross of honour on its red riband
you must lay on my heart;
put my musket in my hand
and gird my sword to my side.

So, like a sentry, I will lie in my grave,
and I will silently listen out
until one day I hear the roar of cannon
and the trot of neighing horses.

Then my Emperor will ride over my grave,
many swords will clash and glitter;
then I will rise, armed, from my grave
to protect the Emperor!'

4 OP. 64/2 [EDUARD MÖRIKE]

Das verlassene Mägdlein

Früh, wann die Hähne krähn,
Eh die Sternlein schwinden,
Muß ich am Herde stehn,
Muß Feuer zünden.

Schön ist der Flamme Schein,
Es springen die Funken.
Ich schaue so darein,
in Leid versunken.

The Deserted Servant-Girl

In the early morning, at cock-crow,
before the stars fade,
I must stand at the range
and light the fire.

The gleam of the flames is lovely,
the sparks fly up –
I stare into emptiness,
lost in my grief.

Plötzlich, da kommt es mir,
Treuloser Knabe,
Daß ich die Nacht von dir
Geträumet habe.

Träne auf Träne dann
Stürzet hernieder;
So kommt der Tag heran –
O ging er wieder!

Suddenly it comes back to me –
you faithless boy! –
that this night
I dreamt of you.

Tear after tear
falls from my eyes;
so the day comes –
if it would only go away again!

5 OP. 79/23 [MÖRIKE]

Er ist's!

Frühling läßt sein blaues Band
Wieder flattern durch die Lüfte;
Süße, wohlbekannte Düfte
Streifen ahnungsvoll das Land.
Veilchen träumen schon,
Wollen balde kommen.
Horch, von fern ein leiser Harfenton!
Frühling, ja du bist's!
Dich hab ich vernommen!

Spring is Here!

Once again spring trails his blue riband
fluttering through the air;
sweet, familiar scents,
full of promise, brush the land.
Violets already dream
of coming soon.
Listen – a harp sounds softly in the distance!
Yes, spring – it is you!
It is you I heard!

6 OP. 39 [JOSEF VON EICHENDORFF]

Liederkreis

(1) In der Fremde

Aus der Heimat hinter den Blitzen rot
Da kommen die Wolken her.
Aber Vater und Mutter sind lange tot,
Es kennt mich dort keiner mehr.
Wie bald, ach wie bald kommt die stille
    Zeit,
Da ruhe ich auch; und über mir
Rauscht die schöne Waldeinsamkeit,
Und keiner kennt mich mehr hier?

Song Cycle

(1) In Foreign Parts

The clouds come from my homeland
behind the red lightning,
but father and mother have long been dead,
and no one there knows me now.
How soon will that quiet time come
when I too shall rest, and
the lovely, lonely forests rustle above me
and no one here will know me?

(2) Intermezzo

Dein Bildnis wunderselig
Hab ich im Herzensgrund,
Das sieht so frisch und fröhlich
Mich an zu jeder Stund.

(2) Intermezzo

I bear your beautiful likeness
in the depths of my heart.
Gaily and brightly it looks at me
at every hour of the day.

Mein Herz still in sich singet
Ein altes, schönes Lied,
Das in die Luft sich schwinget
Und zu dir eilig zieht.

My heart sings softly to itself
an old and lovely song
that wings itself into the air
and flies swiftly to you.

(3) *Waldesgespräch*

Es ist schon spät, es ist schon kalt,
Was reitst du einsam durch den Wald?
Der Wald ist lang, du bist allein,
Du schöne Braut! ich führ dich heim!

'Groß ist der Männer Trug und List,
Vor Schmerz mein Herz gebrochen ist,
Wohl irrt das Waldhorn her und hin,
O flieh! Du weißt nicht, wer ich bin.'

So reich geschmückt ist Roß und Weib,
So wunderschön der junge Leib;
Jetzt kenn ich dich – Gott steh mir bei!
Du bist die Hexe Lorelei.

'Du kennst mich wohl – von hohem Stein
Schaut still mein Schloß tief in den Rhein.
Es ist schon spät, es ist schon kalt,
Kommst nimmermehr aus diesem Wald!'

(3) *Dialogue in the Woods*

It is late already, it is cold;
why do you ride through the woods alone?
The woods are long, you are alone –
You lovely bride – I will take you home.

'Great is the guile and the cunning of men;
grief has broken my heart.
The horn is sounding, now here, now there.
O fly! you cannot know who I am.'

Horse and rider are so finely arrayed,
your young body is so beautiful;
now I know you – may God protect me!
You are the witch Lorelei.

'Yes, you know me. From its high rock
my castle looks deep into the Rhine.
It is late already, it is cold –
you will never leave these woods.'

(4) *Die Stille*

Es weiß und rät es doch keiner,
Wie mir so wohl ist, so wohl!
Ach, wüßt es nur einer, nur einer,
Kein Mensch es sonst wissen soll!

So still ist's nicht draußen im Schnee,
So stumm und verschwiegen sind
Die Sterne nicht in der Höh,
Als meine Gedanken sind.

Ich wünscht, ich wär ein Vöglein
Und zöge über das Meer,
Wohl über das Meer und weiter,
Bis daß ich im Himmel wär!

Es weiß und rät es doch keiner,
Wie mir so wohl ist, so wohl!
Ach, wüßt es nur einer, nur einer,
Kein Mensch es sonst wissen so

(4) *Stillness*

No one knows, no one can guess
how happy I feel!
If only one other knew it,
no one else should.

The snow outside is not so still,
the stars in the heavens are not
so mute and silent
as my thoughts are.

I wish I were a little bird
and could fly across the sea –
across the sea and beyond,
until I reached heaven!

No one knows, no one can guess
how happy I feel!
If only one other knew it,
no one else should.

(5) *Mondnacht*

Es war, als hätt der Himmel,
Die Erde still geküßt,
Daß sie im Blütenschimmer
Von ihm nur träumen müßt.

Die Luft ging durch die Felder,
Die Ähren wogten sacht,
Es rauschten leis die Wälder,
So sternklar war die Nacht.

Und meine Seele spannte
Weit ihre Flügel aus,
Flog durch die stillen Lande,
Als flöge sie nach Haus.

(5) *Moonlit Night*

It was as if heaven
had softly kissed the earth,
so that earth, with its shining blossoms,
must dream only of heaven.

The breeze passed through the fields,
the corn swayed gently,
the woods rustled softly,
the night was bright with stars.

And my soul spread
wide its wings
and flew through the silent land
as if it were flying home.

(6) *Schöne Fremde*

Es rauschen die Wipfel und schauern,
Als machten zu dieser Stund
Um die halb versunkenen Mauern
Die alten Götter die Rund.

Hier hinter den Myrtenbäumen
In heimlich dämmernder Pracht,
Was sprichts du wirr, wie in Träumen,
Zu mir, phantastische Nacht?

Es funkeln auf mich alle Sterne
Mit glühendem Liebesblick,
Es redet trunken die Ferne
Wie von künftigem großen Glück!

(6) *A Lovely Foreign Land*

The tree-tops rustle and shudder
as though at this hour
the ancient gods were making the round
of the half-ruined walls.

Here, under the myrtles,
in secret, twilit splendour –
what are you saying to me, fantastic night?
I hear it vaguely, as in a dream.

All the stars shine down on me
with fiery glances of love,
and the distance speaks with ecstasy
of some great happiness to come.

(7) *Auf einer Burg*

Eingeschlafen auf der Lauer
Oben ist der alte Ritter;
Drüben gehen Regenschauer,
Und der Wald rauscht durch das Gitter.

Eingewachsen Bart und Haare,
Und versteinert Brust und Krause,
Sitzt er viele hundert Jahre
Oben in der stillen Klause.

Draußen ist es still und friedlich,
Alle sind ins Tal gezogen,
Waldesvögel einsam singen
In den leeren Fensterbogen.

(7) *In a Castle*

Up there, at his look-out,
the old knight has fallen asleep.
The rain is showering down
and the forest rustles through the portcullis.

With his beard and hair grown into each
    other,
his breast and his ruff turned to stone,
he has sat up there in his silent cell
many hundreds of years.

Outside all is still and peaceful,
everyone has gone down into the valley.
Lonely woodbirds sing
in the empty window-arches.

Eine Hochzeit fährt da unten
Auf dem Rhein im Sonnenscheine,
Musikanten spielen munter,
Und die schöne Braut, die weinet.

On the sunlit Rhine down there
a wedding-party sails by;
musicians strike up merrily,
and the lovely bride weeps.

(8) *In der Fremde*

Ich hör die Bächlein rauschen
Im Walde her und hin,
Im Walde, in dem Rauschen
Ich weiß nicht, wo ich bin.

Die Nachtigallen schlagen
Hier in der Einsamkeit,
Als wollten sie was sagen
Von der alten schönen Zeit.

Die Mondesschimmer fliegen,
Als säh ich unter mir
Das Schloß im Tale liegen,
Und ist doch so weit von hier!

Als müßte in dem Garten
Voll Rosen weiß und rot,
Meine Liebste auf mich warten,
Und ist doch so lange tot.

(8) *In Foreign Parts*

I hear the brooks rippling
all through the forest;
amid these forest-murmurs
I know not where I am.

The nightingales are calling
through this solitude
as if they wanted to tell
of beautiful times long past.

The moonbeams flicker
as if I saw below me
the castle in the valley –
yet it lies so far from here!

As though in the garden
full of white and red roses
my love were awaiting me –
yet she died long ago.

(9) *Wehmut*

Ich kann wohl manchmal singen,
Als ob ich fröhlich sei,
Doch heimlich Tränen dringen,
Da wird das Herz mir frei.

Es lassen Nachtigallen,
Spielt draußen Frühlingsluft,
Der Sehnsucht Lied erschallen
Aus ihres Kerkers Gruft.

Da lauschen alle Herzen,
Und alles ist erfreut,
Doch keiner fühlt die Schmerzen,
Im Lied das tiefe Leid.

(9) *Sadness*

It is true – I can sing at times
as though I were happy;
but secretly tears well up
to relieve my heavy heart.

When spring breezes play outside
nightingales sing
their song of longing
from their gloomy prison.

Then all hearts listen,
and all are glad;
yet no one feels the pain
and the deep grief in the song.

(10) *Zwielicht*

Dämmrung will die Flügel spreiten,
Schaurig rühren sich die Bäume,
Wolken ziehn wie schwere Träume –
Was will dieses Graun bedeuten?

(10) *Twilight*

Dusk is about to spread its wings,
the trees shudder and stir,
clouds drift by like heavy dreams –
what means this fear as the world grows
grey?

Hast ein Reh du lieb vor andern,
Laß es nicht alleine grasen,
Jäger ziehn im Wald und blasen,
Stimmen hin und wieder wandern.

Hast du einen Freund hienieden,
Trau ihm nicht zu dieser Stunde,
Freundlich wohl mit Aug' und Munde,
Sinnt er Krieg im tück'schen Frieden.

Was heut gehet müde unter,
Hebt sich morgen neugeboren.
Manches geht in Nacht verloren –
Hüte dich, sei wach und munter!

(11) *Im Walde*

Es zog eine Hochzeit den Berg entlang,
Ich hörte die Vögel schlagen,
Da blitzten viel Reiter, das Waldhorn klang
Das war ein lustiges Jagen!

Und eh ich's gedacht, war alles verhallt,
Die Nacht bedecket die Runde;
Nur von den Bergen noch rauschet der
    Wald,
Und mich schauert's im Herzensgrunde.

(12) *Frühlingsnacht*

Überm Garten durch die Lüfte
Hört ich Wandervögel ziehn,
Das bedeutet Frühlingsdüfte,
Unten fängt's schon an zu blühn.

Jauchzen möcht ich, möchte weinen,
Ist mir's doch, als könnt's nicht sein!
Alte Wunder wieder scheinen
Mit dem Mondesglanz herein.

Und der Mond, die Sterne sagen's,
Und im Traume rauscht's der Hain,
Und die Nachtigallen schlagen's:
Sie ist deine, sie ist dein!

If you have a favourite deer,
let it not graze alone!
Hunters are moving through the woods,
    blowing their horns,
voices call – now here, now there.

If you have a friend on this earth
Do not trust him at this hour!
He may smile at you with eyes and lips,
but in false peace he thinks of war.

What wearily goes to its rest today
will rise tomorrow, new-born.
But much can be lost in the night –
be wary and watchful!

(11) *In the Woods*

A wedding-party passed by the hill-side;
I heard the birds singing;
many horsemen flashed by, the horn
    sounded –
it was a merry hunt!

And before I realized it, all was gone.
Night covers all around
only the forest still soughs from the moun-
    tain –
and my heart shudders within me.

(12) *Spring Night*

I heard the migrant birds
fly through the skies over the garden.
That means spring is here, with its sweet
    scents!
The flowers are beginning to bloom.

I want to rejoice, I want to weep:
I can hardly believe it true!
Old marvels shine down again
with the moonlight.

And the moon and stars say it,
the wood whispers it in its dream,
the nightingales sing it:
'She is yours!'

7 OP. 42 [ADALBERT VON CHAMISSO]

Frauen = Liebe und = Leben   *Woman's Love and Woman's Life*

(1)

Seit ich ihn gesehen,
Glaub ich blind zu sein;
Wo ich hin nur blicke,
Seh ich ihn allein;
Wie im wachen Traume
Schwebt sein Bild mir vor,
Taucht aus tiefstem Dunkel,
Heller nur empor.

Sonst ist licht – und farblos
Alles um mich her,
Nach der Schwestern Spiele
Nicht begehr ich mehr,
Möchte lieber weinen,
Still im Kämmerlein;
Seit ich ihn gesehen,
Glaub ich blind zu sein.

(2)

Er, der Herrlichste von allen,
Wie so milde, wie so gut!
Holde Lippen, klares Auge,
Heller Sinn und fester Mut.

So wie dort in blauer Tiefe,
Hell und herrlich, jener Stern,
Also er an meinem Himmel,
Hell und herrlich, hehr und fern.

Wandle, wandle deine Bahnen,
Nur betrachten deinen Schein,
Nur in Demut ihn betrachten,
Selig nur und traurig sein!

Höre nicht mein stilles Beten,
Deinem Glücke nur geweiht;
Darfst mich niedre Magd nicht kennen,
Hoher Stern der Herrlichkeit!

Nur die Würdigste von allen
Darf beglücken deine Wahl,
Und ich will die Hohe segnen,
Segnen viele tausendmal.

Will mich freuen dann und weinen,
Selig, selig bin ich dann;
Sollte mir das Herz auch brechen,
Brich, O Herz, was liegt daran?

(1)

Since first I saw him
I think myself blind;
wherever I look
I see only him.
As in a waking dream
his image floats before me;
in blackest darkness
it stands out the more brightly.

All else around me
is without colour and light;
I take no more pleasure
in my sisters' games;
I would rather weep quietly
in my little room;
since first I saw him
I think myself blind.

(2)

He, the most wonderful of men,
how tender he is, how kind!
Gentle lips, bright eyes,
a clear mind and firm courage.

As that star shines brightly and gloriously
in the deep blue,
so he shines in my heaven,
bright and glorious, exalted and remote.

Follow your course –
I will only gaze on your brightness,
look at it humbly
and be happy and sad!

Do not hear the silent prayer
I offer up for your happiness;
you must not know this lowly handmaid,
my glorious, distant star!

Only the worthiest
may be made happy by your choice,
and I will bless her
many thousand times.

Then I will rejoice and weep,
then I am happy, happy;
Even if my heart should break –
break, heart – what does it matter!

(3)
Ich kann's nicht fassen, nicht glauben,
Es hat ein Traum mich berückt;
Wie hätt er doch unter allen
Mich Arme erhöht und beglückt?

Mir war's, er habe gesprochen:
'Ich bin auf ewig dein',
Mir war's – ich träume noch immer,
Es kann ja nimmer so sein.

O laß im Traume mich sterben,
Gewieget an seiner Brust,
Den seligsten Tod mich schlürfen
In Tränen unendlicher Lust.

(4)
Du Ring an meinem Finger,
Mein goldenes Ringelein,
Ich drücke dich fromm an die Lippen,
Dich fromm an das Herze mein.

Ich hatt ihn ausgeträumet,
Der Kindheit friedlich schönen Traum,
Ich fand allein mich, verloren
Im öden, unendlichen Raum.

Du Ring an meinem Finger
Da hast du mich erst belehrt,
Hast meinem Blick erschlossen
Des Lebens unendlichen, tiefen Wert.

Ich will ihm dienen, ihm leben,
Ihm angehören ganz,
Hin selber mich geben und finden
Verklärt mich in seinem Glanz.

Du Ring an meinem Finger,
Mein goldenes Ringelein,
Ich drücke dich fromm an die Lippen
Dich fromm an das Herze mein.

(5)
Helft mir, ihr Schwestern,
Freundlich mich schmücken,
Dient der Glücklichen heute mir,
Windet geschäftig
Mir um die Stirne
Noch der blühenden Myrte Zier.

Als ich befriedigt,
Freudigen Herzens,
Sonst dem Geliebten im Arme lag,

(3)
I cannot grasp it, I cannot believe it;
a dream must be deceiving me.
How, out of all the others,
could he have honoured and blessed me?

I thought I heard him say:
'I am yours for ever.'
I thought – but I must be still dreaming,
for surely it could not be.

O let me die in this dream;
cradled against his heart
let me drink in most delicious death
with tears of unending joy.

(4)
Ring on my finger,
little golden ring –
devoutly I press you to my lips
and to my heart.

The peaceful, blissful dream of childhood
had ended,
and I found myself alone, lost
in a dreary, limitless waste.

Ring on my finger,
you taught me;
you opened my eyes
to the limitless, inexhaustible value of life.

I will serve him, live for him,
belong wholly to him;
I will give myself to him and find myself
transfigured by his brightness.

Ring on my finger,
little golden ring –
devoutly I press you to my lips
and to my heart.

(5)
Sisters, be kind, help
to adorn me,
serve me today in my happiness.
Busily twine
about my brow
the blossoming myrtle.

When, up till now, I lay, satisfied
and with joy in my heart
in the arms of my love,

Immer noch rief er,
Sehnsucht im Herzen,
Ungeduldig den heutigen Tag.

he still wished, impatiently
and with longing in his heart,
for this day.

Helft mir, ihr Schwestern,
Helft mir verscheuchen
Eine törichte Bangigkeit,
Daß ich mit klarem
Aug ihn empfange,
Ihn, die Quelle der Freudigkeit.

Help me, sisters,
to banish
a foolish fear,
that I may receive him
with an unclouded eye –
him, the source of my joy.

Bist, mein Geliebter,
Du mir erschienen,
Giebst du mir, Sonne, deinen Schein?
Laß mich in Andacht,
Laß mich in Demut,
Laß mich verneigen dem Herren mein.

My beloved,
Have you appeared to me?
Sun, do you shine on me?
In devotion
and humility
I bow to my lord.

Streuet ihm, Schwestern,
Streuet ihm Blumen,
Bringet ihm knospende Rosen dar,
Aber euch, Schwestern,
Grüß ich mit Wehmut
Freudig scheidend aus eurer Schar.

Sisters, strew
flowers before him,
offer him rose buds.
But you, sisters,
I bid a sad farewell
as I joyfully leave you.

(6)
Süßer Freund, du blickest
Mich verwundert an,
Kannst es nicht begreifen,
Wie ich weinen kann;
Laß der feuchten Perlen
Ungewohnte Zier
Freudighell erzittern
In dem Auge mir.

(6)
Sweet friend, you look at me
in wonder,
and cannot understand
why I weep.
Let the unaccustomed
pearly drops
tremble, joyously bright,
in my eye.

Wie so bang mein Busen,
Wie so wonnevoll!
Wüßt ich nur mit Worten,
Wie ich's sagen soll;
Komm und birg dein Antlitz
Hier an meiner Brust,
Will in's Ohr dir flüstern
Alle meine Lust.

How anxious my heart is,
how full of bliss!
If I only knew how
to say it in words;
come, hide your face
here on my breast,
that I may whisper in your ear
what gives me joy.

Weißt du nun die Tränen,
Die ich weinen kann,
Sollst du nicht sie sehen,
Du geliebter Mann?
Bleib an meinem Herzen,
Fühle dessen Schlag,
Daß ich fest und fester
Nur dich drücken mag.

Do you know now
why I weep?
Should you not see my tears,
my beloved?
Rest against my heart,
feel how it beats,
that I may press you against me
closer and closer.

Hier an meinem Bette
Hat die Wiege Raum,
Wo sie still verberge
Meinen holden Traum;
Kommen wird der Morgen,
Wo der Traum erwacht,
Und daraus dein Bildnis
Mir entgegen lacht.

Here by my bed
there is room for a cradle,
which may silently hide
my blissful dream.
The day will come
when the dream comes true
and your image
smiles up at me.

(7)

An meinem Herzen, an meiner Brust,
Du meine Wonne, du meine Lust!
Das Glück ist die Liebe, die Lieb ist das
   Glück,
Ich hab's gesagt und nehm's nicht zurück.
Hab überschwenglich mich geschätzt
Bin überglücklich aber jetzt.
Nur die da säugt, nur die da liebt
Das Kind, dem sie die Nahrung giebt;
Nur eine Mutter weiß allein
Was lieben heißt und glücklich sein.
O, wie bedaur' ich doch den Mann,
Der Mutterglück nicht fühlen kann!
Du lieber, lieber Engel, du
Du schauest mich an und lächelst dazu!
An meinem Herzen, an meiner Brust,
Du meine Wonne, du meine Lust!

(7)

At my heart, at my breast –
you my joy, my delight!
Happiness is love, love happiness –
I have said it and say so still.
I thought myself boundlessly happy,
but now I am happier still.
Only a mother who nurses
and loves the child she feeds,
only a mother can know
what it means to love and be happy.
How sorry I am for men
who cannot feel a mother's bliss!
Sweet angel,
you look at me and smile!
At my heart, at my breast –
you my joy, my delight!

(8)

Nun hast du mir den ersten Schmerz getan,
Der aber traf.
Du schläfst, du harter, unbarmherz'ger
   Mann,
Den Todesschlaf.

(8)

Now, for the first time, you have hurt me,
but this hurt is cruel.
Hard, pitiless man, you are sleeping
the sleep of death.

Es blicket die Verlaßne vor sich hin,
Die Welt ist leer.
Geliebet hab ich und gelebt, ich bin
Nicht lebend mehr.

Left all alone, I gaze before me;
the world is empty.
I have loved, I have lived,
and now I have no more life.

Ich zieh mich in mein Innres still zurück,
Der Schleier fällt,
Da hab ich dich und mein verlornes Glück,
Du meine Welt!

Softly I draw back into myself;
the veil falls.
There I am with you and my lost happiness –
you, my whole world!

8 OP. 48 [HEINE]

Dichterliebe

(1)
Im wunderschönen Monat Mai,
Als alle Knospen sprangen,
Da ist in meinem Herzen
Die Liebe aufgegangen.

Im wunderschönen Monat Mai,
Als alle Vögel sangen,
Da hab ich ihr gestanden
Mein Sehnen und Verlangen.

(2)
Aus meinen Tränen sprießen
Viel blühende Blumen hervor,
Und meine Seufzer werden
Ein Nachtigallenchor.

Und wenn du mich lieb hast, Kindchen,
Schenk ich dir die Blumen all,
Und vor deinem Fenster soll klingen
Das Lied der Nachtigall.

(3)
Die Rose, die Lilie, die Taube, die Sonne,
Die liebt ich einst alle in Liebeswonne.
Ich lieb sie nicht mehr, ich liebe alleine
Die Kleine, die Feine, die Reine, die Eine;
Sie selber, aller Liebe Wonne
Ist Rose und Lilie und Taube und Sonne.

(4)
Wenn ich in deine Augen seh,
So schwindet all mein Leid und Weh;
Doch wenn ich küsse deinen Mund,
So werd ich ganz und gar gesund.

Wenn ich mich lehn an deine Brust,
Kommt's über mich wie Himmelslust;
Doch wenn du sprichst: Ich liebe dich!
So muß ich weinen bitterlich.

(5)
Ich will meine Seele tauchen
In den Kelch der Lilie hinein;
Die Lilie soll klingend hauchen
Ein Lied von der Liebsten mein.

A Poet's Love

(1)
In the lovely month of May,
when all the buds opened,
love unfolded
in my heart.

In the lovely month of May,
when all the birds sang,
I confessed to her
my longing and desire.

(2)
From my tears
many blossoms spring,
and my sighs become
a choir of nightingales.

And if you will love me, child,
I will give you all the flowers,
and at your window
the nightingale shall sing.

(3)
The rose, the lily, the dove, the sun –
all these I once loved with passionate joy.
I love them no longer; I love only her
who is so small, so gentle, so pure, so
    unique;
she herself, the joy of all passion,
is rose, and lily, and dove, and sun.

(4)
When I look into your eyes
all my pain and sorrow vanish;
but when I kiss your lips
I have all my health again.

When I lay my head on your breast
heavenly bliss steals over me;
but when you say: 'I love you'
I must weep bitterly.

(5)
I will plunge my soul
into the lily's cup;
the lily shall resound and breathe forth
a song of my love.

Das Lied soll schauern und beben,
Wie der Kuß von ihrem Mund,
Den sie mir einst gegeben
In wunderbar süßer Stund.

(6)
Im Rhein, im heiligen Strome,
Da spiegelt sich in den Welln,
Mit seinem großen Dome,
Das große heilige Köln.

Im Dom da steht ein Bildnis,
Auf goldenem Leder gemalt;
In meines Lebens Wildnis
Hat's freundlich hinein gestrahlt.

Es schweben Blumen und Englein
Um unsre liebe Frau;
Die Augen, die Lippen, die Wänglein,
Die gleichen der Liebsten genau.

(7)
Ich grolle nicht, und wenn das Herz auch
bricht,
Ewig verlornes Lieb! Ich grolle nicht.
Wie du auch strahlst in Diamantenpracht,
Es fällt kein Strahl in deines Herzens Nacht.

Das weiß ich längst. Ich sah dich ja im
Traume,
Und sah die Nacht in deines Herzens Raume,
Und sah die Schlang, die dir am Herzen
frißt,
Ich sah, mein Lieb, wie sehr du elend bist.

(8)
Und wüßten's die Blumen, die kleinen,
Wie tief verwundet mein Herz,
Sie würden mit mir weinen,
Zu heilen meinen Schmerz.

Und wüßten's die Nachtigallen,
Wie ich so traurig und krank,
Sie ließen fröhlich erschallen
Erquickenden Gesang.

Und wüßten sie mein Wehe,
Die goldenen Sternelein,
Sie kämen aus ihrer Höhe,
Und sprächen Trost mir ein.

The song shall quiver and tremble
like the kiss from her lips —
the kiss she once gave me
in a wondrously sweet hour.

(6)
In the waves of the Rhine, that sacred
stream,
is mirrored
the great and holy city of Cologne
with its great cathedral.

In the cathedral stands a picture
painted on golden leather;
it sent friendly beams
into my life's wilderness.

Flowers and angels
hover about Our Lady;
her eyes, lips, and cheeks
are just like those of my love.

(7)
I bear no grudge, though my heart is
breaking,
O love for ever lost! I bear no grudge.
Though you glitter with splendid diamonds
no ray illuminates the darkness of your heart.

This I have long known. For I saw you in a
dream,
and saw the night that reigns in your heart,
and saw the serpent that feeds on your heart:
I saw, my love, how wretched you are.

(8)
If the little flowers only knew
how sorely my heart is wounded,
they would weep with me
to heal my anguish.

And if the nightingales knew
how sad and sick I am,
they would gaily sound
their refreshing song.

And if the golden stars
but knew my sorrow
they would come from their heights
to comfort me.

Sie alle können's nicht wissen,
Nur eine kennt meinen Schmerz;
Sie hat ja selbst zerrissen,
Zerrissen mir das Herz.

(9)
Das ist ein Flöten und Geigen,
Trompeten schmettern darein;
Da tanzt wohl den Hochzeitsreigen
Die Herzallerliebste mein.

Das ist ein Klingen und Dröhnen,
Ein Pauken und ein Schalmein;
Dazwischen schluchzen und stöhnen
Die lieblichen Engelein.

(10)
Hör ich das Liedchen klingen,
Das einst die Liebste sang,
So will mir die Brust zerspringen
Von wildem Schmerzendrang.

Es treibt mich ein dunkles Sehnen
Hinaus zur Waldeshöh,
Dort löst sich auf in Tränen
Mein übergroßes Weh.

(11)
Ein Jüngling liebt ein Mädchen,
Die hat einen andern erwählt;
Der andre liebt eine andre,
Und hat sich mit dieser vermählt.

Das Mädchen nimmt aus Ärger
Den ersten besten Mann,
Der ihr in den Weg gelaufen;
Der Jüngling ist übel dran.

Es ist eine alte Geschichte,
Doch bleibt sie immer neu;
Und wem sie just passieret,
Dem bricht das Herz entzwei.

(12)
Am leuchtenden Sommermorgen
Geh ich im Garten herum.
Es flüstern und sprechen die Blumen,
Ich aber wandle stumm.

Es flüstern und sprechen die Blumen,
Und schaun mitleidig mich an:
'Sei unsrer Schwester nicht böse,
Du trauriger, blasser Mann!'

All these cannot know my grief;
it is known to one alone –
for she herself
has broken my heart.

(9)
What fluting and fiddling
and braying of trumpets!
My love is dancing
her wedding round.

Amid the tinkling and blaring,
the drumming and piping,
the dear little angels
sob and sigh.

(10)
When I hear the little song
that my love once sang,
a wild anguish
strains to break my heart.

A dark longing drives me
to the wooded heights;
my overwhelming grief
there melts into tears.

(11)
A young man loves a girl
whose choice fell on another.
This other loves yet another
and marries her.

Out of spite the girl takes
the first likely fellow
that comes along;
the young man is in a sad plight.

This is an old story,
yet it remains ever new;
and when it happens to someone
it breaks his heart.

(12)
On a bright summer morning
I walk in the garden.
The flowers whisper and speak,
but I walk in silence.

The flowers whisper and speak,
and look pityingly at me:
'Be not angry with our sister,
you sad, pale man!'

(13)
Ich hab im Traum geweinet,
Mir träumte, du lägest im Grab.
Ich wachte auf, und die Träne
Floß noch von der Wange herab.

Ich hab im Traum geweinet,
Mir träum', du verließest mich.
Ich wachte auf, und ich weinte
Noch lange bitterlich.

Ich hab im Traum geweinet,
Mir träumte, du wärst mir noch gut.
Ich wachte auf, und noch immer
Strömt meine Tränenflut.

(14)
Allnächtlich im Traume seh ich dich,
Und sehe dich freundlich grüßen,
Und laut aufweinend stürz ich mich
Zu deinen süßen Füssen.

Du siehest mich an wehmütiglich
Und schüttelst das blonde Köpfchen;
Aus deinen Augen schleichen sich
Die Perlentränentröpfchen.

Du sagst mir heimlich ein leises Wort,
Und gibst mir den Strauß von Zypressen.
Ich wache auf, und der Strauß ist fort,
Und's Wort hab ich vergessen.

(15)
Aus alten Märchen winkt es
Hervor mit weißer Hand,
Da singt es und da klingt es
Von einem Zauberland;

Wo bunte Blumen blühen
Im goldnen Abendlicht,
Und lieblich duftend glühen,
Mit bräutlichem Gesicht;

Und grüne Bäume singen
Uralte Melodein,
Die Lüfte heimlich klingen,
Und Vögel schmettern drein;

Und Nebelbilder steigen
Wohl aus der Erd hervor,
Und tanzen luft'gen Reigen
Im wunderlichen Chor;

(13)
In my dream I wept;
I dreamt you were lying in your grave.
I awoke, and a tear
still flowed from my cheek.

In my dream I wept;
I dreamt you deserted me.
I awoke, and still I wept
long and bitterly.

In my dream I wept;
I dreamt you loved me still.
I awoke, and my tears
are flowing still.

(14)
Nightly I see you in my dreams
and receive your kindly greeting,
and weeping aloud I cast myself
at your dear feet.

You look at me sadly
and shake your fair head;
pearly tear-drops
steal from your eyes.

Secretly you whisper a word in my ear
and give me a cypress wreath.
I wake, and the wreath is gone
and I have forgotten the word.

(15)
A white hand beckons
from old tales;
a singing and ringing tells
of an enchanted land;

where bright flowers bloom
in the golden light of evening,
with sweet scents
and glowing, bridal faces.

There green trees rustle
ancient melodies,
the air resounds softly,
and birds sing merrily,

and misty images rise
from the earth,
dancing their airy round
in strange concert.

Und blaue Funken brennen
An jedem Blatt und Reis,
Und rote Lichter rennen
Im irren, wirren Kreis;

Und laute Quellen brechen
Aus wildem Marmorstein,
Und seltsam in den Bächen
Strahlt fort der Widerschein.

Ach, könnt ich dorthin kommen,
Und dort mein Herz erfreun,
Und aller Qual entnommen,
Und frei und selig sein!

Ach! jenes Land der Wonne,
Das seh ich oft im Traum,
Doch kommt die Morgensonne,
Zerfließt's wie eitel Schaum.

(16)
Die alten, bösen Lieder,
Die Träume bös und arg,
Die laßt uns jetzt begraben,
Holt einen großen Sarg.

Hinein leg ich gar manches,
Doch sag ich noch nicht was;
Der Sarg muß sein noch größer
Wie's Heidelberger Faß.

Und holt eine Totenbahre,
Und Bretter fest und dick;
Auch muß sie sein noch länger,
Als wie zu Mainz die Brück.

Und holt mir auch zwölf Riesen,
Die müssen noch stärker sein,
Als wie der starke Christoph,
Im Dom zu Köln am Rhein.

Die sollen den Sarg forttragen,
Und senken in's Meer hinab;
Denn solchem großen Sarge
Gebührt ein großes Grab.

Wißt ihr, warum der Sarg wohl
So groß und schwer mag sein?
Ich senkt auch meine Liebe
Und meinen Schmerz hinein.

Blue sparks burn
on every leaf and twig,
red flames whirl
in a strange wild circle,

and murmuring springs gush
from wild marble rocks,
and the brooks show
strange reflections.

If I could only go there
and gladden my heart,
be relieved of my anguish
and be happy and free!

That land of bliss
I often see in my dreams;
but with the morning sun
it dissolves like foam.

(16)
The bad old songs,
the bad, wicked dreams —
let us bury them.
Fetch a large coffin.

I will put many things in the coffin,
but will not yet say what they are.
It must be larger
than the Great Tun of Heidelberg.

And fetch a bier
with thick, strong boards.
The bier must be longer
than the bridge at Mainz.

And fetch me twelve giants;
they must be stronger
than the strong Saint Christopher
in Cologne Cathedral.

They must bear the coffin away
and bury it deep in the sea;
for so large a coffin
must have a large grave.

Do you know why the coffin
should be so large and so heavy?
I laid all my love
and my grief into it.

FRANZ (FERENCZ) LISZT

Born at Raiding in Hungary on 22 October 1811, the son of a steward on the Esterházy estates. He soon attracted attention as a pianist – giving his first concert at the early age of nine – and received a thorough musical training at Vienna and Paris. He became famous throughout Europe as an interpreter of other men's work as well as his own, and spent most of his life on concert tours – he was *the* piano virtuoso of his age as Paganini was *the* virtuoso of the violin. In 1848 he settled (with Princess Caroline Sayn-Wittgenstein, who had fallen in love with him during his tour of Russia and Poland) at Weimar, where he guided the fortunes of opera and orchestra until 1861. After 1861, he lived alternately in Rome, Budapest, and Weimar, becoming a secular priest (the *Abbé* Liszt) in 1865. He died at Beyreuth on 31 June 1886, on a visit to his daughter Cosima who had married Richard Wagner. Liszt wrote over fifty songs, two oratorios, four masses, two piano concertos, and a large number of compositions for solo piano, including *Hungarian Rhapsodies*, *Années de pèlerinage*, and *Consolations*, and many transcriptions of operas, symphonies, and songs.

Liszt once described Schubert's songs as 'miniature operas' – a description far more appropriate to his own, which are often (like his setting of Heine's 'Lorelei') too elaborate for their text. They are chiefly remarkable for bold harmonic progressions (bolder even than anything attempted by Schumann) and for a colouristic use of the piano which makes that instrument sing like an orchestra. His finest works are not the great theatrical show-pieces like 'Kennst du das Land,' but more intimate lyrical songs like 'Blume und Duft' (to a text by Hebbel) and – above all – the strange and subtle 'Glocken von Marling', written in 1874 and full of uncannily modern departures from accepted tonality.

I GROVE 273 [HEINE]

Lorelei

Ich weiß nicht, was soll es bedeuten
Daß ich so traurig bin;
Ein Märchen aus alten Zeiten
Das kommt mir nicht aus dem Sinn.

Die Luft ist kühl und es dunkelt,
Und ruhig fließt der Rhein;
Der Gipfel des Berges funkelt
Im Abendsonnenschein.

Die schönste Jungfrau sitzet
Dort oben wunderbar,
Ihr goldnes Geschmeide blitzet
Sie kämmt ihr goldenes Haar.

Sie kämmt es mit goldenem Kamme
Und singt ein Lied dabei;
Das hat eine wundersame
  Gewaltige Melodei.

Lorelei

I do not know why
I should be so sad;
a tale of times past
haunts my mind.

The air is cool, it is growing dark,
and the Rhine flows calmly by;
the mountain-top sparkles
in the evening sunshine.

A beautiful woman is sitting
up there in strange splendour;
her golden jewels flash brightly,
she is combing her golden hair.

She combs it with a golden comb
and sings a song
that has a strange
powerful melody.

Den Schiffer im kleinen Schiffe
ergreift es mit wildem Weh,
Er schaut nicht die Felsenriffe,
Er schaut nur hinauf in die Höh.

Ich glaube, die Wellen verschlingen
Am Ende Schiffer und Kahn;
Und das hat mit ihrem Singen
Die Lorelei getan.

The boatman in his little skiff
is seized with wild anguish;
he does not see the reefs,
he only looks to the heights.

I think the waves
swallow boatman and boat in the end;
and that the Lorelei has done
with her singing.

2 GROVE 320 [NIKOLAUS LENAU]

Die drei Zigeuner

Drei Zigeuner fand ich einmal
Liegen an einer Weide,
Als mein Fuhrwerk mit müder Qual
Schlich durch sandige Heide.

Hielt der eine für sich allein
In den Händen die Fiedel,
Spielt', umglüht vom Abendschein,
Sich ein lustiges Liedel.

Hielt der zweite die Pfeif' im Mund,
Blickte nach seinem Rauche,
Froh, als ob er vom Erdenrund
Nichts zum Glücke mehr brauche.

Und der dritte behaglich schlief,
Und sein Zymbal am Baum hing;
Über die Saiten der Windhauch lief,
Über sein Herz ein Traum ging.

An den Kleidern trugen die drei
Löcher und bunte Flicken;
Aber sie boten trotzig frei
Spott den Erdengeschicken.

Dreifach haben sie mir gezeigt,
Wenn das Leben uns nachtet,
Wie man's verschläft, verraucht, vergeigt,
Und es dreifach verachtet.

[Nach den Zigeunern lange noch
Mußt ich schaun im Weiterfahren,
Nach den Gesichtern dunkelbraun,
nach den schwarzlockigen Haaren.]

The Three Gipsies

I once saw three gipsies
lying by a willow-tree,
as my carriage wearily dragged itself
over a sandy heath.

One of them sat apart and held
a fiddle in his hands;
as the evening sun glowed around him
he played himself a merry song.

The second had a pipe in his mouth
and watched its smoke;
he seemed glad, needing nothing more on
     earth
to complete his happiness.

The third slept comfortably,
his dulcimer hung on the tree;
the wind brushed its strings
and a dream passed over his heart.

Their clothes showed
Holes and colourful patches;
but, bold and free, they scorned
all that fate might have in store.

They showed me three ways
of facing the dark side of life:
One may sleep it away, smoke it away,
     fiddle it away –
and despise it, like those three.

[For a long time I had to look back to those
     gipsies
after I had driven on:
back to their dark-brown faces
and their black curly hair.]

3 GROVE 328 [EMIL KUH]

'Ihr Glocken von Marling'

Ihr Glocken von Marling, wie braust ihr so
    hell!
Ein wohliges Lauten, als sänge der Quell.
Ihr Glocken von Marling, ein heil'ger
    Gesang
Umwallet wie schützend den weltlichen
    Klang.
Nehmt mich in die Mitte der tönenden
    Flut –
Ihr Glocken von Marling, behütet mich gut!

'Bells of Marling'

Bells of Marling, how brightly you ring out!
Your sound is sweet, like a bubbling spring.
Bells of Marling, your sacred song
embraces protectively the sounds of this
    earth.
Take me into the midst of your sounding
    flood –
bells of Marling, keep me from harm!

RICHARD WAGNER

Born at Leipzig on 22 May 1813, Wagner soon moved to Dresden, where his stepfather introduced him to the world of opera. He acquired a musical education and obtained posts with various operatic troupes and companies (Würzburg 1833, Magdeburg 1834, Riga 1837); then migrated to Paris, where he received a call to Dresden as *Hofkapellmeister* in 1841. In 1849, however, he was forced to flee to Switzerland after taking part in an abortive revolutionary rising; and there many of his greatest works were either written (*Tristan und Isolde*) or conceived and sketched (*Die Meistersinger, Der Ring des Nibelungen*). It was at Zürich, too, that he met, and fell in love with, Mathilde Wesendonk (see p. 189). In 1864 after staying at Biebrich and Vienna, Wagner was called to Munich by the new king of Bavaria, Ludwig II, who was forced by his ministers to dismiss Wagner from Munich in 1865, but who continued to support him generously until his death. From 1866 to 1871 Wagner lived and worked at Triebschen near Lucerne, after 1871 in Bayreuth, where his festival theatre was opened in 1876. He died at Venice on 13 February 1883. Wagner is best known for his operas and the *Siegfried Idyll* for small orchestra; but he also left a symphony, nine concert overtures, three marches for orchestra, a string quartet, several choral works, and seven settings of words from Goethe's *Faust*.

Wagner did not write many songs: the most notable are his early setting of Heine's 'Die beiden Grenadiere' (in a French translation) which, like the better known Schumann setting, introduces the tune of 'La Marseillaise'; and the five 'Wesendonk' songs which are sketches for *Tristan und Isolde*. But Wagner derived much inspiration from the German *Lied* – notably from the ballads of Loewe, which he greatly admired; and he has himself pointed out that the whole of *Der fliegende Holländer* unfolded from the germ of Senta's ballad, a song which bears unmistakable witness to Loewe's influence. In his turn Wagner – through his theory and practice – profoundly influenced the development of the *Lied*: the songs of Hugo Wolf and those of Gustav Mahler show clearly the veneration these composers felt for Wagner's musical and poetic principles.

1857–8 [MATHILDE WESENDONK]

| Fünf Gedichte für eine Frauen-stimme und Klavier | Five 'Wesendonk' Songs |

(1) *Der Engel*   (1) *The Angel*

In der Kindheit frühen Tagen
Hört ich oft von Engeln sagen,
Die des Himmels hehre Wonne
Tauschen mit der Erdensonne,

Daß, wo bang ein Herz in Sorgen
Schmachtet vor der Welt verborgen,
Daß, wo still es will verbluten,
Und vergehn in Tränenfluten,

In early childhood
I often heard tell of angels
who left the pure bliss of heaven
to come where earth's sun shines.

Where there is a sorrowful heart
that hides its grief from the world,
that bleeds silently
and dissolves in tears,

Daß, wo brünstig sein Gebet
Einzig um Erlösung fleht,
Da der Engel niederschwebt,
Und es sanft gen Himmel hebt.

Ja, es stieg auch mir ein Engel nieder,
Und auf leuchtendem Gefieder
Führt er, ferne jedem Schmerz,
Meinen Geist nun himmelwärts!

that fervently prays
for deliverance –
there the angel will fly down
and waft it gently to heaven.

Yes, an angel descended to me also,
and on shining wings
he bears my spirit – freed from all pain –
towards heaven.

(2) *Stehe still!*

Sausendes, brausendes Rad der Zeit,
Messer du der Ewigkeit;
Leuchtende Sphären im weiten All,
Die ihr umringt den Weltenball;
Urewige Schöpfung, halte doch ein,
Genug des Werdens, laß mich sein!

Halte an dich, zeugende Kraft,
Urgedanke, der ewig schafft!
Hemmet den Atem, stillet den Drang,
Schweigend nur eine Sekunde lang!
Schwellende Pulse, fesselt den Schlag;
Ende, des Wollens ew'ger Tag!

Daß in selig süßem Vergessen
Ich mög alle Wonne ermessen!

Wenn Auge in Auge wonnig trinken,
Seele ganz in Seele versinken;
Wesen in Wesen sich wiederfindet,
Und alles Hoffens Ende sich kündet,
Die Lippe verstummt in staunendem
    Schweigen,
Keinen Wunsch mehr will das Innre zeugen:
Erkennt der Mensch des Ew'gen Spur,
Und löst dein Rätsel, heil'ge Natur!

(2) *Stand Still!*

Rushing, roaring wheel of time,
you that measure eternity;
shining spheres in the vast universe,
you that encircle our earthly sphere –
pause, eternal creation;
enough of *becoming*, let me *be*!

Hold   yourselves   back,   you   generative
        powers,
Primal Thought that must ever create!
Stop all breath, silence every urge,
let there be peace for but one moment!
Swelling pulses, restrain your beating –
end, eternal day of the Will!

Then, in sweet forgetfulness
I may taste the full measure of my joy.

When eye blissfully gazes into eye,
soul drowns in soul;
when being finds itself in being
and all hopes are near their goal;
when lips are mute in silent amazement
and the soul wishes for nothing more –
then man sees Eternity's footprints
and solves your riddle, divine Nature!

(3) *Im Treibhaus*

Hochgewölbte Blätterkronen,
Baldachine von Smaragd,
Kinder ihr aus fernen Zonen,
Saget mir, warum ihr klagt?

Schweigend neiget ihr die Zweige,
Malet Zeichen in die Luft,
Und der Leiden stummer Zeuge
Steiget aufwärts, süßer Duft.

(3) *In the Greenhouse*

You high-arching leafy crowns,
you emerald canopies,
you children of distant climes –
why do you lament?

Silently you incline your branches
and make signs in the air,
and a sweet scent rises
as mute witness to your sorrows.

Weit in sehnendem Verlangen
Breitet ihr die Arme aus,
Und umschlinget wahnbefangen
Öder Leere nicht'gen Graus.

Wohl, ich weiß es, arme Pflanze;
Ein Geschicke teilen wir,
Ob umstrahlt von Licht und Glanze,
Unsre Heimat ist nicht hier!

Und wie froh die Sonne scheidet
Von des Tages leerem Schein,
Hüllet der, der wahrhaft leidet,
Sich in Schweigens Dunkel ein.

Stille wird's, ein säuselnd Weben
Füllet bang den dunklen Raum:
Schwere Tropfen seh ich schweben
An der Blätter grünem Saum.

(4) Schmerzen

Sonne, weinest jeden Abend
Dir die schönen Augen rot,
Wenn im Meeresspiegel badend
Dich erreicht der frühe Tod;

Doch erstehst in alter Pracht,
Glorie der düstren Welt,
Du am Morgen neu erwacht,
Wie ein stolzer Siegesheld!

Ach, wie sollte ich da klagen,
Wie, mein Herz, so schwer dich sehn,
Muß die Sonne selbst verzagen,
Muß die Sonne untergehn?

Und gebieret Tod nur Leben,
Geben Schmerzen Wonne nur:
O wie dank ich, daß gegeben
Solche Schmerzen mir Natur!

(5) Träume

Sag, welch wunderbare Träume
Halten meinen Sinn umfangen,
Daß sie nicht wie leere Schäume
Sind in ödes Nichts vergangen?

Träume, die in jeder Stunde,
Jedem Tage schöner blühn,
Und mit ihrer Himmelskunde
Selig durchs Gemüte ziehn!

Longingly
you spread wide your wings,
and embrace, deluded,
a horrid emptiness.

I know your grief, poor plant,
for our fate is alike;
though the light shines brightly around us,
this is not our home.

And just as the sun is glad to leave
the empty brightness of day,
so true suffering
assumes the dark mantle of silence.

It grows quiet, an anxious soughing
fills the dark room:
I see heavy drops hanging
from the green-edged leaves.

(4) Agonies

Every evening, Sun, you redden
your lovely eyes with weeping,
when, bathing in the sea,
you are surprised by an early death;

but you rise again in your old splendour,
and halo the dark world
when you wake in the morning
as a conquering hero.

Why should I then complain,
why should my heart be heavy –
if the sun itself must lose heart,
if the sun itself must go down?

And if only death gives birth to life,
if only agony brings bliss –
then I thank Nature
for giving me such agony!

(5) Dreams

What strange dreams are these
that enfold my spirit
and have not melted like bubbles
into dull nothingness?

Dreams that flower more fairly
with every hour of the day,
that float through my mind and bring
blissful intimations of heaven?

Träume, die wie hehre Strahlen
In die Seele sich versenken,
Dort ein ewig Bild zu malen:
Allvergessen, Eingedenken!

Träume, wie wenn Frühlingssonne
Aus dem Schnee die Blüten küßt,
Daß zu nie geahnter Wonne
Sie der neue Tag begrüßt,

Daß sie wachsen, daß sie blühen,
Träumend spenden ihren Duft,
Sanft an deiner Brust verglühen,
Und dann sinken in die Gruft.

Dreams that penetrate the soul
with glorious rays
and there paint a never-fading image:
forgetfulness of all, remembrance of one!

Dreams that are like the spring sun
which charms blossoms from the snow,
so that the new days may greet them
with unimagined bliss,

and they grow, flower,
spread their scent as in a dream,
fade softly against your breast
and sink into their grave.

ROBERT FRANZ

Born at Halle on 28 June 1815 (his family name being Knauth); studied music, despite the opposition of his father, at Dessau, and returned to his native town in 1837. His life was uneventful: he became principal of the academy of music at Halle in 1841, lectured and directed musical activities at Halle University, until deafness forced him to retire in 1867. The remaining years of his life he spent in retirement on a small pension, editing older musical (especially choral) works. He died at Halle on 24 October 1892. His works include over 300 songs, church music, and choral compositions.

Since the death of Elisabeth Schumann, Franz is hardly sung at all in our concert halls. This is not surprising, though many of his songs have a late romantic charm of their own: for Franz tends to be unadventurous in his key-relationships and (for most modern tastes) too uncompromisingly four-square in his melodic lines. He favoured above all the strophic song with few modifications, taking German folk-songs and hymns as his models. His most successful settings have texts by Heine and Mörike: these have a simple inwardness that contrasts with the complexities of Schumann's and Wolf's readings of these poets. He was highly respected by Schumann, Liszt, and Brahms; Brahms tried to persuade the great singer Julius Stockhausen to include Franz's songs in his recitals, and Liszt, in an essay devoted to his work, commended him as a 'psychic colourist' who sacrificed 'effect' to the expression of a gentle inner vision and perspicuity of form.

1 OP. 14/5 [LENAU]

Liebesfrühling

Ich sah den Lenz einmal
Erblühn im schönsten Tal;
Ich sah der Liebe Licht
Im schönsten Angesicht.

Und wandl' ich nun allein
Im Frühling durch den Hain,
Erscheint aus jedem Strauch
Ihr Angesicht mir auch.

Und seh ich sie am Ort
Wo längst der Frühling fort,
So sprießt ein Lenz und schallt
Um ihre süße Gestalt.

Love's Spring

Once I saw the Spring
fill the loveliest valley with blossoms;
I saw the light of love
in the loveliest face.

And now, when I walk alone
through the springtime woods,
in every hedge
I see her face too.

And when I see her in a place
from which spring has departed,
then a new spring blossoms and resounds
about her sweet form.

2 OP. 28/2 [MÖRIKE]

Ein Stündlein wohl vor Tag

Derweil ich schlafend lag,
Ein Stündlein wohl vor Tag,
Sang vor dem Fenster auf dem Baum
Ein Schwälblein mir, ich hört es kaum
Ein Stündlein wohl vor Tag.

Just before daybreak

While I lay sleeping,
just before daybreak,
a swallow sang softly (I scarcely heard it)
on the tree outside my window,
just before daybreak.

'Hör an, was ich dir sag,
Dein Schätzlein ich verklag:
Derweil ich dieses singen tu
Herzt er ein Lieb in guter Ruh,
Ein Stündlein wohl vor Tag.'

O weh! nicht weiter sag!
O still! nichts hören mag!
Flieg ab, flieg ab von meinem Baum!
Ach, Lieb und Treu ist wie ein Traum
Ein Stündlein wohl vor Tag.

'Hear what I have to tell you,
I accuse your sweetheart:
now while I sing to you
he holds another in his arms,
just before daybreak.'

Tell me no more!
I do not want to hear!
Fly away, fly from my tree!
Love and faithfulness are like a dream
just before daybreak.

JOHANNES BRAHMS

Born at Hamburg on 7 May 1833. Brahms's father was a double-bass player in the Hamburg Symphony Orchestra and saw to it that his son received the best musical education that was to be had locally. He became an accomplished pianist (occasionally practising his art in taverns and dancing-saloons in order to earn his keep); and his compositions aroused the interest first of the violinist Joseph Joachim and then that of Robert Schumann, who hailed his work in the *Neue Zeitschrift für Musik*. In 1858 he worked in Detmold as director of music, then as conductor of a ladies' choir at Hamburg; in 1862 he visited Vienna for the first time and settled there in 1863. For a short time he directed the Viennese *Singakademie*, but from 1864 onwards he made his living solely as composer and conductor of his own works. Brahms died at Vienna on 3 April 1897. Besides almost 200 songs for voice and piano accompaniment, Brahms published seven volumes of folk-song arrangements, six works for chorus and orchestra (including settings of Goethe, Schiller, and Hölderlin), a *German Requiem*, four symphonies, two concert overtures, two piano concertos, three string quartets, and a great deal of other chamber music and music for solo piano.

Brahms was a North German with the characteristic tendency of North Germans to melancholy and introspection; but he made his home in the south, where melancholy is diffused through a lighter, gayer atmosphere. Both these poles appear in his songs: the dark longings of his Klaus Groth settings are offset by the spirited rhythms of the *Zigeunerlieder*. As his models Brahms recognized Schubert and folk-song: he favoured the modified strophic form and gave primacy (in contrast to Schumann as well as Hugo Wolf) to the vocal line over the accompaniment. When judging other men's songs, he would often cover the upper stave of the piano accompaniment and look only at vocal line and bass. Nietzsche scoffed that his work showed 'the melancholy of impotence'; but this often-repeated criticism takes no account either of the gaiety of such songs as 'Vergebliches Stäandchen' or the passion and power of his last work, the *Four Serious Songs*. For all his conscious classicism and academicism, Brahms forged for himself a musical language as distinctive as that of Hugo Wolf: Arnold Schoenberg, in a famous essay, hailed him as a spiritual ancestor, a 'great progressive', 'a great innovator in the realm of musical language'.

I OP. 32/9 [GEORG FRIEDRICH DAUMER]

'*Wie bist du, meine Königin*'

'*What Delight you Give, Queen of my Heart!*'

Wie bist du, meine Königin,
Durch sanfte Güte wonnevoll!
Du lächle nur, Lenzdüfte wehn
Durch mein Gemüte, wonnevoll!

Frisch aufgeblühter Rosen Glanz,
Vergleich ich ihn dem deinigen?
Ach, über alles, was da blüht,
Ist deine Blüte wonnevoll!

What delight you give, queen of my heart,
with your gentle goodness!
If you but smile, spring wafts sweet odours
through my soul, filling it with delight.

Can even the glow of roses that have just
    bloomed
be compared with yours?
Beyond all that flowers
your bloom brings delight.

Durch tote Wüsten wandle hin,
Und grüne Schatten breiten sich,
Ob fürchterliche Schwüle dort
Ohn Ende brüte, wonnevoll!

Laß mich vergehn in deinem Arm!
Es ist in ihm ja selbst der Tod,
Ob auch die herbste Todesqual
Die Brust durchwüte, wonnevoll!

Should you walk through desert wastes
where sultry heat for ever broods,
green trees would at once spread their shade,
giving delight.

Let me die in your arms!
There even death, though it should rage
through the heart with fearful pangs,
would bring delight.

2 OP. 33/9 [LUDWIG TIECK]

'Ruhe, Süßliebchen, im Schatten' (aus 'Die schöne Magelone')

'Sweet Darling, Rest in the Shade' (from the cycle The Fair Magelone)

Ruhe, Süßliebchen, im Schatten
Der grünen dämmernden Nacht,
Es säuselt das Gras auf den Matten,
Es fächelt und kühlt dich der Schatten,
Und treue Liebe wacht.
Schlafe, schlaf ein,
Leiser rauscht der Hain,
Ewig bin ich dein.

Schweigt, ihr versteckten Gesänge,
Und stört nicht die süßeste Ruh,
Es lauscht der Vögel Gedränge,
Es ruhn die lauten Gesänge,
Schließ, Liebchen, dein Auge zu.
Schlafe, schlaf ein,
Im dämmernden Schein,
Ich will dein Wächter sein.

Murmelt fort, ihr Melodien,
Rausche nur, du stiller Bach,
Schöne Liebesphantasien
Sprechen in den Melodien,
Zarte Träume schwimmen nach.
Durch den flüsternden Hain
Schwärmen goldene Bienelein
Und summen zum Schlummer dich ein.

Sweet darling, rest in the shade
of this green, translucent night;
the grass soughs in the meadows,
the leaves fan you and cool you,
and faithful love watches.
Sleep, sleep,
the woods rustle more softly,
I am yours for ever.

Be still, you hidden songsters,
and do not disturb her sweet rest.
The thronging birds listen,
their loud song is hushed –
my darling, close your eyes.
Sleep, sleep
in the twilight
I will guard you.

Whisper your harmonious song,
sing on, gentle brook;
beautiful thoughts of love
speak through these melodies,
gentle dreams follow.
Through the murmuring grove
golden bees swarm
and hum you to sleep.

3 OP. 43/1 [JOSEF WENZIG]

Von ewiger Liebe

Eternal Love

Dunkel, wie dunkel in Wald und in Feld!
Abend schon ist es, nun schweiget die Welt.
Nirgend noch Licht und nirgend noch
      Rauch,
Ja, und die Lerche sie schweiget nun auch.

How dark it is in the woods and fields!
It is evening, and the world is still.
No more light, no more smoke –
and even the lark is silent now.

Kommt aus dem Dorfe der Bursche heraus,
Gibt das Geleit der Geliebten nach Haus,
Führt sie am Weidengebüsche vorbei,
Redet so viel und so mancherlei:

'Leidest du Schmach und betrübest du dich,
Leidest du Schmach von andern um mich,
Werde die Liebe getrennt so geschwind,
Schnell wie wir früher vereiniget sind.
Scheide mit Regen und scheide mit Wind,
Schnell wie wir früher vereiniget sind.'

Spricht das Mägdelein, Mägdelein spricht:
'Unsere Liebe sie trennet sich nicht!
Fest ist der Stahl und das Eisen gar sehr,
Unsere Liebe ist fester noch mehr.

'Eisen und Stahl, man schmiedet sie um,
Unsere Liebe, wer wandelt sie um?
Eisen und Stahl, sie können zergehn,
Unsere Liebe muß ewig bestehn!'

A lad comes from the village,
seeing his sweetheart home.
He leads her past the willow-copse
and speaks of many things:

'If you are abused and distressed,
if people abuse you for my sake –
then let our bond of love be severed
as quickly as it was tied;
let us part in wind and rain
as swiftly as we came together.'

The girl says:
'Our love cannot be severed!
Steel is strong, and iron too,
but our love is stronger.

'Iron and steel can be changed in the forge,
but who can change our love?
Iron and steel can be melted down,
but our love must endure for ever.'

4 OP. 43/2 [LUDWIG HÖLTY]

Die Mainacht

Wann der silberne Mond durch die Ge-
    sträuche blinkt,
Und sein schlummerndes Licht über den
    Rasen streut,
Und die Nachtigall flötet,
Wandl' ich traurig von Busch zu Busch.

*

Überhüllet von Laub girret ein Taubenpaar
Sein Entzücken mir vor; aber ich wende
    mich,
Suche dunklere Schatten,
Und die einsame Träne rinnt.

Wann, o lächelndes Bild, welches wie
    Morgenrot
Durch die Seele mir strahlt, find ich auf
    Erden dich?
Und die einsame Träne
Bebt mir heißer die Wang herab!

May Night

When the silvery moon gleams through the
    bushes
and casts his sleeping light on the grass,
when the nightingale calls –
then I wander sadly from bush to bush.

*

A pair of turtle-doves, hidden among the
    leaves,
coo down their ecstasy; but I turn away,
seeking gloomier shadows,
and tears of loneliness steal into my eyes.

When, O smiling vision that shines
like the dawn through my soul, shall I find
    you on earth?
And the lonely tear
trembles, scalding, down my cheek.

5 OP. 47/1 [DAUMER]

Botschaft

Wehe, Lüftchen, lind und lieblich
Um die Wange der Geliebten,
Spiele zart in ihrer Locke,
Eile nicht hinwegzufliehn!

Tut sie dann vielleicht die Frage,
Wie es um mich Armen stehe;
Sprich: 'Unendlich war sein Wehe,
Höchst bedenklich seine Lage;

Aber jetzo kann er hoffen
Wieder herrlich aufzuleben,
Denn du, Holde,
Denkst an ihn.'

Message

Gentle breeze, blow softly and sweetly
about my love's cheek,
play softly with her tresses
and do not hurry away.

If she should chance to ask
how I, poor wretch, am faring,
you must answer: 'His anguish was infinite,
his plight gave cause for great anxiety,

but now he can hope
to delight in life again:
for you, dear one,
are thinking of him.'

6 OP. 49/4 [TRADITIONAL, ARR. SCHERER]

Wiegenlied

Guten Abend, gut Nacht,
Mit Rosen bedacht,
Mit Näglein besteckt,
Schlupf unter die Deck:
Morgen früh, wenn Gott will,
Wirst du wieder geweckt.

Guten Abend, gut Nacht,
Von Englein bewacht,
Die zeigen im Traum
Dir Christkindleins Baum:
Schlaf nun selig und süß,
Schau im Traum's Paradies.

Lullaby

Good evening, good night,
slip under your coverlet
adorned with roses,
bedecked with pinks;
tomorrow, if God wills it,
you will wake again.

Good evening, good night,
guarded by angels:
in your dream they will show you
the Christ-child's tree.
Sleep sweetly now
and see Paradise in your dream.

7 OP. 63/8 [KLAUS GROTH]

'O wüßt ich doch den Weg zurück'

O wüßt ich doch den Weg zurück,
Den lieben Weg zum Kinderland!
O warum sucht' ich nach dem Glück
Und ließ der Mutter Hand?

O wie mich sehnet auszuruhn,
Von keinem Streben aufgeweckt,
Die müden Augen zuzutun,
Von Liebe sanft bedeckt!

'O Could I but Find the Way Back!'

O could I but find the way back,
the dear way to the land of childhood!
Why did I search for happiness
and leave my mother's hand?

Oh, how I long to rest
unmolested by striving,
to close my tired eyes
gently covered by love!

Und nichts zu forschen, nichts zu spähn,
Und nur zu träumen leicht und lind;
Der Zeiten Wandel nicht zu sehn,
Zum zweiten Mal ein Kind!

O zeig mir doch den Weg zurück,
Den lieben Web zum Kinderland!
Vergebens such ich nach dem Glück,
Ringsum ist öder Strand!

To cease all searching and peering,
to know nothing but gentle dreams;
not to see times change –
to be a child for the second time!

O show me the way back,
the dear way back to childhood!
Vainly I search for happiness,
on the desolate shore all around.

8 op. 84/4 [TRADITIONAL]

Vergebliches Ständchen

'Guten Abend, mein Schatz, guten Abend,
    mein Kind!
Ich komm aus Lieb zu dir,
Ach, mach mir auf die Tür,
Mach mir auf die Tür!'

Mein' Tür ist verschlossen, ich laß dich
    nicht ein;
Mutter die rät mir klug,
Wärst du herein mit Fug,
Wär's mit mir vorbei.

'So kalt ist die Nacht, so eisig der Wind;
Daß mir das Herz erfriert,
Mein Lieb erlöschen wird.
Öffne mir, mein Kind!'

Löschet dein Lieb, laß sie löschen nur!
Löschet sie immerzu,
Geh heim zu Bett, zur Ruh;
Gute Nacht, mein Knab!

Vain Serenade

'Good evening, my darling, good evening,
    my child!
Love brings me to you –
please open your door;
open the door!'

My door is locked, I will not let you in;
my mother has given me good advice.
If I gave you the right to come in
all would be up with me!

'The night is cold, the wind so icy
that my very heart will freeze
and my love will go out –
Open the door, my love!'

If your love goes out – let it!
If it goes out
you can go home to bed.
Good night, my lad!

9 op. 86/2 [HERMANN ALLMERS]

Feldeinsamkeit

Ich ruhe still im hohen grünen Gras
Und sende lange meinen Blick nach oben,
Von Grillen rings umschwirrt ohn Unterlaß,
Von Himmelsbläue wundersam umwoben.

Die schönen weißen Wolken ziehn dahin
Durchs tiefe Blau, wie schöne stille Träume;
Mir ist, als ob ich längst gestorben bin
Und ziehe selig mit durch ew'ge Räume.

Solitude in Summer Fields

Silently I rest in the tall green grass
and look steadily upwards;
crickets sing ceaselessly about me,
the blue of the sky encompasses me
    strangely.

The lovely white clouds drift
through the deep blue like lovely still
    dreams.
It is as though I had died long ago
and were now drifting with the clouds
    through eternal space.

10 OP. 94/4 [HANS SCHMIDT]

Sapphische Ode

Rosen brach ich nachts mir am dunklen
    Hage;
Süßer hauchten Duft sie als je am Tage;
Doch verstreuten reich die bewegten Äste
Tau, der mich näßte.

Auch der Küsse Duft mich wie nie berückte,
Die ich nachts vom Strauch deiner Lippen
    pflückte:
Doch auch dir, bewegt im Gemüt gleich
    jenen,
Tauten die Tränen.

Sapphic Ode

I gathered roses from the dark hedge by
    night;
the scent they breathed was sweeter than by
    day.
But when I stirred the branches they
    showered upon me
a profusion of dew.

The fragrant kisses too, which I gathered by
    night
from the rose-bush of your lips, enchanted
    as never before.
But you also, when your soul was stirred
shed the dew of tears.

11 OP. 96/1 [HEINE]

'Der Tod, das ist die kühle Nacht'

Der Tod, das ist die kühle Nacht,
Das Leben ist der schwüle Tag.
Es dunkelt schon, mich schläfert,
Der Tag hat mich müd gemacht.

Über mein Bett erhebt sich ein Baum,
Drin singt die junge Nachtigall;
Sie singt von lauter Liebe,
Ich hör es sogar im Traum.

'Death is the Cool Night'

Death is the cool night,
Life the sultry day.
It is growing dark, I grow sleepy:
the day has tired me.

A tree rises above my bed,
the young nightingale sings in its branches;
it sings only of love –
I hear it even in my dream.

12 OP. 105/2 [HERMANN LINGG]

Immer leiser wird mein Schlummer

Immer leiser wird mein Schlummer,
Nur wie Schleier liegt mein Kummer
Zitternd über mir.
Oft im Traume hör ich dich
Rufen drauß vor meiner Tür,
Niemand wacht und öffnet dir,
Ich erwach und weine bitterlich.

Ja, ich werde sterben müssen,
Eine andre wirst du küssen,
Wenn ich bleich und kalt.
Eh die Maienlüfte wehn,

My Slumber Grows Ever Softer

My slumber grows ever softer,
my grief now lies lightly upon me,
trembling like a veil.
In my dream I often hear you
calling outside my door.
No one wakes to open the door.
I awake and weep bitterly.

Yes, I must die,
you will kiss another
when I am pale and cold.
Before the May breezes blow,

Eh die Drossel singt im Wald:
Willst du mich noch einmal sehn,
Komm, o komme bald!

before the thrush sings in the wood
if you want to see me once more,
come, come soon!

13 OP. 105/4 [DETLEV VON LILIENCRON]

Auf dem Kirchhofe

Der Tag ging regenschwer und sturmbewegt,
Ich war an manch vergeßnem Grab gewesen,
Verwittert Stein und Kreuz, die Kränze alt,
Die Namen überwachsen, kaum zu lesen.

Der Tag ging sturmbewegt und regen-
schwer,
Auf allen Gräbern fror das Wort: Gewesen.
Wie sturmestot die Särge schlummerten,
Auf allen Gräbern taute still: Genesen.

In the Churchyard

The day was heavy with rain and rough with
storms;
I had stood by many forgotten graves
with weather-beaten stones and crosses,
faded wreaths,
and names so overgrown they could scarcely
be read.

The day was rough with storms and heavy
with rain;
the cold graves proclaimed: 'All is past.'
As the coffins slumbered, dead in the storm,
still dew on the graves proclaimed: 'All is
made well.'

14 FROM BRAHMS'S VERSION OF GERMAN FOLK-SONGS [DEUTSCHE VOLKSLIEDER, 1894]

No. 6: Trennung (Schwäbisch)

Dort unten im Tale
Läuft's Wasser so trüb,
Und i kann dir's net sagen,
i hab di so lieb.

'Sprichst allweil von Liebe;
Sprichst allweil von Treu,
Und a bissele Falschheit
Is auch wohl dabei.'

Und wenn i dir's zehnmal sag,
Daß i di lieb und mag,
Und du willst nit verstehn,
Muß i halt weitergehn.

Für die Zeit, wo du gliebt mi hast,
Da dank i dir schön,
Und i wünsch, daß dir's anderswo
Besser mag gehn.

Parting (Swabian dialect)

Down there in the valley
the brook runs so dully,
and I cannot tell you
how much I love you.

'You always speak of love,
you always say you are faithful,
but I am sure you are
just a little bit false.'

If I tell you ten times
that I love you and want you,
and you still won't understand me –
it is time for me to go.

For the time that you loved me
I thank you from my heart,
and I hope you may fare
better elsewhere.

No. 15 'Schwesterlein'

Schwesterlein, Schwesterlein, wann gehn wir
    nach Haus?
'Morgen wenn die Hahnen krähn,
Wolln wir nach Hause gehn,
Brüderlein, Brüderlein, dann gehn wir nach
    Haus.'

Schwesterlein, Schwesterlein, wohl ist es
    Zeit.
'Mein Liebster tanzt mit mir,
Geh ich, tanzt er mit ihr,
Brüderlein, Brüderlein, laß du mich heut.'

Schwesterlein, Schwesterlein, was bist du
    blaß?
'Das macht der Morgenschein
Auf meinen Wängelein,
Brüderlein, Brüderlein, die vom Taue naß.'

Schwesterlein, Schwesterlein, du wankest so
    matt?
'Suche die Kammertür,
Suche mein Bettlein mir
Brüderlein, es wird fein unterm Rasen sein.'

No. 25 'Mein Mädel hat einen Rosenmund'

Mein Mädel hat einen Rosenmund,
Und wer ihn küßt, der wird gesund;
O du! o du! o du!
O du schwarzbraunes Mägdelein,
Du la la la la!
Du läßt mir keine Ruh!

Dein Augen sind wie die Nacht so schwarz,
Wenn nur zwei Sternlein funkeln drin;
O du, usw.

Du Mädel bist wie der Himmel gut,
Wenn er über uns blau sich wölben tut;
O du, usw.

No. 33 'Och Mod'r, ich well en Ding han' (Kölnisch)

Och Mod'r, ich well en Ding han!
'Wat för en Ding, ming Hetzenskind?'
En Ding, en Ding.

'Sister, Dear Sister'

Sister, dear sister, when are we going home?
'Tomorrow at cock-crow
we shall go home;
then, brother, we shall go home.'

Sister, dear sister, it is time to go.
'My love is dancing with me –
if I go, he will dance with her;
dear brother, let me be tonight.'

Sister, dear sister, why are you so pale?
'It is the morning light
shining on my cheeks
that are wet with dew.'

Sister, dear sister, why this tired stumbling?
'Help me to the door of my room,
help me to my bed –
All shall be well, dear brother, under the turf.'

'My Girl Has Rosy Lips'

My girl has rosy lips,
who kisses them, will be cured of all ills.
O you
nut-brown maid,
you
give me no peace.

Your eyes are as black as the night
when it twinkles with only two stars;
O you, etc.

You are as good as the blue sky
that arches above us;
O you, etc.

'Mother, I Want Something!' (Cologne dialect)

Mother, I want something!
'What do you want, my darling?'
A thing, a thing.

'Wells de dann e Pöppchen han?'
Nä, Moder, nä!
Ehr sitt kein gode Moder,
Ehr könnt dat Ding nit rode!
Wat dat Kind för'n Ding well han,
Dingderlingdingding!

Och Mod'r, ich well en Ding han!
'Wat för en Ding, ming Hetzenskind?'
En Ding, en Ding.
'Wells de dann e Ringelchen han?
Nä, Moder, nä, usw.

Och Mod'r, ich well en Ding han!
'Wat för en Ding, ming Hetzenskind?'
En Ding, en Ding.
'Wells de dann a Kleidchen han?'
Nä, Moder, nä, usw.

Och Mod'r, ich well en Ding han!
'Wat für en Ding, ming Hetzenskind?'
En Ding, en Ding.
'Wells de dann eine Mann han?'
Jo, Moder, jo!
Ehr sitt en gode Moder,
Ehr künnt dat Ding wohl rode,
Wat dat Kind för'n Ding well han,
Dingderlingdingding!

'Do you want a doll?'
No, mother, no,
you are not a good mother,
you can't guess what things your child
     wants,
a thing-de-ring-ding-ding.

Mother, I want something!
'What do you want, my darling?'
A thing, a thing.
'Do you want a ring?'
No, mother, no, etc.

Mother, I want something!
'What do you want, my darling?'
A thing, a thing.
'Do you want a new dress?'
No, mother, no, etc.

Mother, I want something!
'What do you want, my darling?'
A thing, a thing.
'Do you want a husband?'
Yes, mother, yes!
You are a good mother,
you can guess what thing your child wants,
a thing-de-ring-ding-ding.

15 OP. 103 [TRANSLATION ATTRIBUTED TO HUGO CONRAT]

Zigeunerlieder

(1)
He, Zigeuner, greife in die Saiten ein!
Spiel das Lied vom ungetreuen Mägdelein!
Laß die Saiten weinen, klagen, traurig bange,
Bis die heiße Träne netzet diese Wange!

(2)
Hochgetürmte Rimaflut,
Wie bist du so trüb;
An dem Ufer klag ich
Laut nach dir, mein Lieb!

Wellen fliehen, Wellen strömen,
Rauschen an dem Strand heran zu mir.
An dem Rimaufer laß mich
Ewig weinen nach ihr!

Gipsy Songs

(1)
Gipsy, sound your strings
and play the song of the faithless girl!
Let your lamenting strings be full of fear and
     sadness
until tears scald my cheek!

(2)
How turbid, O Rima,
are your flooding waters!
I stand on the bank, and sadly
I call for you, my love.

The waves come and go,
flooding towards me on the shore.
On the banks of the Rima
Let me ever weep for her.

(3)
Wißt ihr, wenn mein Kindchen am aller-
    schönsten ist?
Wenn ihr süßes Mündchen scherzt und lacht
    und küßt.
Mägdelein, du bist mein, inniglich küß ich
    dich,
Dich erschuf der liebe Himmel einzig nur
    für mich!

Wißt ihr, wann mein Liebster am besten mir
    gefällt?
Wenn in seinen Armen er mich umschlungen
    hält.
Schätzelein, du bist mein, inniglich küß ich
    dich,
Dich erschuf der liebe Himmel einzig nur für
    mich!

(4)
Lieber Gott, du weißt, wie oft bereut ich hab,
Daß ich meinem Liebsten einst ein Küßchen
    gab.
Herz gebot, daß ich ihn küssen muß,
Denk, solang ich leb, an diesen ersten Kuß.

Lieber Gott, du weißt, wie oft in stiller Nacht
Ich in Lust und Leid an meinen Schatz
    gedacht.
Lieb ist süß, wenn bitter auch die Reu,
Armes Herze bleibt ihm ewig, ewig treu.

(5)
Brauner Bursche führt zum Tanze
Sein blauäugig schönes Kind;
Schlägt die Sporen keck zusammen,
Csardasmelodie beginnt.

Küßt und herzt sein süßes Täubchen,
Dreht sie, führt sie, jauchzt und springt;
Wirft drei blanke Silbergulden
Auf das Zimbal, daß es klingt.

(6)
Röslein dreie in der Reihe blühn so rot,
Daß der Bursch zum Mädel gehe, ist kein
    Verbot!
Lieber Gott, wenn das verboten wär,

(3)
Do you know when my sweetheart is
    loveliest?
When her sweet lips banter and laugh and
    kiss.
You are mine, sweet girl, I kiss you with all
    my heart;
heaven made you only for me.

Do you know when I love my sweetheart
    most?
When he clasps me tight in his arms.
Darling, you are mine, I kiss you with all
    my heart;
heaven made you only for me.

(4)
You know, dear God, how often I repented
giving my sweetheart (once) a little kiss.
My heart told me to kiss him,
and as long as I live I shall remember that
    first kiss.

You know, dear God, how often in the still
    night
I thought of my darling with pleasure and
    pain.
Love is sweet, though repentance is bitter;
my poor heart will ever be faithful to him.

(5)
The brown lad leads
his lovely, blue-eyed sweetheart to the
    dance,
His spurs clash boldly together
As the Czardas strikes up.

He embraces and kisses his sweet dove
leads her, spins her around, leaps full of joy,
he throws three shining silver florins
that make the dulcimer ring.

(6)
Three little red roses bloom side by side –
lads are not forbidden to go to their
    lasses!
Dear God, if that were forbidden

Ständ die schöne weite Welt schon längst
  nicht mehr;
Ledig bleiben Sünde wär!

this beautiful wide world would no longer
  exist.
To remain single – *that* would be a sin!

Schönstes Städtchen in Alföld ist Ketsch-
  kemet,
Dort gibt es gar viele Mädchen schmuck und
  nett!
Freunde, sucht euch dort ein Bräutchen aus,
Freit um ihre Hand und gründet euer Haus,
Freudenbecher leeret aus.

The loveliest town in Alföld is called
  Kecskemét;
it holds many fine, trim girls.
Friends, look for a bride there,
woo her and found a family –
drink the full cup of joy!

(7)
Kommt dir manchmal in den Sinn, mein
  süßes Lieb,
Was du einst mit heil'gem Eide mir gelobt?
Täusch mich nicht, verlaß mich nicht,
Du weißt nicht, wie lieb ich dich hab,
Lieb du mich, wie ich dich,
Dann strömt Gottes Huld auf dich herab!

(7)
Sweet darling, do you sometimes remember
what you vowed to me with a sacred oath?
Do not deceive me, do not desert me,
you know how much I love you.
Love me as I love you,
and God's grace will shine on you.

(8)
Rote Abendwolken ziehn am Firmament,
Sehnsuchtsvoll nach dir,
Mein Lieb, das Herze brennt,
Himmel strahlt in glühnder Pracht,
Und ich träum bei Tag und Nacht
Nur allein
Von dem süßen Liebchen mein.

(8)
Red clouds drift along the sky
longingly towards you.
My love, my heart is burning.
The heavens shine in flaming glory,
and day and night I dream
only
of my sweet love.

16 OP. 121 [LUTHER'S TRANSLATION OF THE BIBLE]

Vier ernste Gesänge

Four Serious Songs

(1)
Denn es gehet dem Menschen wie dem Vieh;
wie dies stirbt, so stirbt er auch; und haben
alle einerlei Odem; und der Mensch hat
nichts mehr denn das Vieh; denn es ist alles
eitel.

Es fährt alles an einen Ort; es ist alles von
Staub gemacht und wird wieder zu Staub.

Wer weiß, ob der Geist des Menschen
aufwärts fahre, und der Odem des Viehes
unterwärts unter die Erde fahre?

Darum sahe ich, daß nichts bessers ist, denn
daß der Mensch fröhlich sei in seiner Arbeit,

(1)
For that which befalleth the sons of men befalleth beasts; even one thing befalleth them;
as the one dieth, so dieth the other; yea, they
have all one breath; so that a man hath no
preeminence above a beast: for all is vanity.

All go unto one place; all are of the dust,
and all turn to dust again.

Who knoweth the spirit of man that goeth
upward, and the spirit of the beast that goeth
downward to the earth?

Wherefore I perceive that there is nothing
better, than that a man should rejoice in his

denn das ist sein Teil. Denn wer will ihn dahin bringen, daß er sehe, was nach ihm geschehen wird?

(2)
Ich wandte mich und sahe an alle, die Unrecht leiden unter der Sonne; und siehe da waren Tränen derer die Unrecht litten, und hatten keinen Tröster; und die ihnen Unrecht täten waren zu mächtig, daß sie keinen Tröster haben konnten.

Da lobte ich die Toten, die schon gestorben waren, mehr als die Lebendigen, die noch das Leben hatten;

Und der noch nicht ist, ist besser, als alle Beide, und des Bösen nicht inne wird, das unter der Sonne geschieht.

(3)
O Tod, wie bitter bist du, wenn an dich gedenket ein Mensch, der gute Tage und genug hat und ohne Sorge lebet; und dem es wohl geht in allen Dingen und noch wohl essen mag!

O Tod, wie wohl tust du dem Dürftigen, der da schwach und alt ist, der in allen Sorgen steckt, und nichts Bessers zu hoffen noch zu erwarten hat!

(4)
Wenn ich mit Menschen= und mit Engels=zungen redete, und hätte der Liebe nicht, so wär ich ein tönend Erz, oder eine klingende Schelle.

Und wenn ich weissagen könnte, und wüßte alle Geheimnisse und alle Erkenntnis; und hätte allen Glauben, also daß ich Berge versetzte; und hätte der Liebe nicht, so wäre ich nichts.

Und wenn ich alle meine Habe den Armen gäbe, und ließe meinen Leib brennen und hätte der Liebe nicht, so wäre mir's nichts nütze.

own works; for that is his portion: for who shall bring him to see what shall be after him?

Eccles. iii. 19–22

(2)
So I returned, and considered all the oppressions that are done under the sun: and behold the tears of such as were oppressed, and they had no comforter; and on the side of their oppressors there was power; but they had no comforter.

Wherefore I praised the dead which are already dead more than the living which are yet alive.

Yea, better is he than both they, which hath not yet been, who hath not seen the evil work that is done under the sun.

Eccles. iv 1–3

(3)
O death, how bitter is the remembrance of thee to a man that liveth at rest in his possessions, unto the man that hath nothing to vex him, and that hath prosperity in all things: yea, unto him that is yet able to receive meat!

O death, acceptable is thy sentence unto the needy, and unto him whose strength faileth, that is now in the last age, and is vexed with all things, and to him that despaireth, and hath lost patience!

Ecclus. xli 1, 2

(4)
Though I speak with the tongues of men and of angels, and have not charity, I am become as sounding brass, or a tinkling cymbal.

And though I have the gift of prophecy, and understand all mysteries, and all knowledge; and though I have all faith, so that I could remove mountains, and have not charity, I am nothing.

And though I bestow all my goods to feed the poor, and though I give my body to be burned, and have not charity, it profiteth me nothing.

1 Cor. xiii 1–3

Wir sehen jetzt durch einen Spiegel in einem dunkeln Worte; dann aber von Angesicht zu Angesichte. Jetzt erkenne ich's stückweise; dann aber werd ich's erkennen, gleichwie ich erkennet bin.

For now we see through a glass, darkly; but then face to face: now I know in part; but then shall I know even as also I am known.

Nun aber bleibet Glaube, Hoffnung, Liebe, diese drei; aber die Liebe ist die größeste unter ihnen.

And now abideth faith, hope, charity, these three; but the greatest of these is charity.

1 Cor. xiii 12–13

HUGO WOLF

Born at Windischgrätz (in the Austrian Steiermark) on 13 March 1860, the son of a furrier who was also an enthusiastic amateur musician. He soon showed great aptitude for music and an equally great impatience of discipline: he failed to finish his courses first at a local school, then at the Vienna conservatoire. Attempting to earn his own living as a music teacher, he found in Vienna friends and patrons who helped and furthered him whenever his pride would permit them to do so. An engagement as second conductor at Salzburg ended after only three months. From 1884 to 1887 Wolf acted as music critic of the Vienna *Salonblatt*, in which capacity he showed himself as a brilliant but unbridled polemicist who saw all the virtues of Wagner and none of the virtues of Brahms. Wolf composed his songs in a frenzy of enthusiasm – several songs a day, whole volumes in a few weeks – which was usually followed by long periods of depression and inactivity. In 1897 he showed unmistakable signs of mental illness; after a brief spell in a sanatorium he was discharged as cured, but he soon had a relapse which led to his incarceration (in October 1898) in an asylum near Vienna, where he died on 22 February 1903. His works include the Mörike, Eichendorff, Goethe, Italian, and Spanish song-books as well as over one hundred other songs, of which he himself published thirty-one; one completed opera (*Der Corregidor*), the symphonic poem *Penthesilea* (inspired by Kleist), the *Italian Serenade* for small orchestra or string quartet, and a handful of other instrumental and choral works. He also orchestrated twenty-three of his songs.

Wolf introduced into the *Lied* the harmonic innovations and declamatory principles of Wagner's operas. More than any other composer he respected his texts: every nuance, every inflexion of their speech-melody, generally finds its counterpart in the vocal line of his songs, while the accompaniments are usually built up out of one or two tiny phrases which are expanded and developed on symphonic principles. Wolf is a master of concentration (notably in the songs of his *Italienisches Liederbuch*, which seldom take up more than a page of music) and a master of melodic invention (gestures and figures, moods and thoughts, are all transformed into unforgettable melody). Each of his song-books has its own distinctive and unmistakable atmosphere, yet in all of them can be heard Wolf's own voice and accent. No one but Schubert has made so powerful a contribution to the art of the *Lied* – and not even Schubert has married poetry and music as perfectly as did Wolf in the best of his 'poems for voice and piano'.

I FROM THE MÖRIKE-LIEDER [COMP. 1888]

(1) *Verborgenheit*

Laß, o Welt, o laß mich sein!
Locket nicht mit Liebesgaben,
Laßt dies Herz alleine haben
Seine Wonne, seine Pein!

Was ich traure, weiß ich nicht,
Es ist unbekanntes Wehe;
Immerdar durch Tränen sehe
Ich der Sonne liebes Licht.

(1) *Withdrawal*

Let me be, O world!
Do not tempt me with gifts of love,
Let this heart keep to itself
its joy and its sorrow.

I do not know what I mourn for,
it is an unknown grief;
only through tears I see
the sun's dear light.

Oft bin ich mir kaum bewußt,
Und die helle Freude zücket
Durch die Schwere, so mich drücket,
Wonniglich in meiner Brust.

Laß, o Welt, o laß mich sein!
Locket nicht mit Liebesgaben,
Laßt dies Herz alleine haben
Seine Wonne, seine Pein!

Often (I am hardly conscious of it)
bright joy flashes
through the gloom that oppresses me,
bringing rapture to my heart.

Let me be, O world!
Do not tempt me with gifts of love,
Let this heart keep to itself
its joy and its sorrow.

(2) *Der Gärtner*

Auf ihrem Leibrößlein,
So weiß wie der Schnee,
Die schönste Prinzessin
Reit't durch die Allee.

Der Weg, den das Rößlein
Hintanzet so hold,
Der Sand, den ich streute,
Er blinket wie Gold!

Du rosenfarb's Hütlein
Wohl auf und wohl ab,
O wirf eine Feder,
Verstohlen herab!

Und willst du dagegen
Eine Blüte von mir,
Nimm tausend für eine,
Nimm alle dafür!

(1) *The Gardener*

On her favourite
snow-white horse
the loveliest princess
rides down the avenue.

On the path, along which the horse
prances so prettily,
the sand I strewed
sparkles like gold.

Little rose-coloured hat
bobbing up and down –
please throw me down a feather
when no one is looking!

And if, in return,
you want one of my flowers –
take a thousand for your one,
take them all!

(3) *Auf ein altes Bild*

In grüner Landschaft Sommerflor,
Bei kühlem Wasser, Schilf, und Rohr,
Schau, wie das Knäblein Sündelos
Frei spielet auf der Jungfrau Schoss!
Und dort im Walde wonnesam,
Ach, grünet schon des Kreuzes Stamm!

(3) *Lines on an Old Picture*

In a green landscape veiled in summer air,
beside cool water, reeds and rushes,
see the infant Jesus, free from sin,
playing gaily on the Virgin's lap!
And there, in those delightful woods
the tree of the cross is already in leaf.

(4) *Schlafendes Jesuskind*

Sohn der Jungfrau, Himmelskind! am Boden,
Auf dem Holz der Schmerzen eingeschlafen,
Das der fromme Meister, sinnvoll spielend,
Deinen leichten Träumen unterlegte;
Blume du, noch in der Knospe dämmernd
Eingehüllt die Herrlichkeit des Vaters!

(4) *The Christchild Asleep*

Son of the Virgin, heavenly child! fallen asleep
on the ground, on the wood of your agony,
which the pious artist, in meaningful play,
laid under your lightly dreaming form;
O flower, with the Father's glory
still hidden in the bud!

O wer sehen könnte, welche Bilder
Hinter dieser Stirne, diesen schwarzen
Wimpern sich in sanftem Wechsel malen!
[Sohn der Jungfrau, Himmelskind!]

If one could but see the images
that pass and gently change behind
that forehead and these dark lashes!
[Son of the Virgin, heavenly child!]

(5) *An die Geliebte*

Wenn ich, von deinem Anschaun tief
    gestillt,
Mich stumm an deinem heilgen Wert
    vergnüge,
Dann hör ich recht die leisen Atemzüge
Des Engels, welcher sich in dir verhüllt.

Und ein erstaunt, ein fragend Lächeln quillt
Auf meinem Mund, ob mich kein Traum
    betrüge,
Daß nun in dir, zu ewiger Genüge,
Mein kühnster Wunsch, mein einzger, sich
    erfüllt?

Von Tiefe dann zu Tiefen stürzt mein Sinn,
Ich höre aus der Gottheit nächtger Ferne
Die Quellen des Geschicks melodisch
    rauschen.

Betäubt kehr ich den Blick nach oben hin,
Zum Himmel auf – da lächeln alle Sterne;
Ich knie, ihrem Lichtgesang zu lauschen.

(5) *To the Beloved*

When looking at you has made me deeply
    content
and I delight, silently, in your sacred worth –
then I can hear the gentle breathing
of the angel hidden within you.

And an amazed, questioning smile rises
to my lips: 'Does not a dream deceive me?
Is my boldest, my only wish to be fulfilled
in you – am I to be for ever satisfied?'

My soul then plunges from depth to depth;
In God's dark distances I hear
the springs of fate rippling melodiously.

Stunned I raise my eyes
to the heavens – there all the stars are smiling
I kneel to listen to their song of light.

(6) *Denk es, o Seele!*

Ein Tännlein grünet wo,
Wer weiß, im Walde,
Ein Rosenstrauch, wer sagt,
In welchem Garten?
Sie sind erlesen schon,
Denk es, o Seele,
Auf deinem Grab zu wurzeln
Und zu wachsen.

Zwei schwarze Rößlein weiden
Auf der Wiese,
Sie kehren heim zur Stadt
In muntern Sprüngen.
Sie werden schrittweis gehn
Mit deiner Leiche;
Vielleicht, vielleicht noch eh
An ihren Hufen
Das Eisen los wird,
Das ich blitzen sehe!

(6) *O Soul, Remember This!*

A little fir tree is growing, who
knows where, in the wood,
a rose-bush in who can tell
in what garden.
Already they are ordained –
O soul, remember this! –
to strike root and to grow
on your grave.

Two little black horses are grazing
in the meadow,
they come home to the village
with happy curvetings.
They will go at foot-pace
with your corpse;
perhaps, perhaps even before
on their hooves
the horseshoe loosens
that I can see gleaming!

(7) *Der Feuerreiter*

Sehet ihr am Fensterlein
Dort die rote Mütze wieder?
Nicht geheuer muß es sein,
Denn er geht schon auf und nieder.
Und auf einmal welch Gewühle
Bei der Brücke nach dem Feld!
Horch! das Feuerglöcklein gellt:
Hinterm Berg,
Hinterm Berg
Brennt es in der Mühle!

Schaut, da sprengt er wütend schier
Durch das Tor, der Feuerreiter,
Auf dem rippendürren Tier,
Als auf einer Feuerleiter!
Querfeldein, durch Qualm und Schwüle,
Rennt er schon und ist am Ort!
Drüben schallt es fort und fort:
Hinterm Berg,
Hinterm Berg
Brennt es in der Mühle!

Der so oft den roten Hahn
Meilenweit von fern gerochen,
Mit des heil'gen Kreuzes Span
Freventlich die Glut besprochen –
Weh! dir grinst vom Dachgestühle
Dort der Feind im Höllenschein.
Gnade Gott der Seele dein!
Hinterm Berg,
Hinterm Berg
Rast er in der Mühle!

Keine Stunde hielt es an,
Bis die Mühle borst in Trümmer;
Doch den kecken Reitersmann
Sah man von der Stunde nimmer.
Volk und Wagen im Gewühle
Kehren heim von all dem Graus;
Auch das Glöcklein klinget aus:
Hinterm Berg,
Hinterm Berg
Brennt's! –

Nach der Zeit ein Müller fand
Ein Gerippe samt der Mützen
Aufrecht an der Kellerwand
Auf der beinern Mähre sitzen:

(7) *The Fire-Rider*

Do you see the red cap again,
there, at that window?
Something must be wrong,
he is walking up and down!
And suddenly: what thronging crowds
near the bridge, making for the field!
Listen to the shrill fire-bell:
Behind the hill,
behind the hill,
the mill is on fire!

Look – there he comes, frenziedly galloping
through the gate: the Fire Rider
straddling his skinny mount
like a fire-ladder!
Across the fields he rides through smoke and
    sultry heat;
he has already reached his goal!
The bell over there rings on and on:
Behind the hill,
behind the hill,
The mill is on fire!

You, who so often smelt a blaze
a mile off, who with a splinter from the Holy
    Cross
wickedly conjured the fire –
now from the rafters the foul fiend
grins at you amid the flames of hell.
God have mercy on your soul!
Behind the hill,
behind the hill,
he is raging in the mill!

It did not take an hour
for the mill to break in pieces;
but from that hour the bold rider
was never seen again.
Thronging crowd and carriages
turn home after all this horror;
the bell too stops ringing:
Behind the hill,
behind the hill,
a fire . . . !

Some time after a miller found
a skeleton with the cap
sitting upright against the cellar wall
on the fleshless mare.

Feuerreiter, wie so kühle
Reitest du in deinem Grab!
Husch! da fällt's in Asche ab.
Ruhe wohl,
Ruhe wohl
Drunten in der Mühle!

Fire-rider, how coldly
you are riding in your grave!
Hush – now it all falls to ashes.
Rest,
rest
down there in the mill!

2 FROM THE EICHENDORFF-LIEDER [COMP. 1886–8]

(1) *Der Musikant*

Wandern lieb ich für mein Leben,
Lebe eben, wie ich kann,
Wollt ich mir auch Mühe geben,
Paßt es mir doch gar nicht an.

Schöne alte Lieder weiß ich;
In der Kälte, ohne Schuh,
Draußen in die Saiten reiß ich,
Weiß nicht, wo ich abends ruh!

Manche Schöne macht wohl Augen,
Meinet, ich gefiel ihr sehr,
Wenn ich nur was wollte taugen,
So ein armer Lump nicht wär.

Mag dir Gott ein'n Mann bescheren,
Wohl mit Haus und Hof versehn!
Wenn wir zwei zusammen wären,
Möcht mein Singen mir vergehn.

(1) *The Minstrel*

I dearly love a roving life,
I live as I can.
Even if I tried to take trouble
my nature would not let me.

I know lovely old songs;
without shoes, out in the cold
I pluck my strings,
and never know where I shall rest at night.

Many a lovely girl makes eyes at me,
fancying she could like me well
if only I were good for something,
and not such a poor rascal!

May God send you a husband
with a good house and home!
If we two were together
I should soon sing no more.

(2) *Verschwiegene Liebe*

Über Wipfel und Saaten
In den Glanz hinein –
Wer mag sie erraten,
Wer holte sie ein?
Gedanken sich wiegen,
Die Nacht ist verschwiegen,
Gedanken sind frei.

Errät es nur eine,
Wer an sie gedacht
Beim Rauschen der Haine,
Wenn niemand mehr wacht
Als die Wolken, die fliegen –
Mein Lieb ist verschwiegen
Und schön wie die Nacht.

(2) *Love That Keeps Its Council*

Over tree-tops and cornfields
into the gleaming light –
who may guess at them?
Who could overtake them?
Thoughts float gently,
the night keeps her counsel –
Thoughts are free.

If only *one* could guess
who has been thinking of her
while the woods rustle
and no one is awake
except the clouds that fly past –
my love keeps her council
and is lovely as the night.

(3) *Das Ständchen*

Auf die Dächer zwischen blassen
Wolken schaut der Mond herfür,
Ein Student dort auf den Gassen
Singt vor seiner Liebsten Tür.

Und die Brunnen rauschen wieder
Durch die stille Einsamkeit,
Und der Wald vom Berge nieder,
Wie in alter, schöner Zeit.

So in meinen jungen Tagen
Hab ich manche Sommernacht
Auch die Laute hier geschlagen
Und manch lust'ges Lied erdacht.

Aber von der stillen Schwelle
Trugen sie mein Lieb zur Ruh,
Und du, fröhlicher Geselle,
Singe, sing nur immer zu!

(3) *The Serenade*

Between pale clouds
the moon peers on the rooftops;
A student there in the street
sings before his sweetheart's door.

And again the fountains are plashing
through the silent solitude,
again the trees rustle from the wooded
        mountains
as in former, happier times.

Just so in my young days
(on many a summer night)
I plucked my strings here
and thought out many a joyful song.

But from the silent threshold
my love has been borne to her rest.
And you, my gay friend,
sing on, sing ever on!

3 FROM THE GOETHE-LIEDER [COMP. 1888–9]

(1) *Harfenspieler Lieder*

(1) Songs of the Harper (from Goethe's *Wilhelm Meister's Apprenticeship*)

(1)
Wer sich der Einsamkeit ergibt,
Ach! der ist bald allein;
Ein jeder lebt, ein jeder liebt,
Und läßt ihn seiner Pein.

Ja! laßt mich meiner Qual!
Und kann ich nur einmal
Recht einsam sein,
Dann bin ich nicht allein

Es schleicht ein Liebender lauschend sacht,
Ob seine Freundin allein?
So überschleicht bei Tag und Nacht
Mich Einsamen die Pein,

Mich Einsamen die Qual.
Ach werd ich erst einmal
Einsam im Grabe sein,
Da läßt sie mich allein!

(i)
Who gives himself over to solitude
is soon alone;
everyone lives and loves
and leaves him to his pain.

Yes, leave me to my anguish!
And once I can be
really by myself,
then I am not alone.

A lover stalks softly and listens,
to find out if his love is alone.
Just so by day and by night,
when I am by myself

pain and anguish steal over me.
When once I shall lie
in the grave by myself –
then anguish will leave me alone.

(ii)
An die Türen will ich schleichen,
Still und sittsam will ich stehn,
Fromme Hand wird Nahrung reichen,
Und ich werde weiter gehn.

Jeder wird sich glücklich scheinen,
Wenn mein Bild vor ihm erscheint,
Eine Träne wird er weinen,
Und ich weiß nicht, was er weint.

(iii)
Wer nie sein Brot mit Tränen aß,
Wer nie die kummervollen Nächte
Auf seinem Bette weinend saß,
Der kennt euch nicht, ihr himmlischen
    Mächte.

Ihr führt ins Leben uns hinein,
Ihr laßt den Armen schuldig werden,
Dann überlaßt ihr ihn der Pein;
Denn alle Schuld rächt sich auf Erden.

(2) *Lieder der Mignon*

(i)
Heiß mich nicht reden, heiß mich schweigen!
Denn mein Geheimnis ist mir Pflicht;
Ich möchte dir mein ganzes Innre zeigen,
Allein das Schicksal will es nicht.

Zur rechten Zeit vertreibt der Sonne Lauf
Die finstre Nacht, und sie muß sich erhellen;
Der harte Fels schließt seinen Busen auf,
Mißgönnt der Erde nicht die tiefverborgnen
    Quellen.

Ein jeder sucht im Arm des Freundes Ruh,
Dort kann die Brust in Klagen sich ergießen;
Allein ein Schwur drückt mir die Lippen zu.
Und nur ein Gott vermag sie aufzuschließen.

(ii)
Nur wer die Sehnsucht kennt,
Weiß, was ich leide!
Allein und abgetrennt
Von aller Freude,
Seh ich ans Firmament

(ii)
I will steal to the doors
and stand in humble silence;
charitable hands will give me food,
and I will go on my way.

Everyone who sees me
will think his own lot fortunate;
he will shed a tear –
and I do not know why he weeps.

(iii)
Who never watered his bread with tears,
who never sat, through long, miserable
    nights
weeping on his bed –
he does not know you, heavenly powers.

You lead us into life,
you let the poor wretch incur guilt
and then you leave him to his pain –
for all guilt, on earth, draws vengeance on
    itself.

(2) *Mignon's Songs* (from *Wilhelm
    Meister's Apprenticeship*)

(i)
Do not bid me speak – bid me be silent!
To keep my secret is my duty.
I would like to show you all my mind;
but fate will not have it so.

At the appointed time the sun's course dis-
    pels
nocturnal darkness, and it must grow bright;
the hard rock opens its bosom
and does not grudge the earth the deeply
    hidden springs.

Everyone seeks rest in the arms of a friend,
where the heart can pour out its laments;
but my lips are sealed by an oath
and only a god may open them.

(ii)
Only he who knows longing
knows what I suffer!
Alone and cut off
from all joy
I look to the firmament

Nach jener Seite.
Ach! der mich liebt und kennt
Ist in der Weite.
Es schwindelt mir, es brennt
Mein Eingeweide.
Nur wer die Sehnsucht kennt,
Weiß, was ich leide!

on yonder side.
He who loves and knows me
is far away.
I am giddy, my vitals
burn.
Only he who knows longing
knows what I suffer!

(iii)
So laßt mich scheinen, bis ich werde;
Zieht mir das weiße Kleid nicht aus!
Ich eile von der schönen Erde
Hinab in jenes feste Haus.

(iii)
Let me appear an angel until I become one!
Do not take my white robe from me.
I am hurrying from the lovely earth
to the solid dwelling you know of.

Dort ruh ich eine kleine Stille,
Dann öffnet sich der frische Blick;
Ich lasse dann die reine Hülle,
Den Gürtel und den Kranz zurück.

There, for a while, I will rest in silence;
then, refreshed, my eyes will open;
I shall leave the pure white raiment,
the girdle and the wreath behind.

Und jene himmlischen Gestalten,
Sie fragen nicht nach Mann und Weib,
Und keine Kleider, keine Falten
Umgeben den verklärten Leib.

And those heavenly forms
will not ask if I am man or woman,
and no clothes, no folds
will encumber my transfigured body.

Zwar lebt ich ohne Sorg und Mühe,
Doch fühlt ich tiefen Schmerz genung;
Vor Kummer altert ich zu frühe,
Macht mich auf ewig wieder jung!

True, I have lived without trouble or care,
but I felt deep pain enough.
With sorrow I grew old too early,
make me for ever young again!

(iv) '*Kennst du das Land?*'

Kennst du das Land, wo die Zitronen
blühn,
Im dunkeln Laub die Gold-Orangen glühn,
Ein sanfter Wind vom blauen Himmel weht,
Die Myrte still und hoch der Lorbeer steht?
Kennst du es wohl?
Dahin! dahin
Möcht ich mit dir, o mein Geliebter, ziehn.

(iv) '*Do you know the land?*'

Do you know the land where the lemons
blossom?
Where golden oranges glow among the dark
leaves,
a soft breeze blows from the blue sky,
and the still myrtle and the tall laurels grow?
Do you know it?
There, there
I long to go with you, my love.

Kennst du das Haus? Auf Säulen ruht sein
Dach.
Es glänzt der Saal, es schimmert das Gemach,
Und Marmorbilder stehn und sehn mich an:
Was hat man dir, du armes Kind, getan?
Kennst du es wohl?
Dahin! dahin
Möcht ich mit dir, o mein Beschützer, ziehn.

Do you know the house? Its roof rests on
pillars,
the hall gleams, the room glistens,
and marble statues stand and look at me:
'What have they done to you, poor child?'
Do you know it?
There, there
I long to go with you, my protector.

Kennst du den Berg und seinen Wolkensteg?
Das Maultier sucht im Nebel seinen Weg;
In Höhlen wohnt der Drachen alte Brut;
Es stürzt der Fels und über ihn die Flut!
Kennst du ihn wohl?
Dahin! dahin
Geht unser Weg! O Vater, laß uns ziehn!

Do you know the mountain and its cloud-
    girt path?
The mule picks its way in the mist;
caves hold the ancient brood of dragons,
the rock falls sheer and the torrent over it!
Do you know it?
There, there
lies our way – O father, let us go!

(3) *Die Bekehrte*

Bei dem Glanz der Abendröte
Ging ich still den Wald entlang,
Damon saß und blies die Flöte,
Daß es von den Felsen klang,
So la la! . . .

Und er zog mich zu sich nieder,
Küßte mich so hold, so süß.
Und ich sagte: Blase wieder!
Und der gute Junge blies,
So la la! . . .

Meine Ruh ist nun verloren,
Meine Freude floh davon,
Und ich hör vor meinen Ohren
Immer nur den alten Ton,
So la la, le ralla! . . .

(3) *Converted*

In the red glow of sunset
I wandered quietly along the wood.
Damon sat and played his flute
so that it echoed from the rocks,
So la-la . . .

And he drew me down to his side
and kissed me so gently, so sweetly.
I said to him: 'Play once more!'
and the good lad played,
So la-la . . .

Now my peace is lost,
my joy has flown,
and in my ears I hear
nothing but the one old strain:
So la-la . . .

(4) *Anakreons Grab*

Wo die Rose hier blüht, wo Reben um Lor-
    beer sich schlingen,
Wo das Turtelchen lockt, wo sich das
    Grillchen ergötzt,
Welch ein Grab ist hier, das alle Götter mit
    Leben
Schön bepflanzt und geziert? Es ist Ana-
    kreons Ruh.
Frühling, Sommer, und Herbst genoß der
    glückliche Dichter;
Vor dem Winter hat ihn endlich der Hügel
    geschützt.

(4) *Anacreon's Grave*

Here, where the rose blooms and vines twine
    around laurel,
where the turtle-dove calls and the cricket
    loves to be –
what grave is here, that all the gods have
    planted and adorned with life? It is Ana-
    creon's resting-place.
The happy poet enjoyed spring, summer,
    and autumn;
From the winter, at the last, his mound pro-
    tected him.

(5) *Prometheus*

Bedecke deinen Himmel, Zeus,
Mit Wolkendunst
Und übe, dem Knaben gleich,

(5) *Prometheus*

Cover your heavens, Zeus,
with cloudy vapour,
and test your strength, like a boy

Der Disteln köpft,
An Eichen dich und Bergeshöhn;
Mußt mir meine Erde
Doch lassen stehn
Und meine Hütte, die du nicht gebaut,
Und meinen Herd,
Um dessen Glut
Du mich beneidest.

Ich kenne nichts Ärmeres
Unter der Sonn als euch, Götter!
Ihr nähret kümmerlich
Von Opfersteuern
Und Gebetshauch
Eure Majestät
Und darbtet, wären
Nicht Kinder und Bettler
Hoffnungsvolle Toren.

Da ich ein Kind war,
Nicht wußte, wo aus noch ein,
Kehrt ich mein verirrtes Auge
Zur Sonne, als wenn drüber wäre
Ein Ohr, zu hören meine Klage,
Ein Herz wie meins,
Sich des Bedrängten zu erbarmen.

Wer half mir
Wider der Titanen Übermut?
Wer rettete vom Tode mich,
Von Sklaverei?
Hast du nicht alles selbst vollendet,
Heilig glühend Herz?
Und glühtest jung und gut,
Betrogen, Rettungsdank
Dem Schlafenden da droben?

Ich dich ehren? Wofür?
Hast du die Schmerzen gelindert
Je des Beladenen?
Hast du die Tränen gestillet
Je des Geängstigten?
Hat nicht mich zum Manne geschmiedet
Die allmächtige Zeit
Und das ewige Schicksal,
Meine Herrn und deine?

Wähntest du etwa,
Ich sollte das Leben hassen,
In Wüsten fliehen,

beheading thistles
on oaks and mountain peaks;
yet my earth
you have to let stand,
and my hut, which you did not build
and my hearth, whose glow
you envy me.

I know nothing more wretched
under the sun than you, gods!
Scantily you feed
your majesty
on sacrificial tributes
and the breath of prayer,
and you would starve
if children and beggars
were not hopeful fools.

When I was a child,
not knowing where to turn
I raised my puzzled eye
to the sun, as if there were above it
an ear to hear my lamentation,
a heart like my own,
to pity my distress.

Who helped me
against the Titans' insolence?
who saved me from death
and slavery?
Did you not achieve all this yourself,
holy, glowing heart?
And did you not burn –
deceived in your youth and innocence –
with gratitude
for the sleeper up there?

I honour you? What for?
Have you ever relieved my anguish
when I was suffering?
Have you ever dried my tears
when I was terrified?
Was I not forged into a man
by almighty Time
and eternal Fate,
my masters and yours?

Did you perhaps delude yourself
I would come to hate life
and flee into the wilderness

Weil nicht alle
Blütenträume reiften?

Hier sitz ich, forme Menschen
Nach meinem Bilde,
Ein Geschlecht, das mir gleich sei,
Zu leiden, zu weinen,
Zu genießen und zu freuen sich,
Und dein nicht zu achten,
Wie ich!

because the blossoming dreams of my youth
did not all mature?

Here I sit, forming men
in my image,
a race that will resemble me;
to suffer, to weep,
to enjoy and be glad,
and not to heed you –
like me!

(6) *Ganymed*

Wie im Morgenglanze
Du rings mich anglühst,
Frühling, Geliebter!
Mit tausendfacher Liebeswonne
Sich an mein Herz drängt
Deiner ewigen Wärme
Heilig Gefühl,
Unendliche Schöne!

Daß ich dich fassen möcht
In diesen Arm!

Ach, an deinem Busen
Lieg ich, schmachte,
Und deine Blumen, dein Gras
Drängen sich an mein Herz.
Du kühlst den brennenden
Durst meines Busens,
Lieblicher Morgenwind!
Ruft drein die Nachtigall
Liebend nach mir aus dem Nebeltal.

Ich komm, ich komme!
Wohin? Ach, wohin?

Hinauf! Hinauf strebt's.
Es schweben die Wolken
Abwärts, die Wolken
Neigen sich der sehnenden Liebe.
Mir! Mir!
In euerm Schoße
Aufwärts!
Umfangend umfangen!
Aufwärts an deinen Busen,
Alliebender Vater!

(6) *Ganymede*

How you glow all around me
in the morning light
beloved, Spring!
With a thousandfold ecstasy of love
the divine feeling
of eternal warmth
strains against my heart –
unending beauty!

Could I but embrace you
with these arms!

At your breast
I lie languishing,
and your flowers, your grass
press against my heart.
You cool the burning
thirst of my breast,
lovely morning breeze!
The nightingale calls
lovingly towards me out of the misty valley.

I come, I am coming!
Where to, oh, where to?

Upwards! I strive upwards.
The clouds are floating
downwards, the clouds
stoop to yearning love.
To me! to me!
In your lap
upwards!
Embracing, embraced!
Upwards to your bosom,
all-loving father!

4 FROM 'SPANISCHES LIEDERBUCH' [SPANISH POEMS TRANSLATED BY
EMANUEL GEIBEL AND PAUL HEYSE; COMP. 1889–90]

(1) *Der heilige Josef singt*

Nun wandre, Maria,
Nun wandre nur fort.
Schon krähen die Hähne,
Und nah ist der Ort.

Nun wandre, Geliebte,
Du Kleinod mein,
Und balde wir werden
In Bethlehem sein.

Dann ruhest du fein
Und schlummerst dort.
Schon krähen die Hähne
Und nah ist der Ort.

Wohl seh ich, Herrin,
Die Kraft dir schwinden;
Kann deine Schmerzen,
Ach, kaum verwinden.

Getrost! Wohl finden
Wir Herberg dort.
Schon krähen die Hähne
Und nah ist der Ort.

Wär erst bestanden
Dein Stündlein, Marie,
Die gute Botschaft,
Gut lohnt ich sie.

Das Eselein hie
Gäb ich drum fort!
Schon krähen die Hähne,
Komm! Nah ist der Ort.

(1) *St Joseph's Song*

Walk on, Mary,
ever on.
The cocks are already crowing,
and the place is near.

Walk on, my love,
my treasure,
and soon we shall be
in Bethlehem.

There you shall rest
and sleep.
The cocks are already crowing,
and the place is near.

I see – dear wife and lady –
your strength ebbing,
your agony
I can hardly bear.

Have courage! we shall find
some shelter there.
The cocks are already crowing,
and the place is near.

If your hour of pain
were already over, Mary,
I would well reward
the bringer of such good news.

This little ass here
I would gladly give him!
The cocks are already crowing,
come – the place is near!

(2) '*In dem Schatten meiner Locken*'

In dem Schatten meiner Locken
Schlief mir mein Geliebter ein.
Weck ich ihn nun auf? – Ach nein!

Sorglich strählt ich meine krausen
Locken täglich in der Frühe,
Doch umsonst ist meine Mühe,
weil die Winde sie zerzausen.
Lockenschatten, Windessausen
Schläferten den Liebsten ein.
Weck ich ihn nun auf? – Ach nein!

(2) '*In the shadow of my tresses*'

In the shadow of my tresses
my love fell asleep.
Shall I wake him now? No!

Carefully I combed my curly
tresses early every morning;
but my efforts are vain,
for the winds ruffle them.
The shade of my tresses, the rustling of the
    wind
lulled my love to sleep.
Shall I wake him now? No!

Hören muß ich, wie ihn gräme,
Daß er schmachtet schon so lange,
Daß ihm Leben geb und nehme
Diese meine braune Wange,
Und er nennt mich eine Schlange,
Und doch schlief er bei mir ein.
Weck ich ihn nun auf? – Ach nein!

I have to hear how sad he is,
how long he has languished,
how this brown cheek of mine
gives him life and takes it from him;
and he calls me a snake –
yet he fell asleep by my side.
Shall I wake him now? No!

(3) '*Auf dem grünen Balkon*'

Auf dem grünen Balkon mein Mädchen
Schaut nach mir durch's Gitterlein.
Mit den Augen blinzelt sie freundlich,
Mit dem Finger sagt sie mir: Nein!

Glück, das nimmer ohne Wanken
Junger Liebe folgt hienieden,
Hat mir eine Lust beschieden,
Und auch da noch muß ich schwanken.
Schmeicheln hör ich oder Zanken,
Komm ich an ihr Fensterlädchen.
Immer nach dem Brauch der Mädchen
Träuft ins Glück ein bißchen Pein:
Mit den Augen blinzelt sie freundlich,
Mit dem Finger sagt sie mir: Nein!

Wie sich nur in ihr vertragen
Ihre Kälte, meine Glut?
Weil in ihr mein Himmel ruht,
Seh ich Trüb und Hell sich jagen.
In den Wind gehn meine Klagen,
Daß noch nie die süße Kleine
Ihre Arme schlang um meine;
Doch sie hält mich hin so fein –
Mit den Augen blinzelt sie freundlich
Mit dem Finger sagt sie mir: Nein!

(3) '*From her green balcony*'

From her green balcony my love
peeps at me through the trellis.
Her eyes blink kindly,
while her finger says: 'No!'

Fortune, which never, here on earth,
lets the path of young love run smooth,
has given me joy –
but I am kept in doubt.
Now I hear kind words, now reproaches,
when I come to her shuttered window.
With girls it is always like that –
a little pain drops into the cup of happiness.
Her eyes blink kindly,
while her finger says: 'No!'

How can she endure together
her coldness and my fire?
Since she is my heaven
I see darkness chase light, light darkness.
The wind bears away my lament
that my sweet, my dear one
has never yet embraced me.
But she holds me off so gently:
her eyes blink kindly,
while her finger says: 'No!'

5 'ITALIENISCHES LIEDERBUCH' [ITALIAN POEMS TRANSLATED BY PAUL
HEYSE; COMP. 1890–6]

(1)

Auch kleine Dinge können uns entzücken,
Auch kleine Dinge können teuer sein.
Bedenkt, wie gern wir uns mit Perlen
    schmücken;
Sie werden schwer bezahlt und sind nur
    klein.
Bedenkt, wie klein ist die Olivenfrucht,

(1)

Little things can also delight us,
little things may also be precious.
Think how we like to adorn ourselves with
    pearls –
they fetch a high price, yet they are small.
Think how little an olive is,
yet its goodness makes it sought after.

Und wird um ihre Güte doch gesucht.
Denkt an die Rose nur, wie klein sie ist,
Und duftet doch so lieblich, wie ihr wißt.

(2)
Mir ward gesagt, du reisest in die Ferne.
Ach, wohin gehst du, mein geliebtes Leben?
Den Tag, an dem du scheidest, wüßt ich
    gerne;
Mit Tränen will ich das Geleit dir geben.
Mit Tränen will ich deinen Weg befeuchten –
Gedenk an mich, und Hoffnung wird mir
    leuchten!
Mit Tränen bin ich bei dir allerwärts –
Gedenk an mich, vergiß es nicht, mein Herz!

(3)
Ihr seid die Allerschönste weit und breit,
Viel schöner als im Mai der Blumenflor.
Orvietos Dom steigt so voll Herrlichkeit,
Viterbos größter Brunnen nicht empor.
So hoher Reiz und Zauber ist dein eigen,
Der Dom von Siena muß sich vor dir neigen.
Ach, du bist so an Reiz und Anmut reich,
Der Dom von Siena selbst ist dir nicht gleich.

(4)
Gesegnet sei, durch den die Welt entstund;
Wie trefflich schuf er sie nach allen Seiten!
Er schuf das Meer mit endlos tiefem Grund,
Er schuf die Schiffe, die hinübergleiten,
Er schuf das Paradies mit ew'gem Licht,
Er schuf die Schönheit und dein Angesicht.

(5)
Selig ihr Blinden, die ihr nicht zu schauen
Vermögt die Reize, die uns Glut entfachen;
Selig ihr Tauben, die ihr ohne Grauen
Die Klagen der Verlieben könnt verlachen;
Selig ihr Stummen, die ihr nicht den Frauen
Könnt eure Herzensnot verständlich machen;
Selig ihr Toten, die man hat begraben!
Ihr sollt vor Liebesqualen Ruhe haben.

(6)
Wer rief dich denn? Wer hat dich herbestellt?
Wer hieß dich kommen, wenn es dir zur
    Last?
Geh zu dem Liebchen, das dir mehr gefällt,

Think of the rose – how small it is!
But as you know, it smells so sweet.

(2)
They told me you would travel far away.
Where are you going, love of my life?
I would like to know the day you depart;
With tears I will see you on your way,
With tears I will water your path –
Think of me, and hope will shine on me!
With tears I am with you, wherever you go –
think of me, do not forget, dear heart!

(3)
You are the fairest far and near,
lovelier far than the flowers of May.
Not even the Cathedral of Orvieto
or the greatest fountain of Viterbo rises in
    such majesty.
Your attraction, your enchantment are such
That the Cathedral of Siena must bow before
    you.
You are so rich in grace and charm
that not even Siena Cathedral can compare
    with you.

(4)
Blessed be he who created the world;
how excellently he fashioned it on all sides!
He made the sea with its bottomless depths,
he made the ships that glide past,
he made Paradise with its eternal light,
he made beauty and your face.

(5)
Blessed are the blind, who cannot see
the charms that kindle burning desire;
blessed are the deaf, who without shuddering
can laugh at lovers' laments;
blessed are the dumb, who cannot tell
    women
of their heart's anguish;
blessed are the dead in their graves –
they are safe from the torments of love.

(6)
Who called you? Who asked you here?
Who told you to come if you find it such a
    burden?
Go to the sweetheart you like better,

Geh dahin, wo du die Gedanken hast.
Geh nur, wohin dein Sinnen steht und
    Denken!
Daß du zu mir kommst, will ich gern dir
    schenken.
Geh zu dem Liebchen, das dir mehr gefällt!
Wer rief dich denn? Wer hat dich herbestellt?

go where your thoughts are,
go to her you dream and think of!
Please don't come here for *my* sake!
Go to the sweetheart you like better!
Who called you? Who asked you to come?

(7)

Der Mond hat eine schwere Klag erhoben
Und vor dem Herrn die Sache kund gemacht;
Er wolle nicht mehr stehn am Himmel
    droben,
Du habest ihn um seinen Glanz gebracht.
Als er zuletzt das Sternenheer gezählt,
Da hab es an der vollen Zahl gefehlt;
Zwei von den schönsten habest du entwen-
    det:
Die beiden Augen dort, die mich verblendet.

(7)

The moon has brought a heavy charge
before the Lord, and announced
that he no longer wants to stand in the sky:
for you, he said, have robbed him of his
    splendour.
When he last counted the host of stars,
the full number was not there:
two of the loveliest you had taken from him—
those two eyes that have blinded me.

(8)

Nun laß uns Frieden schließen, liebstes
    Leben,
Zu lang ist's schon, daß wir in Fehde liegen.
Wenn du nicht willst, will ich mich dir
    ergeben;
Wie könnten wir uns auf den Tod bekriegen?
Es schließen Frieden Könige und Fürsten,
Und sollten Liebende nicht darnach dürsten?
Es schließen Frieden Fürsten und Soldaten,
Und sollt' es zwei Verliebten wohl mißraten?
Meinst du, daß, was so großen Herrn gelingt,
Ein Paar zufriedner Herzen nicht vollbringt?

(8)

Now let us make peace, my dearest love;
we have quarrelled far too long.
If you refuse, I will surrender to you;
how could we make war to the death?
Kings and princes make peace,
should not lovers crave it?
Princes and soldiers make peace,
should two lovers fail to do likewise?
Do you think what such great lords manage
could not be done by two contented hearts?

(9)

Daß doch gemalt all deine Reize wären,
Und dann der Heidenfürst das Bildnis fände.
Er würde dir ein groß Geschenk verehren,
Und legte seine Kron in deine Hände.
Zum rechten Glauben mußt' sich bekehren
Sein ganzes Reich, bis an sein fernstes Ende.
Im ganzen Lane würd es ausgeschrieben,
Christ soll ein jeder werden und dich lieben.
Ein jeder Heide flugs bekehrte sich
Und wurd ein guter Christ und liebte dich.

(9)

If only a picture were painted of all your
    charms,
and the king of the heathens found it!
He would bestow a great gift on you
and lay his crown in your hands.
His whole kingdom, to its farthest corner,
Would be converted to the true faith.
An edict would be published throughout the
    land
that everyone should turn Christian and love
    you.
Every heathen would straightway be con-
    verted,
would become a good Christian and love you.

(10)
Du denkst mit einem Fädchen mich zu
    fangen,
Mit einem Blick schon mich verliebt zu
    machen?
Ich fing schon andre, die sich höher schwan-
    gen;
Du darfst mir ja nicht traun, siehst du mich
    lachen.
Schon andre fing ich, glaub es sicherlich.
Ich bin verliebt, doch eben nicht in dich.

(10)
You think you can catch me with a thread,
making me love you by just looking at me?
I have caught others whose minds flew
    higher.
Do not trust me when you see me laugh!
I have caught others, just you believe me.
I am in love – but not with you.

(11)
Wie lange schon war immer mein Verlangen:
Ach, wäre doch ein Musikus mir gut!
Nun ließ der Herr mich meinen Wunsch
    erlangen
Und schickt mir einen, ganz wie Milch und
    Blut.
Da kommt er eben her mit sanfter Miene,
Und senkt den Kopf und spielt die Violine.

(11)
How long I have yearned
to have a musician for my lover!
Now the Lord has granted my wish
and sent me one, all pink and white.
Here he comes, with gentle mien,
bows his head and plays the violin.

(12)
Nein, junger Herr, so treibt man's nicht,
    fürwahr;
Man sorgt dafür, sich schicklich zu betragen.
Für alltags bin ich gut genug, nicht wahr?
Doch beßre suchst du dir an Feiertagen.
Nein, junger Herr, wirst du so weiter
    sünd'gen,
Wird dir den Dienst dein Alltagsliebchen
    künd'gen.

(12)
Oh no, young sir, this just won't do;
you will have to behave better than that.
You think me good enough for a workaday
    sweetheart, do you?
But on holidays you look for something
    better.
Oh no, young sir; if you carry on like that
your workaday sweetheart will give you
    notice.

(13)
Hoffärtig seid Ihr, schönes Kind, und geht
Mit Euren Freiern um auf stolzem Fuß.
Spricht man Euch an, kaum daß Ihr Rede
    steht,
Als kostet Euch zuviel ein holder Gruß.
Bist keines Alexanders Töchterlein,
Kein Königreich wird deine Mitgift sein,
Und willst du nicht das Gold, so nimm das
    Zinn;
Willst du nicht Liebe, nimm Verachtung hin.

(13)
You are haughty, you beautiful girl,
and high and mighty with your suitors.
If you are spoken to, you hardly deign to
    answer,
as if a kindly greeting would cost you too
    much effort.
You are not Alexander's daughter,
and won't have a kingdom for your dowry.
If you don't want gold, have dross instead;
if you don't want love, take contempt.

(14)
Geselle, wolln wir uns in Kutten hüllen,
Die Welt dem lassen, den sie mag ergötzen?
Dann pochen wir an Tür um Tür im stillen:
'Gebt einem armen Mönch um Jesu willen.'

(14)
Come, friend, shall we put on monks' robes
and leave the world to those that enjoy it?
Then, quietly, we will knock at one door
    after another:

– O lieber Pater, du mußt später kommen,
Wenn aus dem Ofen wir das Brot genommen,
O lieber Pater, komm nur später wieder,
Ein Töchterlein von mir liegt krank danieder.
– Und ist sie krank, so laßt mich zu ihr gehen,
Daß sie nicht etwa sterbe unversehen.
Und ist sie krank, so laß mich nach ihr schauen,
Daß sie mir ihre Beichte mag vertrauen.
Schließt Tür und Fenster, daß uns keiner störe,
Wenn ich des armen Kindes Beichte höre!

'Give alms to a poor monk, for Jesus' sake!'
– Dear father, you must come later
when the bread is taken from the oven.
Dear father, do come back later,
my young daughter lies sick in bed.
'If she is ill, let me go to her,
else she might die unprepared.
If she is ill, let me see her,
that she may make confession to me.
Close doors and windows, so that no one disturbs us
when I hear the poor child's confession!'

(15)

Mein Liebster ist so klein, daß ohne Bücken
Er mir das Zimmer fegt mit seinen Locken.
Als er ins Gärtlein ging, Jasmin zu pflücken,
Ist er vor einer Schnecke sehr erschrocken.
Dann setzt' er sich ins Haus um zu verschnaufen,
Da warf ihn eine Fliege übern Haufen;
Und als er hintrat an mein Fensterlein,
Stieß eine Bremse ihm den Schädel ein.
Verwünscht sei'n alle Fliegen, Schnaken, Bremsen
Und wer ein Schätzchen hat aus den Maremmen!
Verwünscht sei'n alle Fliegen, Schnaken, Mücken
Und wer sich, wenn er küßt, so tief muß bücken!

(15)

My sweetheart is so small, that without bending down
he sweeps the floor with his curls.
When he went into the garden to pick jasmine
a snail frightened him.
Then he sat down in the house to catch his breath,
and a fly knocked him over;
and when he stepped over to my window,
a gad-fly knocked in his skull.
A curse on all flies, daddy-long-legs, and gad-flies,
and on all who have a sweetheart from Maremma!
A curse on all flies, daddy-long-legs, and midges,
and on all who have to stoop so low for a kiss!

(16)

Ihr jungen Leute, die ihr zieht ins Feld,
Auf meinen Liebsten sollt ihr Achtung geben.
Sorgt, daß er tapfer sich im Feuer hält;
Er war noch nie im Kriege all sein Leben.
Laßt nie ihn unter freiem Himmel schlafen;
Er ist so zart, es möchte sich bestrafen.
Laßt mir ihn ja nicht schlafen unterm Mond;
Er ginge drauf, er ist's ja nicht gewohnt.

(16)

You young men going off to war –
take care of my sweetheart!
See that he is brave under fire;
he has never seen battle before.
Don't let him sleep in the open;
he is so delicate, and might take harm.
Don't let him sleep out of doors –
it would be the end of him, he's not used to it.

(17)

Und willst du deinen Liebsten sterben sehen,
So trage nicht dein Haar gelockt, du Holde.

(17)

And if you would see your lover die,
do not wear your hair in tresses, my gentle love!

Laß von den Schultern frei sie niederwehen;
Wie Fäden sehn sie aus von purem Golde.
Wie goldne Fäden, die der Wind bewegt –
Schön sind die Haare, schön ist, die sie
  trägt!
Goldfäden, Seidenfäden ungezählt –
Schön sind die Haare, schön ist, die sie
  strählt!

Let your hair flow loose from your shoul-
  ders –
it looks like threads of pure gold.
Like golden threads blown by the wind –
the hair is lovely, and lovely she that wears it!
Golden threads, silken threads, without
  number –
the hair is lovely, and lovely is she that combs
  it!

(18)

Heb auf dein blondes Haupt und schlafe
  nicht,
Und laß dich ja vom Schlummer nicht
  betören.
Ich sage dir vier Worte von Gewicht,
Von denen darfst du keines überhören.
Das erste: daß um dich mein Herze bricht,
Das zweite: dir nur will ich angehören,
Das dritte: daß ich dir mein Heil befehle,
Das letzte: dich allein liebt meine Seele.

(18)

Lift up your fair head and do not sleep,
let not sleep lull you.
I have four weighty things to tell you,
of which you must not miss a single one.
First: my heart is breaking for you.
Second: I want to belong only to you.
Third: you are my salvation,
and last: my soul loves none but you.

(19)

Wir haben beide lange Zeit geschwiegen,
Auf einmal kam uns nun die Sprache wieder.
Die Engel Gottes sind herabgeflogen,
Sie brachten nach dem Krieg den Frieden
  wieder.
Die Engel Gottes sind herabgeflogen,
Mit ihnen ist der Frieden eingezogen.
Die Liebesengel kamen über Nacht
Und haben Frieden meiner Brust gebracht.

(19)

For a long time we have both been silent –
and suddenly we found our speech again.
God's angels flew down
and brought back peace after war.
God's angels flew down
and peace entered with them.
The angels of love came in the night
and brought peace to my breast.

(20)

Mein Liebster singt am Haus im Monden-
  scheine,
Und ich muß lauschend hier im Bette liegen.
Weg von der Mutter wend ich mich und
  weine,
Blut sind die Tränen, die mir nicht versiegen.
Den breiten Strom am Bett hab ich geweint,
Weiß nicht vor Tränen, ob der Morgen
  scheint.
Den breiten Strom am Bett weint ich vor
  Sehnen;
Blind haben mich gemacht die blut'gen
  Tränen.

(20)

Outside the house my lover sings in the
  moonlight
and I must lie in my bed and listen.
I turn away from my mother and weep
tears of blood that will not stop flowing.
I have wept a broad stream by my bed,
and cannot see, for tears, if it is day.
A broad stream of tears I have wept with
  longing –
the tears of blood have blinded me.

(21)

Man sagt mir, deine Mutter woll es nicht;
So bleibe weg, mein Schatz, tu ihr den
    Willen.
Ach Liebster, nein! tu ihr den Willen nicht,
Besuch mich doch, tu's ihr zum Trotz, im
    stillen!
Nein, mein Geliebter, folg ihr nimmermehr,
Tu's ihr zum Trotz, komm öfter als bisher!
Nein, höre nicht auf sie, was sie auch sage;
Tu's ihr zum Trotz, mein Lieb, komm alle
    Tage!

(21)

They tell me your mother disapproves;
stay away then, my darling, do as she bids.
No, dearest, no – do not do as she bids,
visit me just the same, despite her, secretly!
No, my love, do not obey her,
defy her, come more often than before!
No, do not listen to her, whatever she may
    say;
defy her, my darling, come every day!

(22)

Ein Ständchen Euch zu bringen kam ich her,
Wenn es dem Herrn vom Haus nicht unge-
    legen.
Ihr habt ein schönes Töchterlein. Es wär
Wohl gut, sie nicht zu streng im Haus zu
    hegen.
Und liegt sie schon im Bett, so bitt ich sehr,
Tut es zu wissen ihr von meinetwegen,
Daß ihr Getreuer hier vorbeigekommen,
Der Tag und Nacht sie in den Sinn genom-
    men,
Und daß am Tag, der vierundzwanzig zählt,
Sie fünfundzwanzig Stunden lang mir fehlt.

(22)

I have come here to sing a serenade,
if the master of the house approves.
You have a beautiful daughter. Perhaps
it would be good not to keep her indoors too
    strictly.
And if she is in bed already, I beg you
to let her know, for my sake,
that her true love has passed this way,
who thinks of her night and day,
and misses her twenty-five hours
out of every twenty-four.

(23)

Was für ein Lied soll dir gesungen werden,
Das deiner würdig sei? Wo find ich's nur?
Am liebsten grüb ich es tief aus der Erden,
Gesungen noch von keiner Kreatur.
Ein Lied, das weder Mann noch Weib bis
    heute
Hört oder sang, selbst nicht die ältesten
    Leute.

(23)

What song can I sing
that would be worthy of you? Where can I
    find one?
I should like best to dig it deep out of the
    earth,
where no creature has ever sung it;
a song that no man or woman, however old,
has ever heard or sung to this day.

(24)

Ich esse nun mein Brot nicht trocken mehr,
Ein Dorn ist mir im Fuße stecken blieben.
Umsonst nach rechts und links blick ich
    umher,
Und keinen find ich, der mich möchte lieben.
Wenn's doch auch nur ein altes Männlein
    wäre,
Das mir erzeigt' ein wenig Lieb und Ehre.
Ich meine nämlich, so ein wohlgestalter,
Ehrbarer Greis, etwa von meinem Alter.
Ich meine, um mich ganz zu offenbaren,
Ein altes Männlein so von vierzehn Jahren.

(24)

I no longer eat my bread dry,
there is a thorn in my flesh.
In vain do I look right and left,
and find no one to love me.
If there were only a little old man
who loved and honoured me a little!
I mean an upstanding
worthy old man of about my age.
I mean, to be quite frank,
a little old man of about fourteen.

(25)

Mein Liebster hat zu Tische mich geladen
Und hatte doch kein Haus mich zu emp-
  fangen,
Nicht Holz noch Herd zum Kochen und zum
  Braten,
Der Hafen auch war längst entzwei ge-
  gangen.
An einem Fäßchen Wein gebrach es auch,
Und Gläser hat er gar nicht im Gebrauch;
Der Tisch war schmal, das Tafeltuch nicht
  besser,
Das Brot steinhart und völlig stumpf das
  Messer.

(25)

My sweetheart invited me to dinner,
yet had no house to receive me.
There was no wood, no hearth for cooking
  and frying,
even the pot was broken in two.
There was no cask of wine,
there were no glasses;
The table was narrow, the table-cloth no
  better,
the bread as hard as stone, and the knife
  quite blunt.

(26)

Ich ließ mir sagen und mir ward erzählt,
Der schöne Toni hungre sich zu Tode;
Seit ihn so überaus die Liebe quält,
Nimmr er auf einen Backzahn sieben Brote.
Nach Tisch, damit er die Verdauung stählt,
Verspeist er eine Wurst und sieben Brote,
Und lindert nicht Tonina seine Pein,
Bricht nächstens Hungersnot und Teurung
  ein.

(26)

I inquired and was told
that handsome Toni is starving himself to
  death.
Ever since love began to torment him
he eats only seven loaves per tooth.
After a meal, to strengthen his digestion,
he eats a sausage and seven loaves more;
and if Tonina will not ease his pain
we shall soon have famine and starvation.

(27)

Schon streck ich aus im Bett die müden
  Glieder,
Da tritt dein Bildnis vor mich hin, du Traute.
Gleich spring ich auf, fahr in die Schuhe
  wieder
Und wandre durch die Stadt mit meiner
  Laute.
Ich sing und spiele, daß die Straße schallt;
So manche lauscht – vorüber bin ich bald.
So manches Mädchen hat mein Lied gerührt,
Indes der Wind schon Sang und Klang ent-
  führt.

(27)

I had already stretched my tired limbs in bed
when suddenly your image, my darling, stood
  before me.
I jump up at once, put my shoes back on,
and wander through the town with my guitar.
The street resounds with my singing and
  playing;
many a girl listens – but I have soon gone
  past.
Many a girl is moved by my song
when the wind has already borne its sound
  away.

(28)

Du sagst mir, daß ich keine Fürstin sei;
Auch du bist nicht auf Spaniens Thron ent-
  sprossen.
Nein, Bester, stehst du auf bei Hahnenschrei,
Fährst du aufs Feld und nicht in Staats-
  karossen.
Du spottest mein um meine Niedrigkeit,
Doch Armut tut dem Adel nichts zuleid.

(28)

You tell me I am no princess;
but you are not Spanish royalty either.
No, my dear: when you rise at cock-
  crow
you go to the field, and not in a coach and
  four.
You mock my humble station;
but poverty is compatible with nobility.

Du spottest, daß mir Krone fehlt und
    Wappen,
Und fährst doch selber nur mit Schusters
    Rappen.

You mock me for having no crown or crest;
but you yourself ride Shanks's pony.

(29)

Wohl kenn ich Euern Stand, der nicht gering.
Ihr brauchtet nicht so tief herabzusteigen,
Zu lieben solch ein arm und niedrig Ding,
Da sich vor Euch die Allerschönsten neigen.
Die schönsten Männer leicht besiegtet Ihr,
Drum weiß ich wohl, Ihr treibt nur Spiel
    mit mir.
Ihr spottet mein, man hat mich warnen
    wollen,
Doch ach, Ihr seid so schön! Wer kann Euch
    grollen?

(29)

I know how high your station is.
You need not stoop to loving
so poor and humble a creature as I am.
You easily conquered the handsomest men –
I know, therefore, you are only trifling with
    me.
You are mocking me, people have tried to
    warn me,
but you are so beautiful – who could be
    angry with you?

(30)

Laß sie nur gehn, die so die Stolze spielt,
Das Wunderkräutlein aus dem Blumenfeld.
Man sieht, wohin ihr blankes Auge zielt,
Da Tag um Tag ein andrer ihr gefällt.
Sie treibt es grade wie Toscanas Fluß,
Dem jedes Berggewässer folgen muß.
Sie treibt es wie der Arno, will mir scheinen:
Bald hat sie viel Bewerber, bald nicht einen.

(30)

Let her go then, if she acts so proud,
as if she were the fairest flower in the field!
What her bright eyes want, is clear;
for every day another man pleases her.
She goes on like Tuscany's river
that every mountain-stream must follow.
She goes on, it seems to me, like the Arno:
now she has many followers, now not one.

(31)

Wie soll ich fröhlich sein und lachen gar,
Da du mir immer zürnest unverhohlen?
Du kommst nur einmal alle hundert Jahr,
Und dann, als hätte man dir's anbefohlen.
Was kommst du, wenn's die Deinen ungern
    sehn?
Gib frei mein Herz, dann magst du weiter-
    gehn.
Daheim mit deinen Leuten leb in Frieden,
Denn was der Himmel will, geschieht
    hienieden.
Halt Frieden mit den Deinigen zu Haus,
Denn was der Himmel will, das bleibt nicht
    aus.

(31)

How can I be gay, how can I laugh,
when you always spurn me so openly?
You only come once in a hundred years –
and then as though it were by order.
Why do you come if your family is against
    it?
Set my heart free and go your ways.
Live in peace at home with your people;
what Heaven ordains, happens here below.
Live at peace at home with your family;
for what Heaven ordains will come to pass.

(32)

Was soll der Zorn, mein Schatz, der dich
    erhitzt?
Ich bin mir keiner Sünde ja bewußt,
Ach, lieber nimm ein Messer wohlgespitzt
Und tritt zu mir, durchbohre mir die Brust.

(32)

Why this hot anger, my love?
I am conscious of no wrong I have
    done.
I had rather you took a sharp knife
and plunged it in my breast.

Und taugt ein Messer nicht, so nimm ein
   Schwert,
Daß meines Blutes Quell gen Himmel fährt.
Und taugt ein Schwert nicht, nimm des
   Dolches Stahl
Und wasch in meinem Blut all meine Qual.

Or if a knife will not serve, take a sword
and let my blood gush to the heavens.
And if not a sword, take a dagger
and let blood wash away my anguish.

(33)

Sterb ich, so hüllt in Blumen meine Glieder;
Ich wünsche nicht, daß ihr ein Grab mir
   grabt.
Genüber jenen Mauern legt mich nieder,
Wo ihr so manchmal mich gesehen habt.
Dort legt mich hin, in Regen oder Wind;
Gern sterb ich, ist's um dich, geliebtes Kind.
Dort legt mich hin in Sonnenschein und
   Regen;
Ich sterbe lieblich, sterb ich deinetwegen.

(33)

If I die, strew my limbs with flowers;
I will not have you dig a grave for me.
Lay me down to face those walls
where you have often seen me.
There let me lie, in wind or rain;
I die gladly if I die for you, dear love.
There let me lie, in sunshine or rain;
dying is beautiful if it is for your sake.

(34)

Und steht Ihr früh am Morgen auf vom
   Bette,
Scheucht Ihr vom Himmel alle Wolken fort,
Die Sonne lockt Ihr auf die Berge dort,
Und Engelein erscheinen um die Wette
Und bringen Schuh und Kleider Euch sofort.
Dann, wenn Ihr ausgeht in die heil'ge Mette,
So zieht Ihr alle Menschen mit Euch fort,
Und wenn Ihr naht der benedeiten Stätte,
So zündet Euer Blick die Lampen an.
Weihwasser nehmt Ihr, macht des Kreuzes
   Zeichen
Und netzet Eure weiße Stirn sodann
Und neiget Euch und beugt die Knie in-
   gleichen –
O wie holdselig steht Euch alles an!
Wie hold und selig hat Euch Gott begabt,
Die Ihr der Schönheit Kron empfangen habt!
Wie hold und selig wandelt Ihr im Leben;
Der Schönheit Palme ward an Euch gegeben.

(34)

When you rise from your bed at dawn
you chase all clouds from the sky,
you lure the sun on to those hills
and angels vie with one another
to bring you your shoes and clothes.
Then, when you go to Mass,
you draw all the people after you,
and when you approach the sanctuary
your glance lights the lamps.
You take holy water, make the sign of the
   cross,
moisten your white brow,
bow down and bend the knee –
How well all this becomes you!
What gracious blessings God has bestowed
   on you
when He gave you the crown of beauty!
How graciously, how blessedly you walk
   through life;
the palm of beauty was bestowed on you.

(35)

Benedeit die sel'ge Mutter,
Die so lieblich dich geboren,
So an Schönheit auserkoren,
Meine Sehnsucht fliegt dir zu!

Du so lieblich von Gebärden,
Du die Holdeste der Erden,
Du mein Kleinod, meine Wonne,
Süße, benedeit bist du!

(35)

Blessed be the happy mother
who bore you and your charms
you paragon of beauty,
all my longing goes out to you!

You with your charming gestures,
you, dearest on earth,
my jewel, my joy –
God has blessed you, my sweet!

Wenn ich aus der Ferne schmachte
Und betrachte deine Schöne,
Siehe wie ich beb und stöhne,
Daß ich kaum es bergen kann!

Und in meiner Brust gewaltsam
Fühl ich Flammen sich empören,
Die den Frieden mir zerstören,
Ach, der Wahnsinn faßt mich an!

Benedeit die sel'ge Mutter,
Die so lieblich dich geboren,
So an Schönheit auserkoren,
Meine Sehnsucht fliegt dir zu!

(36)
Wenn du, mein Liebster, steigst zum Himmel
    auf,
Trag ich mein Herz dir in der Hand entgegen.
So liebevoll umarmst du mich darauf,
Dann wolln wir uns dem Herrn zu Füßen
    legen.
Und sieht der Herrgott unsre Liebes-
    schmerzen,
Macht er ein Herz aus zwei verliebten Herzen,
Zu einem Herzen fügt er zwei zusammen,
Im Paradies, umglänzt von Himmels-
    flammen.

(37)
Wie viele Zeit verlor ich, dich zu lieben!
Hätt ich doch Gott geliebt in all der Zeit.
Ein Platz im Paradies wär mir verschrieben,
Ein Heilger säße dann an meiner Seit.
Und weil ich dich geliebt, schön frisch
    Gesicht,
Verscherzt ich mir des Paradieses Licht,
Und weil ich dich geliebt, schön Veigelein,
Komm ich nun nicht ins Paradies hinein.

(38)
Wenn du mich mit den Augen streifst und
    lachst,
Sie senkst, und neigst das Kinn zum Busen
    dann,
Bitt ich, daß du mir erst ein Zeichen machst,
Damit ich doch mein Herz auch bänd'gen
    kann,

When I languish afar
and look at your beauty –
see how I tremble and groan!
I can hardly hide it.

And in my heart I feel the force
of rebellious flames
that destroy my peace –
madness seizes me!

Blessed be the happy mother
who bore you and your charms;
You paragon of beauty,
all my longing goes out to you!

(36)
When you go up to heaven, my love,
I shall meet you, bearing my heart in my
    hand.
Then you will embrace me lovingly
and we shall throw ourselves at the Lord's
    feet.
And if the Lord sees the anguish of our love,
He will make one heart of our two loving
    hearts.
He will join two hearts into one
in Paradise, amid the radiance of Heaven.

(37)
How much time I have lost in loving you!
If I had spent that time loving God
I would now be sure of a seat in Paradise,
where a saint would sit by my side.
But because I loved you and your lovely
    fresh face
I have forfeited the light of Paradise,
and because I have loved you, my lovely
    violet,
I shall never enter Paradise.

(38)
When you glance at me and laugh,
when you look down and bow your
    head –
I beg you to give me a sign first
that I may keep my heart in check,

Daß ich mein Herz mag bänd'gen, zahm und
  still,
Wenn es vor großer Liebe springen will,
Daß ich mein Herz mag halten in der Brust,
Wenn es ausbrechen will vor großer Lust.

that I may keep it tame and still
when great love makes it leap up,
that I may hold it back in my breast
when in its great joy it wants to break out.

(39)
Gesegnet sei das Grün und wer es trägt!
Ein grünes Kleid will ich mir machen lassen.
Ein grünes Kleid trägt auch die Frühlings-
  aue,
Grün kleidet sich der Liebling meiner Augen.
In Grün sich kleiden ist der Jäger Brauch,
Ein grünes Kleid trägt mein Geliebter auch;
Das Grün steht allen Dingen lieblich an,
Aus Grün wächst jede schöne Frucht heran.

(39)
Blessed be green and he who wears it!
I will have a green dress made.
The meadows too wear green in spring.
My heart's darling wears green.
To wear green is a hunter's custom,
and my love too wears green.
All things look well in green,
all lovely fruit grows from green.

(40)
O wär dein Haus durchsichtig wie ein Glas,
Mein Holder, wenn ich mich vorüberstehle!
Dann säh ich drinnen dich ohn Unterlaß,
Wie blickt ich dann nach dir mit ganzer Seele!
Wie viele Blicke schickte dir mein Herz,
Mehr als da Tropfen hat der Fluß im März!
Wie viele Blicke schickt ich dir entgegen,
Mehr als da Tropfen niedersprühn im Regen!

(40)
If only your house were transparent like
  glass,
when I steal by, my darling!
Then I should always see you,
and with all my soul I would look at you.
My heart would send you more glances
than the river has drops in March.
I would look at you more times
than there are drops in the falling rain.

(41)
Heut nacht erhob ich mich um Mitternacht,
Da war mein Herz mir heimlich fort-
  geschlichen.
Ich frug: Herz, wohin stürmst du so mit
  Macht?
Es sprach: Nur Euch zu sehn, sei es ent-
  wichen.
Nun sieh, wie muß es um mein Lieben stehn:
Mein Herz entweicht der Brust, um dich zu
  sehn!

(41)
Tonight I rose at midnight
and found that my heart had stolen away.
I asked: 'My heart, where are you going so
  fast?'
It answered that it had deserted me only to
  see you.
Now you can see the force of my love:
my heart steals from my breast only to see
  you!

(42)
Nicht länger kann ich singen, denn der
  Wind
Weht stark und macht dem Atem was zu
  schaffen.
Auch fürcht ich, daß die Zeit umsonst
  verrinnt.
Ja wär ich sicher, ging ich jetzt nicht schlafen.
Ja wüßt ich was, würd ich nicht heimspazieren
Und einsam diese schöne Zeit verlieren.

(42)
I can sing no more, for the wind
blows fiercely and takes my breath away.
I fear, too, that I am wasting my time.
If only I were sure of your love, I would not
  go to bed now.
If only I knew, I would not go home
to pass this lovely time alone.

(43)
Schweig einmal still, du garst'ger Schwätzer
    dort!
Zum Ekel ist mir dein verwünschtes Singen.
Und triebst du es bis morgen früh so fort,
Doch würde dir kein schmuckes Lied
    gelingen.
Schweig einmal still und lege dich aufs Ohr!
Das Ständchen eines Esels zög ich vor.

(43)
Do be quiet, you wretched chatterer;
I am sick of your cursed singing.
Even if you went on till tomorrow morning
you would not produce one decent song.
Be quiet and go to bed!
I would rather be serenaded by a donkey.

(44)
O wüßtest du, wie viel ich deinetwegen,
Du falsche Renegatin, litt zur Nacht,
Indes du im verschloßnen Haus gelegen
Und ich die Zeit im Freien zugebracht.
Als Rosenwasser diente mir der Regen,
Der Blitz hat Liebesbotschaft mir gebracht;
Ich habe Würfel mit dem Sturm gespielt,
Als unter deinem Dach ich Wache hielt.
Mein Bett war unter deinem Dach bereitet,
Der Himmel lag als Decke drauf gebreitet,
Die Schwelle deiner Tür, das war mein
    Kissen –
Ich Ärmster, ach, was hab ich ausstehn
    müssen!

(44)
If you only knew, false traitress, how much
for your sake I have suffered tonight,
while you lay in your locked house
and I spent the night in the open.
The rain was my rose-water,
the lightning brought tidings of love;
I played at dice with the storm,
when I kept watch by your roof.
My bed was under your gable,
the sky spread over as a blanket,
your threshold was my pillow –
poor me, how much I had to suffer!

(45)
Verschling der Abgrund meines Liebsten
    Hütte,
An ihrer Stelle schäum ein See zur Stunde.
Bleikugeln soll der Himmel drüber schütten,
Und eine Schlange hause dort im Grunde.
Drin hause eine Schlange gift'ger Art,
Die ihn vergifte, der mir untreu ward.
Drin hause ein Schlange, giftgeschwollen,
Und bring ihm Tod, der mich verraten
    wollen!

(45)
May a chasm swallow up my lover's hut
and a lake well up there!
May Heaven rain bullets of lead over it,
and a snake make its lair there!
Let a poisonous snake infest it,
and sting him who was unfaithful to me.
Let a snake, swollen with venom, dwell there
and kill him who thought to betray me.

(46)
Ich hab in Penna einen Liebsten wohnen,
In der Maremmeneb'ne einen andern,
Einen im schönen Hafen von Ancona,
Zum vierten muß ich nach Viterbo wandern;
Ein andrer wohnt in Casentino dort,
Der nächste lebt mit mir am selben Ort,
Und wieder einen hab ich in Magione,
Vier in La Fratta, zehn in Castiglione.

(46)
I have one lover living in Penna,
another in the plain of Maremma,
one in the beautiful port of Ancona,
to see the fourth, I must wander to Viterbo,
yet another lives over there, in Casentino,
the next in my own town;
I have another in Magione,
four in La Fratta, ten in Castiglione.

6 THREE SONGS FROM POEMS BY MICHELANGELO [TRANSL. WALTER ROBERT-TORNOW; COMP. 1897]

(1)

Wohl denk ich oft an mein vergangnes
   Leben,
Wie es vor meiner Liebe für dich war;
Kein Mensch hat damals acht auf mich
   gegeben,
Ein jeder Tag verloren für mich war;
Ich dachte wohl, ganz dem Gesang zu leben,
Auch mich zu flüchten aus der Menschen
   Schar.
Genannt in Lob und Tadel bin ich heute,
Und, daß ich da bin, wissen alle Leute!

(2)

Alles endet, was entstehet.
Alles, alles rings vergehet,
Denn die Zeit flieht, und die Sonne
Sieht, daß alles rings vergehet,
Denken, Reden, Schmerz, und Wonne;
Und die wir zu Enkeln hatten
Schwanden wie bei Tag die Schatten,
Wie ein Dunst im Windeshauch.
Menschen waren wir ja auch,
Froh und traurig, so wie ihr,
Und nun sind wir leblos hier,
Sind nur Erde, wie ihr sehet.
Alles endet, was entstehet.
Alles, alles rings vergehet.

(3)

Fühlt meine Seele das ersehnte Licht
Von Gott, der sie erschuf? Ist es der Strahl
Von andrer Schönheit aus dem Jammertal,
Der in mein Herz Erinnrung weckend
   bricht?
Ist es ein Klang, ein Traumgesicht,
Das Aug und Herz mir füllt mit einem Mal
In unbegreiflich glüh'nder Qual,
Die mich zu Tränen bringt? Ich weiß es
   nicht.
Was ich ersehne, fühle, was mich lenkt,
Ist nicht in mir: sag mir, wie ich's erwerbe?
Mir zeigt es wohl nur eines Andren Huld;
Darein bin ich, seit ich dich sah, versenkt,
Micht treibt ein Ja und Nein, ein Süß und
   Herbe –
Daran sind, Herrin, deine Augen Schuld.

(1)

True, I often recall my former life
as it was before I loved you;
no one then took notice of me,
every day was lost to me;
I thought to live for song alone
and flee the madding crowd.
Today my name is praised and blamed
and all the world knows I exist!

(2)

All that comes into being, must end.
All, all around us must perish,
for time is flying and the sun sees
that everything passes:
thought, speech, pain, and joy;
and our grandchildren
vanished like shadows by day,
like smoke in the wind.
We too were men,
with joys and sorrows like your own;
and now we are here, lifeless,
are nothing but earth, as you see.
All that comes into being, must end,
all, all around us must perish.

(3)

Does my soul feel the longed-for light
from God who created it? Is it the bright ray
of other beauty from this vale of tears
that breaks into my heart, awakening
   memory?
Is it a sound, a dream-vision
which suddenly fills my eyes and my heart
with inconceivable, searing pain
that makes me weep? I do not know.
What I long for, what I feel, what guides me
is not in me: tell me how to win it!
Sure, only another's favour may reveal it.
Of this I think ever since I saw you.
I am torn between 'Yes' and 'No', sweetness
   and bitterness:
your eyes, dear mistress, are the cause of that.

GUSTAV MAHLER

Born at Kalischt in Bohemia on 7 July 1860, the son of a shopkeeper and publican. Mahler's first musical impressions were the cavalry signals of the Austrian barracks opposite his father's house – their texture and rhythm can be heard again and again in his later symphonies and songs. After schooling at Jihlava and Prague, he entered the Vienna Conservatory, completing his course in 1878. He then became conductor at various theatres and opera houses: at Ljubljana, Olmütz, Kassel, and – in 1885 – Prague. From Prague he moved to Leipzig, thence to Budapest and Hamburg; and in 1897 he achieved the pinnacle of his ambition by becoming musical director of the Vienna Court Opera. He occupied this post with great distinction, but his many enemies and the intrigues inseparable from the administration of opera houses led him to resign in 1907. Mahler then accepted an appointment at the Metropolitan Opera House, New York, and also conducted the New York Philharmonic Society concerts from 1908 onwards. He was already, however, incurably ill, and died in Vienna on 18 May 1911. He left nine completed symphonies and one unfinished; the early cantata *Das klagende Lied*, based on an unsuccessful opera of the same name written in 1880; the song-cycles *Lieder eines fahrenden Gesellen* and *Kindertotenlieder*, many settings of texts from *Des Knaben Wunderhorn* (see below), and five late songs to texts by Friedrich Rückert.

The merits and demerits of Mahler's symphonies are still contested; but few would now deny his greatness and originality as a composer of songs. He began with songs with piano-accompaniments (of these 'Wer hat denn das Liedlein erdacht' has rightly become a universal favourite) but soon found his real field to be the song with orchestra. Some of these later songs are accompanied by orchestras of symphonic dimensions ('Revelge'); but others call for smaller, selective orchestras that exploit, with the greatest subtlety, the colouristic possibilities of different instruments ('Um Mitternacht', for instance, has only wind instruments, timpani, and harp). *Das Lied von der Erde* merges symphony and song: its different sections are held together by a single basic motif (used vertically in the final chord!) in a way which recalls the symphonic variation principle of the nineteenth and anticipates the 'tone-rows' of the twentieth centuries. Schoenberg looked up to Mahler as his great teacher and celebrated him, in an essay devoted to his work, as 'one of the greatest men and artists'.

I FROM 'LIEDER UND GESÄNGE AUS DER JUGENDZEIT' [DES KNABEN WUNDERHORN] (1882)

Um schlimme Kinder artig zu machen

Es kam ein Herr zum Schlößeli
Auf einem schönen Röß'li,
[Kuckuck, kuckuck!]
Da lugt die Frau zum Fenster aus
Und sagt: 'der Mann ist nicht zu Haus,
Und niemand heim als meine Kind
Und's Mädchen ist auf der Wäschewind!'

Der Herr auf seinem Rößeli
Sagt zu der Frau im Schlößeli:
[Kuckuck, kuckuck!]

How to make Naughty Children Good

A gentleman rode up to the castle
on a beautiful little horse.
[Cuckoo, cuckoo!]
The woman peeps out of the window
and says: 'My husband is not at home,
there is no one here but my children,
and the maid is hanging up the clothes!'

The gentleman on his horse
says to the woman in the castle:
[Cuckoo, cuckoo!]

'Sind's gute Kind, sind's böse Kind?
Ach liebe Frau, ach sagt geschwind.'
[Kuckuck, kuckuck!]

'In meiner Tasch für folgsam Kind,
Da hab ich manche Angebind',
[Kuckuck, kuckuck!]
Die Frau, die sagt: 'sehr böse Kind!
Sie folgen Muttern nicht geschwind,
Sind böse, sind böse!'
Die Frau, die sagt: 'sind böse Kind!
Sie folgen der Mutter nicht geschwind!'

Da sagt der Herr: 'so reit ich heim,
Dergleichen Kinder brauch ich kein'!'
[Kuckuck, kuckuck!]
Und reit auf seinem Rößeli
Weit entweg vom Schlößeli!
[Kuckuck, kuckuck!]

'Are the children good or bad?
Dear lady, tell me quickly!'
[Cuckoo, cuckoo!]

'For obedient children I have
many presents in my pocket.'
[Cuckoo, cuckoo!]
The woman says: 'Very naughty children!
They won't do what mother tells them!
They are naughty, naughty!'
The woman says: 'They are naughty children!
They won't do what mother tells them!'

The gentleman says: 'I'll ride home then,
I'll have nothing to do with children like that!'
[Cuckoo, cuckoo!]
And off he rides on his little horse,
far, far away from the castle.
[Cuckoo, cuckoo!]

2 'LIEDER EINES FAHRENDEN GESELLEN' 'SONGS OF A WAYFARER' (1883)

(1)
Wenn mein Schatz Hochzeit macht,
Hab ich meinen traurigen Tag!
Geh ich in mein Kämmerlein, dunkles Kämmerlein!
Weine! Wein! um meinen Schatz, um meinen lieben Schatz!

Blümlein blau! Verdorre nicht!
Vöglein süß! Du singst auf grüner Heide!
Ach! Wie ist die Welt so schön! Ziküth!

Singet nicht, erblühet nicht, Lenz ist ja vorbei!
Alles Singen ist nun aus!
Des Abends, wenn ich schlafen geh,
Denk ich an mein Leid, an mein Leide!

(2)
Ging heut morgen über's Feld,
Tau noch auf den Gräsern hing;
Sprach zu mir der lustge Fink:
'Ei, du! Gelt? Guten Morgen! Ei gelt? Du!
Wird's nicht eine schöne Welt? schöne Welt!?
Zink! Zink! schön und flink!
Wie mir doch die Welt gefällt!'

(1)
My sweetheart's wedding day
is a sad day for me.
Then I go to my little room
and weep for my dear love.

Little blue flower, do not fade;
sweet little bird, you are singing in the green meadow –
how lovely the world is!

Do not sing, do not bloom; for spring is now over
and all singing must end.
In the evening, when I go to rest,
I think of my grief.

(2)
This morning I walked through the field
when dew still hung on the grass.
The merry chaffinch called to me:
'Well? Good morning! Well?
Is the world not growing lovely?
Chirp, chirp! Lovely!
How I like to be in this world!'

Auch die Glockenblum am Feld
Hat mir lustig, guter Ding
Mit dem Glöckchen klinge, kling,
Ihren Morgengruß geschellt:
'Wird's nicht eine schöne Welt? schöne
    Welt!?
Kling! Kling! Schönes Ding!
Wie mir doch die Welt gefällt! Hei-a!'

Und da fing im Sonnenschein
Gleich die Welt zu funkeln an;
Alles, alles, Ton und Farbe gewann im
    Sonnenschein!
Blum und Vogel, groß und klein!
'Guten Tag, guten Tag! Ist's nicht eine
    schöne Welt?
Ei du! Gelt! Schöne Welt!'

Nun fängt auch mein Glück wohl an?
Nein! Nein! Das ich mein, mir nimmer
    blühen kann!

(3)
Ich hab ein glühend Messer, ein Messer in
    meiner Brust.
O weh! o weh!
Das schneid't so tief in jede Freud und jede
    Lust, so tief!
Ach, was ist das für ein böser Gast!
Nimmer hält er Ruh, nimmer hält er Rast,
Nicht bei Tag, nicht bei Nacht, wenn ich
    schlief!
O weh! o weh!

Wenn ich in den Himmel seh,
Seh ich zwei blaue Augen stehn!
O weh! o weh!
Wenn ich im gelben Felde geh,
Seh ich von fern das blonde Haar im Winde
    wehn!
Oh weh! o weh!
Wenn ich aus dem Traum auffahr
Und höre klingen ihr silbern Lachen,
O weh! o weh!
Ich wollt, ich läg auf der schwarzen Bahr,
Könnt nimmer die Augen aufmachen!

(4)
Die zwei blauen Augen von meinem Schatz
Die haben mich in die weite Welt geschickt.

The bluebell in the field,
in gay and happy mood,
rang out
Her morning-greeting towards me:
'Is the world not growing lovely?
Tinkle, tinkle! Lovely!
How I like to be in this world!'

Then, in the sunshine,
the world began to sparkle;
everything grew bright with colour in the
    sunshine,
big flowers, little flowers, big birds, little
    birds,
'Good day, good day! Is not this world
    lovely?
Well? Is it not lovely?'

Will my happiness begin now?
No – my happiness will never flower

(3)
I feel a knife burning in my breast
alas! alas!
which cuts deep into every joy and pleasure.
What an ill guest is this!
He never rests
by day or night, not even when I sleep.
alas! alas!

When I look up to the sky
I see two blue eyes.
alas! alas!
When I walk through the yellow cornfields
I see her fair hair blowing, far off, in the wind.
alas! alas!
When I start from my dream
and hear her silvery laughter,
alas! alas!
then I wish I were lying in my dark grave
and might never open my eyes again.

(4)
My sweetheart's blue eyes
have driven me into the wide world.

Da mußt ich Abschied nehmen vom aller-
liebsten Platz!
O Augen, blau! Warum habt ihr mich
angeblickt?
Nun hab ich ewig Leid und Grämen!

Ich bin ausgegangen in stiller Nacht,
In stiller Nacht wohl über die dunkle Heide.
Hat mir niemand ade gesagt, ade!
Mein Gesell war Lieb und Leide!

Auf der Straße steht ein Lindenbaum,
Da hab ich zum erstenmal im Schlaf geruht.
Unter dem Lindenbaum, der hat seine
Blüten
Über mich geschneit, da wußt ich nicht,
Wie das Leben tut, war alles, ach alles wieder
gut!
Alles! Alles! Lieb und Leid!
Und Welt und Traum!

Then I had to take leave of the place I love
most.
O you blue eyes – why did you look at me?
Now I must ever feel anguish and grief.

In the dark night I set out
over the dark heath.
No one said good-bye to me,
love and sorrow were my only companions.

A lime-tree stands by the road –
there I rested, and slept for the first time.
Lying under the lime-tree that shed its blossoms
over me, I forgot the pain of life,
and all was well again:
all – love and grief,
world and dream.

3 FROM 'LIEDER AUS "DES KNABEN WUNDERHORN"' [ACHIM VON ARNIM
AND CLEMENS BRENTANO] (1888)

(1) *Wer hat dies Liedlein erdacht?*

(1) *Who Thought Up This Song?*

Dort oben am Berg in dem hohen Haus,
Da gucket ein fein's, lieb's Mädel heraus,
Er ist nicht dort daheime!
Es ist des Wirts sein Töchterlein!
Es wohnet auf grüner Heide!

Mein Herzle ist wund!
Komm, Schätzle, mach's g'sund!
Dein schwarzbraune Äuglein,
Die hab'n mich verwund't!

Dein rosiger Mund
Macht Herzen gesund,
Macht Jugend verständig,
Macht Tote lebendig,
Macht Kranke gesund.

Wer hat denn das schön schöne Liedlein
erdacht?
Es haben's drei Gäns übers Wasser gebracht.
Zwei graue und eine weiße!
Und wer das Liedlein nicht singen kann,
Dem wollen sie es pfeifen!

Up there in the mountain, in the tall house,
a dear, pretty girl looks out of the window.
She does not live there;
she is the innkeeper's daughter
and lives in the green meadow.

My heart is sore –
come, sweetheart, make it whole again!
Your dark brown eyes
have wounded me.

Your rosy mouth
heals wounded hearts,
gives wisdom to youth,
life to the dead,
health to the sick.

Who thought up this lovely little song?
Three geese brought it over the water,
two grey ones and a white one!
And if you cannot sing this song
they will whistle it to you.

(2) *Das irdische Leben*

'Mutter, ach Mutter, es hungert mich,
Gib mir Brot, sonst sterbe ich!'
'Warte nur, warte nur, mein liebes Kind!
Morgen wollen wir ernten geschwind!'

Und als das Korn geerntet war,
Rief das Kind noch immerdar:
'Mutter, ach Mutter, es hungert mich,
Gib mir Brot, sonst sterbe ich!'

'Warte nur, warte nur, mein liebes Kind!
Morgen wollen wir dreschen geschwind!'

Und als das Korn gedroschen war,
Rief das Kind noch immerdar:
'Mutter, ach Mutter, es hungert mich,
Gib mir Brot, sonst sterbe ich!'

'Warte nur, warte nur, mein liebes Kind!
Morgen wollen wir backen geschwind!'

Und also das Brot gebacken war,
Lag das Kind auf der Totenbahr!

(3) *Des Antonius von Padua Fischpredigt*

Antonius zur Predigt
Die Kirche find't ledig.
Er geht zu den Flüssen
Und predigt den Fischen.

Sie schlagen mit den Schwänzen,
Im Sonnenschein glänzen.

Die Karpfen mit Rogen
Sind allhier gezogen,
Hab'n d'Mäuler aufrissen,
Sich Zuhör'ns beflissen.

Kein' Predigt niemalen
Den Fischen so g'fallen!

Spitzgoschete Hechte,
Die immerfort fechten,
Sind eilends herschwommen
Zu hören den Frommen.

Auch jene Phantasten,
Die immerfort fasten,
Die Stockfisch ich meine,
zur Predigt erscheinen.

(2) *Life on Earth*

'Mother, oh mother, I am hungry,
give me bread or I shall die.'
'Wait a little, darling child,
tomorrow we will quickly bring in the corn.'

And when the corn had been brought in
the child still went on calling
'Mother, oh mother, I am hungry,
give me bread or I shall die!'

'Wait a little, darling child,
tomorrow we will quickly thresh the corn.'

And when the corn had been threshed,
the child still went on calling
'Mother, oh mother, I am hungry,
give me bread or I shall die!'

'Wait a little, darling child,
tomorrow we will quickly bake.'

And when the bread had been baked
the child lay dead on the bier.

(3) *St Anthony's Sermon to the Fishes*

Coming to preach his sermon,
St Anthony finds the church empty.
He goes to the rivers
to preach to the fishes.

They swish their tails,
gleaming in the sunshine.

Carp full of roe
have come here,
have opened their gullets wide,
listen attentively.

No sermon ever
so pleased the fishes.

Sharp-mouthed pike
that are ever fighting
have quickly swum hither
to hear the pious man.

And those unworldly creatures
that are always fasting –
I mean the cod –
have put in an appearance.

Kein' Predigt niemalen
Den Fischen so g'fallen!

Gut Aale und Hausen,
Die vornehme schmausen,
Die selbst sich bequemen,
Die Predigt vernehmen.

Auch Krebse, Schildkroten,
Sonst langsame Boten,
Steigen eilig vom Grund
Zu hören diesen Mund!

Kein' Predigt niemalen
Den Stockfisch so g'fallen!

Fisch große, Fisch kleine,
Vornehm und gemeine,
Erheben die Köpfe
Wie verständige Geschöpfe.

Auf Gottes Begehren
Die Predigt anhören.

Die Predigt geendet,
Ein jeder sich wendet.
Die Hechte bleiben Diebe,
Die Aale viel lieben.

Die Predigt hat g'fallen,
Sie bleiben wie allen.

Die Krebs gehn zurücke,
Die Stockfisch bleiben dicke,
Die Karpfen viel fressen,
Die Predigt vergessen!

No sermon ever
so pleased the fishes.

Fine eels and sturgeons
that eat sumptuously –
even they took the trouble
to appear for the sermon.

Crabs too, and turtles,
usually so slow,
rise quickly from the bottom
to hear St Anthony preach.

No sermon ever
so pleased the cod.

Big fish, little fish,
smart fish, common fish –
all lift up their heads
like reasonable creatures.

According to God's will
they listen to the sermon.

The sermon over,
they all turn about.
The pike remain thieves,
the eel stay great lovers.

They liked the sermon
but remain as before.

The crabs go backwards,
the cod stay fat,
the carp guzzle a good deal
and forget the sermon!

(4) *Wo die schönen Trompeten
blasen*

(4) *Where the Splendid Trumpets
Blow*

Wer ist denn draußen und wer klopfet an,
Der mich so leise wecken kann?
'Das ist der Herzallerliebste dein;
Steh auf und laß mich zu dir ein!
Was soll ich hier nun länger stehn?
Ich seh die Morgenröt aufgehn,
Die Morgenröt, zwei helle Stern,
Bei meinem Schatz da wär ich gern!
Bei meinem Herzallerliebe.'

Who is out there, who knocks
to wake me so gently?
'It is your own dear love,
get up and let me in!
Why should I stay out here?
I see the red glow of dawn,
the red dawn and two bright stars.
I would like to be with my sweetheart,
with my dear love.'

Das Mädchen stand auf und ließ ihn ein,
Sie heißt ihn auch willkommen sein.
'Willkommen, lieber Knabe mein!
So lang hast du gestanden.'
Sie reicht' ihm auch die schneeweiße Hand.
Von ferne sang die Nachtigall,
Das Mädchen fing zu weinen an.

The girl got up and let him in
and made him welcome.
'Welcome, my own dearest boy!
You have stood out there so long.'
She gave him her snow-white hand.
Far off the nightingale sang
and the girl began to weep.

'Ach, weine nicht, du Liebste mein!
Auf's Jahr sollst du mein eigen sein.
Mein eigen sollst du werden gewiß,
Wie's keine sonst auf Erden ist.
O Lieb auf grüner Erden!
Ich zieh in Krieg auf grüne Heid;
Die grüne Heid, die ist so weit!
Allwo dort die schönen Trompeten blasen,
Da ist mein Haus von grünem Rasen.'

'Do not weep, my dearest!
Within a year you shall be mine.
No one else on earth
will be mine as you shall be,
oh my love on the green earth!
I go to war in green fields,
the green fields stretch so far!
Where the splendid trumpets blow
there is my home of green turf.'

4 FIVE SONGS TO POEMS BY FRIEDRICH RÜCKERT (1902)

(1) 'Ich atmet' einen linden Duft'

(1) 'I breathed a gentle scent of lime'

Ich atmet' einen linden Duft.
Im Zimmer stand
Ein Zweig der Linde
Ein Angebinde
Von lieber Hand.
Wie lieblich war der Lindenduft!

I breathed a gentle scent of lime.
In the room stood
a lime-twig,
the gift
of a dear hand.
How lovely was the scent of lime!

Wie lieblich ist der Lindenduft!
Das Lindenreis
Brachst du gelinde;
Ich atme leis'
Im Duft der Linde
Der Liebe linden Duft.

How lovely is the scent of lime!
The lime-twig
you broke off gently.
Softly I breathe
the scent of lime,
the gentle scent of love.

(2) 'Liebst du um Schönheit'

(2) 'If You Love For Beauty'

Liebst du um Schönheit, o nicht mich liebe!
Liebe die Sonne, sie trägt ein goldnes Haar!
Liebst du um Jugend, o nicht mich liebe!
Liebe den Frühling, der jung ist jedes Jahr!
Liebst du um Schätze, o nicht mich liebe!
Liebe die Meerfrau, sie hat viel Perlen klar!
Liebst du um Liebe, o ja mich liebe!
Liebe mich immer, dich lieb ich immerdar!

If you love for beauty, then do not love me!
Love the sun for its golden hair.
If you love for youth, then do not love me!
Love the spring who is young every year.
If you love for treasure, then do not love me!
Love the mermaid who has many bright
    pearls.
If you love for love – oh then love me!
Love me always as I will always love you!

(3) 'Blicke mir nicht in die Lieder'

Blicke mir nicht in die Lieder!
Meine Augen schlag ich nieder,
Wie ertappt auf böser Tat.
Selber darf ich nicht getrauen
Ihrem Wachsen zuzuschauen,
Deine Neugier ist Verrat.

Bienen, wenn sie Zellen bauen,
Lassen auch nicht zu sich schauen,
Schauen selber auch nicht zu.
Wenn die reichen Honigwaben
Sie zu Tag befördert haben,
Dann vor allen nasche du!

(3) 'Do not Look at My Songs!'

Do not look at my songs before they are
    finished!
I lower my eyes
as though caught in a crime.
Even I myself dare not
look on as they grow –
your curiosity is treason.

When bees build their cells
they too let no one look in
and do not look on themselves.
When they have brought the rich honey-
    combs
to the light of day,
you shall taste them before anyone else!

(4) 'Ich bin der Welt abhanden gekommen'

Ich bin der Welt abhanden gekommen,
Mit der ich sonst viele Zeit verdorben.
Sie hat so lange nichts von mir vernommen
Sie mag wohl glauben, ich sei gestorben.

Es ist mir auch gar nichts daran gelegen,
Ob sie mich für gestorben hält.
Ich kann auch gar nichts sagen dagegen,
Denn wirklich bin ich gestorben der Welt.

Ich bin gestorben dem Weltgetümmel
Und ruh in einem stillen Gebiet.
Ich leb allein in meinem Himmel,
In meinem Lieben, in meinem Lied.

(4) 'Lost To The World'

I am lost to the world
on which I used to waste so much time.
It has heard nothing of me for so long
that it may well think me dead.

I do not care at all
whether it thinks me dead.
Nor can I deny it:
for I have really died to the world.

I have died to the world's tumult
and rest in a realm of quiet:
I live alone in my own heaven,
in my love, in my song.

(5) 'Um Mitternacht'

Um Mitternacht
Hab ich gewacht
Und aufgeblickt zum Himmel;
Kein Stern vom Sterngewimmel
Hat mir gelacht
Um Mitternacht.

Um Mitternacht
Hab ich gedacht
Hinaus in dunkle Schranken.
Es hat kein Lichtgedanken
Mir Trost gebracht
Um Mitternacht.

(5) 'At Midnight'

At midnight
I was awake
and looked up to the heavens;
Not one of the whole host of stars
smiled down to me
at midnight.

At midnight
my thoughts went out
to the bounds of darkness.
No thought of light
brought me comfort
at midnight.

Um Mitternacht
Nahm ich in acht
Die Schläge meines Herzens;
Ein einz'ger Puls des Schmerzens
War angefacht
Um Mitternacht.

At midnight
I heeded
the beating of my heart;
but one pulse of pain
throbbed, burning,
at midnight.

Um Mitternacht
Kämpft ich die Schlacht,
O Menschheit, deiner Leiden;
Nicht konnt ich sie entscheiden
Mit meiner Macht
Um Mitternacht.

At midnight
I fought the battle
of your suffering, mankind!
I could not decide it
with all my strength
at midnight.

Um Mitternacht
Hab ich die Macht
In deine Hand gegeben!
Herr! über Tod und Leben
Du hältst die Wacht!
Um Mitternacht!

At midnight
I resigned all power
into Thy hand.
Lord! Over death and life
Thou keepest watch,
at midnight.

5 'KINDERTOTENLIEDER' 'SONGS ON THE DEATH OF CHILDREN' [RÜCKERT]
   (1902)

(1)
Nun will die Sonne so hell aufgehn,
Als sei kein Unglück die Nacht geschehn.
Das Unglück geschah auch nur mir allein,
Die Sonne, sie scheinet allgemein.

(1)
Now the sun prepares to rise as brightly
as if the night had brought no cause for grief.
The grief was mine alone.
The sun shines for all alike.

Du mußt nicht die Nacht in dir verschränken,
Mußt sie ins ewige Licht versenken.
Ein Lämplein verlosch in meinem Zelt,
Heil sei dem Freudenlicht der Welt!

You must not shut the night into yourself
but drown it in eternal light.
A lamp went out in my tent –
I bless the light that gladdens all the world!

(2)
Nun seh ich wohl, warum so dunkle Flam-
    men
Ihr sprühtet mir in manchem Augenblicke,
O Augen! Gleichsam um voll in einem Blicke
Zu drängen eure ganze Macht zusammen.

(2)
Now I see, O eyes, why you sometimes
flashed such dark flames towards me!
To collect, as it were, all your power
into a single glance.

Doch ahnt ich nicht, weil Nebel mich
    umschwammen,
Gewoben vom verblendenden Geschicke,
Daß sich der Strahl bereits zur Heimat
    schicke,
Dorthin, von wannen alle Strahlen stammen.

But I could not guess, because deluding Fate
had shrouded me in its mists,
that your brightness was already preparing
to return to its home, the source of all light.

Ihr wolltet mir mit eurem Leuchten sagen:
Wir möchten nah dir bleiben gerne,
Doch ist uns das vom Schicksal abge-
    schlagen.

With your shining you wanted to tell me:
We would gladly stay near you,
but fate will not grant our wish.

Sieh uns nur an, denn bald sind wir dir
ferne!
Was dir nur Augen sind in diesen Tagen,
In künft'gen Nächten sind es dir nur Sterne.

Look at us well, soon we will be far from
you!
What in these days you think of as only *eyes*
will be only *stars* to you in nights to come.

(3)
Wenn dein Mütterlein
Tritt zur Tür herein
Und den Kopf ich drehe,
Ihr entgegensehe,
Fällt auf ihr Gesicht
Erst der Blick mir nicht,
Sondern auf die Stelle
Näher nach der Schwelle,
Dort wo würde dein
Lieb Gesichtchen sein,
Wenn du freudenhelle
Trätest mit herein,
Wie sonst, mein Töchterlein.

(3)
When your mother
comes in at the door
and I turn my head
to look at her,
my eyes light first
not on her face
but on the place
nearer the threshold
where your
dear little face would be
if you came, bright-eyed,
into the room with her
as you used to, my little girl.

Wenn dein Mütterlein
Tritt zur Tür herein
Mit der Kerze Schimmer,
Ist es mir, als immer
Kämst du mit herein,
Huschtest hinterdrein
Als wie sonst ins Zimmer.
O du, des Vaters Zelle
Ach zu schnelle
Erloschner Freudenschein!

When your mother
comes in at the door
holding a flickering candle,
I always think
you are coming with her,
you slipped into the room
as you used to do.
O you light of joy,
in your father's cell —
extinguished all too soon!

(4)
Oft denk ich, sie sind nur ausgegangen!
Bald werden sie wieder nach Hause ge-
langen!
Der Tag ist schön! O sei nicht bang!
Sie machen nur einen weiten Gang.

(4)
I often think they have only gone out
and will soon be coming home again.
It is a beautiful day – do not worry,
they have only gone for a long walk.

Ja wohl, sie sind nur ausgegangen
Und werden jetzt nach Hause gelangen.
O sei nicht bang, der Tag ist schön!
Sie machen nur den Gang zu jenen Höhn!

Yes, they have only gone out
and will presently be home again.
Do not worry, it is a beautiful day,
they have taken a walk to those hills there.

Sie sind uns nur vorausgegangen
Und werden nicht wieder nach Haus ge-
langen!
Wir holen sie ein auf jenen Höhn
Im Sonnenschein! Der Tag ist schön
Auf jenen Höhn.

They have only gone before us,
and will not be coming home again.
We will overtake them on those heights
in the sunshine. The day is beautiful
on those heights.

(5)
In diesem Wetter, in diesem Braus,
Nie hätt ich gesendet die Kinder hinaus;
Man hat sie hinausgetragen.
Ich durfte nichts dazu sagen.

In diesem Wetter, in diesem Saus,
Nie hätt ich gelassen die Kinder hinaus,
Ich fürchtete, sie erkranken,
Das sind nun eitle Gedanken.

In diesem Wetter, in diesem Graus,
Nie hätt ich gelassen die Kinder hinaus,
Ich sorgte, sie stürben morgen,
Das ist nun nicht zu besorgen.

In diesem Wetter, in diesem Braus,
Sie ruhn als wie in der Mutter Haus,
Von keinem Sturme erschrecket,
Von Gottes Hand bedecket.

(5)
In such a stormy weather
I would never have sent the children out.
They have been carried out,
and I could do nothing about it.

In such windy weather
I would never have let the children go out.
I would have been afraid they might fall ill.
Now these are idle thoughts.

In this dreadful weather
I would never have let the children go out.
I was afraid they might die the next day:
that fear is now past.

In this stormy weather
they rest as in their mother's house.
No tempest can terrify them,
God's hand covers them.

6 TWO LATE SONGS [DES KNABEN WUNDERHORN]

(1) *Revelge*

Des Morgens zwischen drei'n und vieren
Da müssen wir Soldaten marschieren,
Die Gässlein auf und ab.
Tralali, tralalei, tralalera,
Mein Schätzel sieht herab.

Ach Bruder, jetzt bin ich geschossen,
Die Kugel hat mich schwer getroffen,
Trag mich in mein Quartier!
Tralali ...
Es ist nicht weit von hier!

'Ach Bruder, ich kann dich nicht tragen,
Die Feinde haben uns geschlagen,
Helf dir der liebe Gott!
Tralali ...
Ich muss marschieren bis in Tod.'

Ach Brüder, ihr geht mir ja vorüber
Als wär's mit mir vorbei,
Als wär's mit mir vorbei!
Tralali ...
Ihr tretet mir zu nah!

(1) *Reveille*

In the morning, between three and four
       o'clock,
we soldiers have to march
through the little streets.
Tralali, tralalei, tralalera,
My sweetheart looks down on us.

O my brother, I am wounded,
a bullet has hurt me sorely,
carry me to my quarters!
Tralali ...
It is not far from here!

'No, my brother, I cannot bear you away,
the enemy has beaten us;
may God help you!
Tralali ...
I must march on into my death.'

O my brothers, you pass by me
as though all
were up with me!
Tralali ...
You hurt me too much!

Ich muß wohl meine Trommel rühren,
Sonst werd ich mich verlieren;
Die Brüder dicht gesät,
Die liegen wie gemäht.

I must beat my drum
or I shall lose myself;
my brothers strew the ground
as if they had been mown down.

Er schlägt die Trommel auf und nieder,
Er wecket seine stillen Brüder,
Sie schlagen ihren Feind.
Tralali ...
Ein Schrecken schlägt den Feind!

He beats his drum now up, now down,
he wakes his still brothers –
they beat back the enemy!
Tralali ...
Terror strikes the enemy.

Er schlägt die Trommel auf und nieder,
Da sind sie vor dem Nachtquartier schon
    wieder,
In's Gässlein hell hinaus,
Sie ziehn vor Schätzleins Haus.

He beats his drum, now up, now down,
and there they have reached their quarters
    again.
They march into the bright little street,
before his sweetheart's house.

Des Morgens stehen da die Gebeine,
In Reih und Glied sie stehn wie Leichen-
    steine,
Die Trommel steht voran,
Daß sie ihn sehen kann.

In the morning the dead men stand there
ranged like tombstones –
the drummer stands in the van
so that she can see him.

(2) Der Tamboursg'sell

(2) The Drummer Boy

Ich armer Tamboursg'sell!
Man führt mich aus dem G'wölb!
Wär ich ein Tambour blieben,
Dürft ich nicht gefangen liegen.

Poor drummer boy that I am!
they are leading me from my cell.
If I had stayed a drummer
I would not now be imprisoned.

O Galgen, du hohes Haus,
Du siehst so furchtbar aus!
Ich schau dich nicht mehr an,
Weil i weiß, daß i g'hör dran.

O gallows, you lofty house,
your sight fills me with terror!
I look at you no more
because I know you will claim me.

Wenn Soldaten vorbei marschiern,
Bei mir nit einquartiern.
Wenn sie fragen, wer i g'wesen bin:
Tambour von der Leibkompanie.

When the soldiers march past
they will not seek quarters in my house.
When they ask, who I was, tell them:
a drummer in the colonel's own company.

Gute Nacht, ihr Marmelstein,
Ihr Berg und Hügelein!
Gute Nacht, ihr Offizier,
Korporal und Musketier!

Good night, you marble rocks,
mountains and hills!
Good night, officers,
corporals and musketeers.

Ich schrei mit heller Stimm:
Von Euch ich Urlaub nimm!
Von Euch ich Urlaub nimm!
Gute Nacht! Gute Nacht.

With a loud voice
I take my leave of you.
I take my leave of you!
Good night! Good night!

7 'DAS LIED VON DER ERDE' 'THE SONG OF THE EARTH' [CHINESE POEMS TRANSLATED BY HANS BETHGE] (1908)

(1) *Das Trinklied vom Jammer der Erde*

Schon winkt der Wein im goldnen Pokale,
Doch trinkt noch nicht, erst sing ich euch
  ein Lied!
Das Lied vom Kummer soll auflachend in
  die Seele euch klingen.
Wenn der Kummer naht, liegen wüst die
  Gärten der Seele,
Welkt hin und stirbt die Freude, der Gesang.
Dunkel ist das Leben, ist der Tod.

Herr dieses Hauses!
Dein Keller birgt die Fülle des goldenen
  Weins!
Hier diese Laute nenn ich mein!
Die Laute schlagen und die Gläser leeren,
Das sind die Dinge, die zusammen passen.
Ein voller Becher Weins zur rechten Zeit
Ist mehr wert als alle Reiche dieser Erde!
Dunkel ist das Leben, ist der Tod.

Das Firmament blaut ewig und die Erde
Wird lange fest stehn und aufblühn im Lenz.
Du aber, Mensch, wie lang lebst denn du?
Nicht hundert Jahre darfst du dich ergötzen
An all dem morschen Tande dieser Erde!
Seht dort hinab! Im Mondschein auf den
  Gräbern
Hockt eine wild-gespenstische Gestalt –
Ein Aff ist's! Hört ihr, wie sein Heulen
Hinausgellt in den süßen Duft des Lebens!
Jetzt nehmt den Wein! Jetzt ist es Zeit,
  Genossen!
Leert eure goldnen Becher zu Grund!
Dunkel ist das Leben, ist der Tod!

(1) *Drinking Song of the Earth's Misery*

The wine already beckons in the golden
  goblet,
but do not drink yet – first I will sing you a
  song.
With a burst of laughter the song of sorrow
  shall sound into your soul.
When sorrow draws near, the soul's gardens
  lie waste,
joy and singing wither and die.
Life and death alike are dark.

Master of this house!
Your cellar is filled with golden wine.
This lute I call my own.
Striking the lute and draining the glass
are things that go well together.
A full cup of wine at the right time
is worth more than all the empires of this
  world!
Life and death alike are dark.

The firmament is ever blue and the earth
will long stand firm and blossom in spring.
But you – Man! – how long do you live?
Not even a hundred years may you divert
  yourself
with all the brittle baubles of this earth.
Look down there! In the moonlight
a wild, ghostly form cowers on the graves.
It is a monkey! Do you hear his howling
shrill into the sweet scent of life?
Now take up the wine – now, friends, it is
  time.
Drain your golden goblets!
Life and death alike are dark.

(2) *Der Einsame im Herbst*

Herbstnebel wallen bläulich überm See;
Vom Reif bezogen stehen alle Gräser;
Man meint', ein Künstler habe Staub von
  Jade
Über die feinen Blüten ausgestreut.

(2) *The Lonely Man in Autumn*

Bluish autumn mists drift over the lake,
all the grass is covered with hoarfrost;
one would think an artist had scattered jade-
  dust
over the delicate blossoms.

Der süße Duft der Blumen ist verflogen;
Ein kalter Wind beugt ihre Stengel nieder.
Bald werden die verwelkten, goldnen
    Blätter
Der Lotosblüten auf dem Wasser ziehn.

The flowers' sweet scent is gone;
a cold wind bends their stems.
Soon the withered golden leaves
of the lotus will float by on the water.

Mein Herz ist müde. Meine kleine Lampe
Erlosch mit Knistern; es gemahnt mich an
    den Schlaf.
Ich komm zu dir, traute Ruhestätte!
Ja, gib mir Ruh, ich hab Erquickung not!

My heart is weary. My little lamp
has guttered out, it summons me to sleep.
I come, dear resting-place!
Yes, give me rest, I need to be refreshed.

Ich weine viel in meinen Einsamkeiten.
Der Herbst in meinem Herzen währt zu
    lange.
Sonne der Liebe, willst du nie mehr scheinen,
Um meine bittern Tränen mild aufzutrock-
    nen?

I weep much in my loneliness.
The autumn in my heart endures too long.
Sun of love, will you never shine again
gently to dry my bitter tears?

(3) *Von der Jugend*

(3) *A Song of Youth*

Mitten in dem kleinen Teiche
Steht ein Pavillon aus grünem
Und aus weißem Porzellan.

In the centre of the little pool
stands a pavilion of green
and white porcelain.

Wie der Rücken eines Tigers
Wölbt die Brücke sich aus Jade
Zu dem Pavillon hinüber.

Like a tiger's back
the jade bridge arches
over to the pavilion.

In dem Häuschen sitzen Freunde,
Schön gekleidet, trinken, plaudern,
Manche schreiben Verse nieder.

Friends sit in the little house,
beautifully dressed; they drink and talk,
some are writing verses.

Ihre seidnen Ärmel gleiten
Rückwärts, ihre seidnen Mützen
Hocken lustig tief im Nacken.

Their silk sleeves slide
back, their silk caps
are gaily perched far back on their heads.

Auf des kleinen Teiches stiller
Wasserfläche zeigt sich alles
Wunderlich im Spiegelbilde.

On the little pool's still
surface everything is
strangely mirrored.

Alles auf dem Kopfe stehend
In dem Pavillon aus grünem
Und aus weißem Porzellan;

Everything stands on its head
in the pavilion of green
and white porcelain;

Wie ein Halbmond steht die Brücke,
Umgekehrt der Bogen. Freunde,
Schön gekleidet, trinken, plaudern.

the bridge stands like a half-moon,
its arch inverted. Friends,
beautifully dressed, are drinking, talking.

(4) *Von der Schönheit*

Junge Mädchen pflücken Blumen,
Pflücken Lotosblumen an dem Uferrande.
Zwischen Büschen und Blättern sitzen sie,
Sammeln Blüten in den Schoß und rufen
Sich einander Neckereien zu.
Goldne Sonne webt um die Gestalten
Spiegelt sie im blanken Wasser wider,
Sonne spiegelt ihre schlanken Glieder,
Ihre süßen Augen wider.
Und der Zephir hebt mit Schmeichelkosen
    das Gewebe
Ihrer Ärmel auf, führt den Zauber
Ihrer Wohlgerüche durch die Luft.

O sieh, was tummeln sich für schöne Knaben
Dort an dem Uferrand auf mut'gen Rossen?
Weithin glänzend wie die Sonnenstrahlen,
Schon zwischen dem Geäst der grünen
    Weiden
Trabt das jungfrische Volk einher!
Das Roß des einen wiehert fröhlich auf
Und scheut und saust dahin,
Über Blumen, Gräser, wanken hin die Hufe,
Sie zerstampfen jäh im Sturm die hinge-
    sunknen Blüten,
Hei! Wie flattern im Taumel seine Mähnen,
Dampfen heiß die Nüstern!
Goldne Sonne webt um die Gestalten,
Spiegelt sie im blanken Wasser wider.

Und die schönste von den Jungfraun sendet
Lange Blicke ihm der Sehnsucht nach.
Ihre stolze Haltung ist nur Verstellung.
In dem Funkeln ihrer großen Augen,
In dem Dunkel ihres heißen Blicks
Schwingt klagend noch die Erregung ihres
    Herzens nach.

(5) *Der Trunkene im Frühling*

Wenn nur ein Traum das Leben ist,
Warum dann Müh und Plag?
Ich trinke, bis ich nicht mehr kann,
Den ganzen, lieben Tag!

Und wenn ich nicht mehr trinken kann,
Weil Kehl und Seele voll,

(4) *A Song of Beauty*

Young girls are picking flowers,
picking lotus-flowers by the river-bank.
They sit among bushes and leaves,
gather blossoms in their laps, and call
banteringly one to the other.
The golden sun plays around them,
mirrors them in the shining water.
The sun mirrors their slender limbs
and their sweet eyes.
Caressingly the soft breeze lifts the fabric
of their sleeves, and bears the magic
of their perfumes through the air.

Look now – what handsome boys are these,
    frolicking
by the river-bank on mettlesome horses?
Gleaming in the distance, like the sunbeams,
these supple young men are already canter-
    ing
between the green willow-branches.
One horse neighs merrily,
rears and plunges on;
its hooves fly over flowers and grass,
trampling the fallen blossoms in their stormy
    passage.
How its mane flutters in its frenzy,
how its nostrils steam!
The golden sun plays around these figures,
mirrors them in the shining water.

And the loveliest of the girls
looks after him with longing.
Her proud bearing is only pretence.
The fire of her large eyes,
The darkness of their passionate gaze,
Still throb, lamenting, with the agitation of
    her heart.

(5) *The Drunken Man in Spring*

If life is only a dream
why should there be trouble and care?
I drink till I can drink no more,
the whole day through.

And when I can drink no more
because throat and soul are full,

So tauml' ich bis zu meiner Tür
Und schlafe wundervoll!

Was hör ich beim Erwachen? Horch!
Ein Vogel singt im Baum.
Ich frag ihn, ob schon Frühling sei.
Mir ist als wie im Traum.

Der Vogel zwitschert: Ja! Der Lenz
Ist da, sei kommen über Nacht!
Aus tiefstem Schauen lausch ich auf,
Der Vogel singt und lacht!

Ich fülle mir den Becher neu
Und leer ihn bis zum Grund,
Und singe, bis der Mond erglänzt
Am schwarzen Firmament!

Und wenn ich nicht mehr singen kann,
So schlaf ich wieder ein.
Was geht mich denn der Frühling an?
Laßt mich betrunken sein!

then I stagger to my door
and sleep marvellously well.

What do I hear when I wake? Listen!
A bird sings in the tree.
I ask it if spring has come –
it all seems like a dream.

The bird twitters: 'Yes! Spring
is here, it came over night!'
Lost in gazing, I listen –
the bird sings and laughs!

I replenish my cup
and drain it to the bottom,
and I sing till the moon begins to shine
in the black skies.

And when I can sing no more
I go to sleep again.
What do I care for the spring?
Let me be drunk!

(6) Der Abschied

Die Sonne scheidet hinter dem Gebirge.
In alle Täler steigt der Abend nieder
Mit seinen Schatten, die voll Kühlung sind.
O sieh! Wie eine Silberbarke schwebt
Der Mond am blauen Himmelssee herauf.
Ich spüre eines feinen Windes Wehn
Hinter den dunklen Fichten!
Der Bach singt voller Wohllaut durch das
    Dunkel.
Die Blumen blassen im Dämmerschein.
Die Erde atmet voll von Ruh und Schlaf.
Alle Sehnsucht will nun träumen,
Die müden Menschen gehn heimwärts,
Um im Schlaf vergeßnes Glück
Und Jugend neu zu lernen!
Die Vögel hocken still in ihren Zweigen.
Die Welt schläft ein!

Es wehet kühl im Schatten meiner Fichten.
Ich stehe hier und harre meines Freundes;
Ich harre sein zum letzten Lebewohl.
Ich sehne mich, o Freund, an deiner Seite
Die Schönheit dieses Abends zu genießen.
Wo bleibst du? Du läßt mich lang allein!

(6) The Farewell

The sun goes down behind the mountain,
the evening descends in all the valleys
and brings cooling shades.
Look! like a silver bark
the moon floats up the blue lake of heaven.
I feel a gentle breeze stirring
behind the dark spruce.
Melodiously the brook sings through the
    darkness.
The flowers grow pale in the gloaming.
The earth is breathing full of peace and sleep.
Now all longing turns to dreams,
tired men make for home
to recapture in sleep
forgotten happiness and youth.
The birds cower silently in the branches.
The world is falling asleep.

A cool wind blows in the shadow of my
    spruce.
I stand here waiting for my friend;
I wait to bid him a last farewell.
I long to enjoy the beauty of this evening
by your side, my friend.
Where do you linger? You have left me alone
    so long!

Ich wandle auf und nieder mit meiner Laute
Auf Wegen, die von weichem Grase schwel-
   len.
O Schönheit! O ewigen Liebens– Lebens–
   trunkne Welt!

Er stieg vom Pferd und reichte ihm den
   Trunk
Des Abschieds dar. Er fragte ihn, wohin
Er führe und auch warum es müßte sein.
Er sprach, und seine Stimme war umflort:
   'Du mein Freund,
Mir war auf dieser Welt das Glück nicht
   hold!
Wohin ich geh? Ich geh, ich wandre in die
   Berge.
Ich suche Ruhe für mein einsam Herz.
Ich wandle nach der Heimat, meiner Stätte.
Ich werde niemals in die Ferne schweifen.
Still ist mein Herz und harret seiner Stunde!

Die liebe Erde allüberall
Blüht auf im Lenz und grünt
Auf's neu! Allüberall und ewig
Blauen licht die Fernen!
Ewig . . . ewig . . .'

I wander up and down with my lute
on paths soft with swelling grass.
O beauty! O world intoxicated with eternal
   love and life!

He dismounted and proffered him the cup
in token of farewell. He asked where
he was going and why it had to be.
He said, and his voice trembled: 'O my
   friend,
in this world fortune did not smile on me.
Where I am going? I go into the mountains.
I seek peace for my lonely heart.
I am making for home, for my resting-place.
I will never roam into strange lands.
My heart is still and bides its time.

Everywhere the dear earth
blossoms in spring and grows
green again. Everywhere, for ever,
the distant horizons shine blue and bright.
Ever . . . ever . . .'

RICHARD STRAUSS

Born on 11 June 1864 into the musical atmosphere of Munich, where his father was a horn-player at the court-opera. From the first he haunted opera houses and concert halls. At the age of twenty he was taken on as assistant to Hans von Bülow at the Meiningen opera, and he succeeded Bülow as first conductor in 1885. From Meiningen Strauss went to opera houses at Munich (second conductor, 1887) and Weimar (assistant conductor, 1889); in 1894 he succeeded Bülow again, this time as conductor of the Berlin Philharmonic Orchestra. He stayed in Berlin until 1919, when he became director of the Vienna State Opera. In 1924 Strauss retired to Garmisch in the Bavarian highlands, which was to remain his home (with brief interruptions) for twenty-five years. He died at Garmisch on 8 September 1949. His works include sixteen operas, two ballets, two symphonies, ten symphonic poems, a violin concerto, an oboe concerto, two horn concertos, and over 150 songs.

Strauss's greatest contribution to vocal music are his operas – notably those written in collaboration with one of Austria's greatest poets, Hugo von Hofmannsthal (including *Elektra, Der Rosenkavalier, Ariadne auf Naxos*, and *Die Frau ohne Schatten*) and that which has the relation of words and music as its subject: *Capriccio*; but his songs too, hindered though many of them are by banal texts, have rightly won many friends in the concert hall. Chief among these songs are early works like 'Ständchen', 'Ruhe, meine Seele', and 'Morgen', which unite a bewitching melody with harmonic boldness; more subtle mood-pictures like 'Traum durch die Dämmerung'; the haunting setting, for bass voice, of C. F. Meyer's 'Im Spätboot' (which no one, alas, ever sings); and the translucent orchestral songs with texts by Hesse and Eichendorff (*Vier letzte Lieder*). With these 'Last Songs', which include a deliberate reminiscence of his earlier tone-poem *Death and Transfiguration (Tod und Verklarung)*, Strauss took his leave of the world.

I OP. 17/2 [ADOLF VON SCHACK]

Ständchen

Mach auf, mach auf, doch leise, mein Kind,
Um keinen vom Schlummer zu wecken.
Kaum murmelt der Bach, kaum zittert im
  Wind
Ein Blatt an den Büschen und Hecken.
Drum leise, mein Mädchen, daß nichts sich
  regt,
Nur leise die Hand auf die Klinke gelegt.

Mit Tritten wie Tritte der Elfen so sacht,
Um über die Blumen zu hüpfen,
Flieg leicht hinaus in die Mondscheinnacht,
Zu mir in den Garten zu schlüpfen.
Rings schlummern die Blüten am rieselnden
  Bach
Und duften im Schlaf; nur die Liebe ist wach.

Serenade

Open up, my love, but softly
so that no one wakes.
The brook hardly murmurs, the breeze
  hardly moves
a leaf in the bushes and hedges.
Be still then, my love, so that nothing should
  stir;
lay your hand gently on the latch.

With steps as soft as those with which elves
leap over flowers
fly swiftly out into the moonlit night,
slip into the garden to join me.
The flowers slumber by the rippling brook
wafting out their fragrance in sleep – only
  love is awake.

Sitz nieder, hier dämmert's geheimnisvoll
Unter den Lindenbäumen,
Die Nachtigall uns zu Häupten soll
Von unseren Küssen träumen
Und die Rose, wenn sie am Morgen erwacht,
Hoch glühn von den Wonneschauern der
　　Nacht.

Sit here in the mysterious twilight
of these lime-trees;
the nightingale above us shall
dream of our kisses,
and the rose, when it wakes in the morning,
shall glow with the stormy bliss of the night.

2 OP. 27/1 [KARL HENCKELL]

Ruhe, meine Seele

Rest, my soul

Nicht ein Lüftchen regt sich leise,
Sanft entschlummert ruht der Hain;
Durch der Blätter dunkle Hülle
Stiehlt sich lichter Sonnenschein.

Not a breeze is stirring,
the woods lie gently asleep;
through dark, covering leaves
bright sunshine is stealing.

Ruhe, ruhe, meine Seele,
Deine Stürme gingen wild,
Hast getobt und hast gezittert,
Wie die Brandung, wenn sie schwillt!

Rest, rest, my soul;
shaken by tempests
you raged and quivered
like wild breakers on the shore.

Diese Zeiten sind gewaltig
Bringen Herz und Hirn in Not –
Ruhe, ruhe, meine Seele,
Und vergiß, was dich bedroht!

These are mighty times,
troubling heart and brain –
rest, rest, my soul,
and forget what threatens you.

3 OP. 27/4 [JOHN HENRY MACKAY]

Morgen

Tomorrow

Und morgen wird die Sonne wieder scheinen
Und auf dem Wege, den ich gehen werde,
Wird uns, die Glücklichen, sie wieder einen
Inmitten dieser sonnenatmenden Erde ...

And tomorrow the sun will shine again
and on the path we walk in our happiness
it will again unite us
in the midst of this sun-breathing earth. ...

Und zu dem Strand, dem weiten, wogen-
　　blauen,
Werden wir still und langsam niedersteigen,
Stumm werden wir uns in die Augen schauen,
Und auf uns sinkt des Glückes stummes
　　Schweigen. ...

And to the wide shore with its blue waves
we shall again descend, slow and still,
mutely we shall look into each other's eyes
and the silence of happiness will again sink
　　upon us. ...

4 OP. 29/1 [OTTO JULIUS BIERBAUM]

Traum durch die Dämmerung

Weite Wiesen im Dämmergrau;
Die Sonne verglomm, die Sterne ziehn,
Nun geh ich hin zu der schönen Frau,
Weit über Wiesen im Dämmergrau,
Tief in den Busch von Jasmin.

Durch Dämmergrau in der Liebe Land;
Ich gehe nicht schnell, ich eile nicht;
Mich zieht ein weiches samtenes Band
Durch Dämmergrau in der Liebe Land,
In ein blaues mildes Licht.
[Ich gehe nicht schnell, ich eile nicht;
Durch Dämmergrau in der Liebe Land,
In ein mildes, blaues Licht.]

Dreaming in the Twilight

Wide meadows in the grey twilight;
the sun has faded, the stars move in the
    heavens;
I walk towards the lovely woman
far over the meadows in the grey twilight
deep in the jasmine bushes.

Through the grey twilight to the land of
    love;
I do not walk fast, I do not hurry;
A soft, velvet thread draws me
through the grey twilight to the land of love,
into a gentle blue light.
[I do not walk fast, I do not hurry;
through the grey twilight to the land of love,
into a gentle blue light.]

5 OP. 36/3 [DES KNABEN WUNDERHORN]

Hat gesagt – bleibt's nicht dabei

Mein Vater hat gesagt,
Ich soll das Kindlein wiegen,
Er will mir auf den Abend
Drei Gaggeleier sieden;
Sied't er mir drei,
Ißt er mir zwei
Und ich mag nicht wiegen
Um ein einziges Ei.

Mein' Mutter hat gesagt,
Ich soll die Mägdlein verraten,
Sie wollt mir auf den Abend
Drei Vögelein braten.
Brat' sie mir drei,
Ißt sie mir zwei
Um ein einzig Vöglein
Treib ich kein Verräterei.

Mein Schätzlein hat gesagt,
Ich sollt sein gedenken,
Er wollt mir auf den Abend
Drei Küßlein auch schenken.
Schenkt er mir drei,
Bleibt's nicht dabei.
Was kümmert mich's Vöglein,
Was schiert mich das Ei!

Promises made and broken

My father has asked me
to mind the baby;
he would boil me three duck-eggs
in the evening.
If he boils me three,
He'll eat two himself:
and I won't mind the baby
for just one egg.

My mother has asked me
to tell on the maids;
she would fry me in the evening
three little fowls.
If she fries me three,
she'll eat two herself;
and for just one little fowl
I won't be a tell-tale.

My sweetheart has told me
to think of him;
he would, in the evening,
give me three kisses.
If he gives me three,
he won't stop at those –
what do I care for fowls,
what do I care for eggs!

6 op. 39/4 [RICHARD DEHMEL]

Befreit

Du wirst nicht weinen. Leise,
Leise wirst du lächeln und wie zur Reise
Geb ich dir den Blick und Kuß zurück.
Unsere lieben vier Wände,
Du hast sie bereitet,
Ich habe sie dir zur Welt geweitet;
   o Glück!

Dann wirst du heiß meine Hände fassen
Und wirst mir deine Seele lassen,
Läßt unsern Kindern mich zurück.
Du schenktest mir dein ganzes Leben,
Ich will es ihnen wieder geben;
   o Glück!

Es wird sehr bald sein, wir wissen's beide;
Wir haben einander befreit vom Leide,
So geb ich dich der Welt zurück.
Dann wirst du mir nur noch im Traum
   erscheinen,
Und mich segnen und mit mir weinen;
   o Glück!

Release

You will not weep. Gently,
gently you will smile, and as before a journey
I shall return your glance and your kiss.
You have cared for
the room we love,
I made it a wide world for you;
   you my happiness!

Then, ardently, you will seize my hands
and leave me your soul.
You will leave me to care for our children.
You gave up your whole life to me,
I will give it back to them;
   you my happiness!

It will be very soon, we both know it.
We freed each other from suffering,
and I will give you back to the world.
Soon you will appear to me only in my
   dreams,
you will bless me and weep with me;
   you my happiness!

7 op. 41/1 [RICHARD DEHMEL]

Wiegenlied

Träume, du mein süßes Leben,
Von dem Himmel, der die Blumen bringt.
Blüten schimmern da, die leben
Von dem Lied, das deine Mutter singt.

Träume, Knospe meiner Sorgen,
Von dem Tage, da die Blume sproß;
Von dem hellen Blütenmorgen,
Da dein Seelchen sich der Welt erschloß.

Träume, Blüte meiner Liebe,
Von der stillen, von der heil'gen Nacht,
Da die Blume seiner Liebe
Diese Welt zum Himmel mir gemacht.

Lullaby

Dream, my sweet, my life,
of the heavens bringing flowers.
There are shining blossoms that live
by your mother's song.

Dream, you bud grown from my cares,
of the day the flower unfolded;
of the morning bright with blossoms
on which your soul opened to the world.

Dream, you blossom of my love,
of the still, the holy night,
when the flower of his love
made this world my heaven.

8 OP. 56/3 [CONRAD FERDINAND MEYER]

Im Spätboot

Aus der Schiffsbank mach ich meinen Pfühl.
Endlich wird die heiße Stirne kühl!

O wie süß erkaltet mir das Herz!
O wie weich verstummen Lust und Schmerz!

Über mir des Rohres schwarzer Rauch
Wiegt und biegt sich in des Windes Hauch.

Hüben hier und wieder drüben dort
Hält das Boot an manchem kleinen Port:

Bei der Schiffslaterne kargem Schein
Steigt ein Schatten aus und niemand ein.

Nur der Steurer noch, der wacht und steht!
Nur der Wind, der mir im Haare weht!

Schmerz und Lust erleiden sanften Tod.
Einen Schlummrer trägt das dunkle Boot.

Last Boat Across

I make the ship's bench my pillow.
At last my burning forehead is cooled!

How sweetly the heart grows colder,
how softly joy and anguish are stilled!

Above me the black smoke from the chimney
bends and wavers in the breeze.

On this side of the lake and on that
the boat stops at many a little halt;

by the dim gleam of the ship's lantern
a shadow disembarks and no one comes on
    board.

Only the steersman stands on watch;
only the wind ruffles my hair.

Anguish and joy die a gentle death.
The dark boat bears a sleeper away.

9 OP. 69/5 [HEINE]

Schlechtes Wetter

Das ist ein schlechtes Wetter,
Es regnet und stürmt und schneit;
Ich sitze am Fenster und schaue
Hinaus in die Dunkelheit.

Da schimmert ein einsames Lichtchen,
Das wandelt langsam fort;
Ein Mütterchen mit dem Laternchen
Wankt über die Straße dort.

Ich glaube, Mehl und Eier
Und Butter kaufte sie ein;
Sie will einen Kuchen backen
Für's große Töchterlein.

Die liegt zu Haus[e] im Lehnstuhl
Und blinzelt schläfrig ins Licht;
Die goldnen Locken wallen
Über das süße Gesicht.

Rough Weather

The weather is rough today:
rain, storm, and sleet!
I sit at my window and peer
out into the darkness.

A lone little light glimmers out there,
wandering slowly on:
a little old woman with a lantern
hobbles across the street.

I think she has been shopping,
buying flour, eggs, and butter
to bake a cake
for her grown-up daughter.

The daughter sits at home, in the arm-chair,
winking sleepily into the light;
her golden curls fall
about her sweet face.

10 OP. POSTH. [HERMANN HESSE AND JOSEF VON EICHENDORFF]

Vier letzte Lieder

(1) *Beim Schlafengehen* (Hesse)

Nun der Tag mich müd gemacht,
Soll mein sehnliches Verlangen
Freundlich die gestirnte Nacht
Wie ein müdes Kind empfangen.

Hände, laßt von allem Tun,
Stirn, vergiß du alles Denken,
Alle meine Sinne nun
Wollen sich in Schlummer senken.

Und die Seele unbewacht,
Will in freien Flügen schweben,
Um im Zauberkreis der Nacht
Tief und tausendfach zu leben.

(2) *September* (Hesse)

Der Garten trauert,
Kühl sinkt in die Blumen der Regen.
Der Sommer schauert
Still seinem Ende entgegen.

Golden tropft Blatt um Blatt
Nieder vom hohen Akazienbaum.
Sommer lächelt erstaunt und matt
In den sterbenden Gartentraum.

Lange noch bei den Rosen
Bleibt er stehn, sehnt sich nach Ruh.
Langsam tut er die (großen)
Müdgewordnen Augen zu.

(3) *Frühling* (Hesse)

In dämmrigen Grüften
Träumte ich lang
Von deinen Bäumen und blauen Lüften,
Von deinem Duft und Vogelgesang.

Nun liegst du erschlossen
In Gleiß und Zier,
Von Licht übergossen
Wie ein Wunder vor mir.

Four Last Songs

(1) *Going to Sleep*

Now the day has tired me,
I yearn for the starry night.
May she receive me kindly,
Like a tired child!

Hands, leave your doing,
Brain, leave your thinking –
all my senses
would now sink into slumber.

And the unwatched soul
wants to soar up freely
to live a thousand times more intensely
in the magic circle of night.

(2) *September*

The garden mourns,
the cool rain sinks into the flowers.
The summer shudders
silently towards its end.

Leaf after golden leaf
drops from the tall acacia.
The summer smiles, astonished and weary,
into the garden's dying dream.

Long he remains standing
by the roses, yearning for rest.
Slowly he closes his (large)
eyes that have grown so tired.

(3) *Spring*

In twilit valleys
I have long dreamt
of your trees and blue skies,
your perfumes and your bird-song.

Now you lie visibly before me
in shining splendour,
flooded with light,
like a miracle.

Du kennst mich wieder,
Du lockest mich zart,
Es zittert durch all meine Glieder
Deine selige Gegenwart!

You know me again,
you lure me gently,
your happy presence
trembles through all my limbs!

(4) *Im Abendrot* (Eichendorff)

(4) *In the Sunset Glow*

Wir sind durch Not und Freude
Gegangen Hand in Hand:
Vom Wandern ruhen wir beide
Nun überm stillen Land.

Through troubles and joys
we have gone hand in hand;
now we both rest from our wanderings
high over the still countryside.

Rings sich die Täler neigen,
Es dunkelt schon die Luft,
Zwei Lerchen nur noch steigen
Nachträumend in den Duft.

The valleys descend round about us;
the skies are already growing dark.
Only two larks, remembering a dream,
are rising into the haze.

Tritt her und laß sie schwirren,
Bald ist es Schlafenszeit,
Daß wir uns nicht verirren
In dieser Einsamkeit.

Come, let them fly –
soon it is time to sleep.
We must not go astray
in this loneliness.

O weiter, stiller Friede!
So tief im Abendrot,
Wie sind wir wandermüde –
Ist dies etwa der Tod?

O wide, still peace!
So deep in the sunset glow,
how weary we are with wandering –
can this be death?

ARNOLD SCHOENBERG

Born in Vienna on 13 September 1874. Became, in 1894, a pupil of Alexander Zemlinsky, whose sister he married. Richard Strauss took an interest in his work, and obtained for him a scholarship (*Lisztstipendium*) and a teaching post in Berlin. Lived in Berlin from 1901 to 1914, and came into touch with the leading artists and writers of the Expressionist movement (he was himself a painter of more than average talent, and directed for a time the musical activities of an influential literary cabaret). In 1908 he broke away from traditional harmony and evolved what he called 'atonic' music, written in no definite key but with several tonic centres. *Das Buch der hängenden Gärten* belongs to this period. In 1914 Schoenberg returned to Vienna, and served for a time in the Austrian army. After the First World War he experimented with new forms of tonal organization and evolved the 'twelve-tone row', seen in its full perfection in the *Serenade* (Opus 24) of 1921–3. From now on most of his work is based on a pattern of twelve notes, serving as a 'tonal reservoir' from which all material used in a particular composition is drawn. In 1924 Schoenberg accepted a call to resume his teaching in Berlin; but the coming of Hitler in 1933 drove him from Germany. He emigrated at first to Paris, then to the U.S.A., where he taught at the University of California from 1936 to 1944. He died at Los Angeles on 14 July 1951. His works include the symphonic poem *Pélleas und Mélisande*, the string sextet *Verklärte Nacht*, a number of string quartets and 'chamber symphonies', compositions in which speech and music blend in new ways (*Pierrot Lunaire*, *Gurrelieder*, *A Survivor from Warsaw*), a monodrama (*Erwartung*, 1909) and an unfinished opera, *Moses und Aaron*.

'With the George-songs,' Schoenberg wrote in 1910 about his *Buch der hängenden Gärten*, 'I succeeded for the first time in approaching an ideal of expression and form which floated before me for years. . . . I am conscious, now, of having broken through the barriers of a past aesthetic.' Here are nearly all the features that made Schoenberg's vocal music seem so difficult to its first hearers: the break with tonality (though several tonic centres may be distinguished); the absence of those recurrent 'themes' that bind together the accompaniments of Mahler and Wolf (though it is still possible to find thematic links between the eleventh and fifteenth song); the predominance of chords deemed 'dissonant' in earlier musical thought; the sudden leaps of the singing voice; the novel counterpoint that replaces nineteenth-century harmony; the independent movement of horizontal melody over vertical chords; the compression of musical ideas into the shortest possible space. These innovations have delayed the acceptance of Schoenberg's songs into the *Lieder* repertoire; but they should not prove a permanent bar to the realization that *Das Buch der hängenden Gärten* is one of the peaks of twentieth-century vocal music.

OP. 15 [STEFAN GEORGE]

Fünfzehn Gedichte aus 'Das Buch der hängenden Gärten'	Fifteen Poems from 'The Book of the Hanging Gardens'
(1)	(1)
Unterm schutz von dichten blättergründen	Protected by leafy thickets
Wo von sternen feine flocken schneien ·	where stars shed fine flakes,
Sachte stimmen ihre leiden künden ·	where gentle voices lament,
Fabeltiere aus den braunen schlünden	where fabulous beasts spit rays of water
Strahlen in die marmorbecken speien ·	from brown gullets into marble basins,

Draus die kleinen bäche klagend eilen:
Kamen kerzen das gesträuch entzünden ·
Weisse formen das gewässer teilen.

from which, lamenting, little brooks hasten –
candles came to illuminate the bushes,
white forms divided the waters.

(2)
Hain in diesen paradiesen
Wechselt ab mit blütenwiesen
Hallen · buntbemalten fliesen.
Schlanker störche schnäbel kräuseln
Teiche die von fischen schillern ·
Vögel-reihen matten scheines
Auf den schiefen firsten trillern
Und die goldnen binsen säuseln –
Doch mein traum verfolgt nur eines.

(2)
In these Gardens of Eden
woods alternate with flowery meadows,
and these with porticos and coloured tiles.
The beaks of slender storks ruffle
ponds that glisten with fish.
Rows of softly gleaming birds
trill on the sloping gables,
and the golden reeds sough.
But my dream pursues one single goal.

(3)
Als neuling trat ich ein in dein gehege
Kein staunen war vorher in meinen mienen ·
Kein wunsch in mir eh ich dich blickte rege.
Der jungen hände faltung sieh mit huld ·
Erwähle mich zu denen die dir dienen
Und schone mit erbarmender geduld
Den der noch strauchelt auf so fremdem stege.

(3)
As a novice I entered your domain;
my face showed no wonder before,
no wish stirred in me before I saw you.
Look with favour on these folded hands,
take me among those who serve you,
and indulge, with patience and pity,
one who yet stumbles on unfamiliar paths.

(4)
Da meine lippen reglos sind und brennen
Beacht ich erst wohin mein fuss geriet:
In andrer herren prächtiges gebiet.
Noch war vielleicht mir möglich mich zu
        trennen ·
Da schien es dass durch hohe gitterstäbe
Der blick vor dem ich ohne lass gekniet
Mich fragend suchte oder zeichen gäbe.

(4)
Only now that my lips burn without moving
I notice where my foot has strayed:
in the splendid domain of other masters.
Yet I might, perhaps, still have torn myself
        away –
but I seemed to see, through tall trellises,
that glance before which I knelt unceasingly
seeking me or giving me a sign.

(5)
Saget mir auf welchem pfade
Heute sie vorüberschreite –
Dass ich aus der reichsten lade
Zarte seidenweben hole ·
Rose pflücke und viole ·
Dass ich meine wange breite ·
Schemel unter ihrer sohle.

(5)
Tell me on which path
she will pass today –
that I may fetch, from the richest shrine,
a delicate silken web,
that I may gather roses and violets,
that I may make of my cheek
a stool for her feet.

(6)
Jedem werke bin ich fürder tot.
Dich mir nahzurufen mit den sinnen ·
Neue reden mit dir auszuspinnen ·
Dienst und lohn gewährung und verbot ·
Von allen dingen ist nur dieses not

(6)
Now I am lost to all other labour.
To call you to me with all my senses,
to think of new things to say to you,
service and reward, licence and refusal –
only this is needful;

Und weinen dass die bilder immer fliehen
Die in schöner finsternis gediehen –
Wann der kalte klare morgen droht.

(7)

Angst und hoffen wechselnd mich beklem-
   men ·
Meine worte sich in seufzer dehnen ·
Mich bedrängt so ungestümes sehnen
Dass ich mich an rast und schlaf nicht kehre
Dass mein lager tränen schwemmen
Dass ich jede freude von mir wehre
Dass ich keines freundes trost begehre.

(8)

Wenn ich heut nicht deinen leib berühre
Wird der faden meiner seele reissen
Wie zu sehr gespannte sehne.
Liebe zeichen seien trauerflöre.
Mir der leidet seit ich dir gehöre.
Richte ob mir solche qual gebühre ·
Kühlung sprenge mir dem fieberheissen
Der ich wankend draussen lehne.

(9)

Streng ist uns das glück und spröde ·
Was vermocht ein kurzer kuss?
Eines regentropfens guss
Auf gesengter bleicher öde
Die ihn ungenossen schlingt ·
Neue labung missen muss
Und vor neuen gluten springt.

(10)

Das schöne beet betracht ich mir im harren ·
Es ist umzäunt mit purpurn-schwarzem
   dorne
Drin ragen kelche mit geflecktem sporne
Und sammtgefiederte geneigte farren
Und flockenbüschel wassergrün und rund
Und in der mitte glocken weiss und mild –
Von einem odem ist ihr feuchter mund
Wie süsse frucht vom himmlischen gefild.

(11)

Als wir hinter dem beblümten tore
Endlich nur das eigne hauchen spürten
Warden uns erdachte seligkeiten?

and to weep because images
that flourished in beautiful darkness
should take flight when the cold, clear morning threatens.

(7)

Fear and hope oppress me in turn;
my words are lengthened into sighs.
Such violent longing besets me
that I care for neither rest nor sleep,
that tears drench my couch,
that I drive all joy from me,
and want no friend to console me.

(8)

If I do not touch your body today
the thread of my soul will break
like a bow-string drawn too tight.
Let signs of love be veils of sorrow
for me, who suffer since I belong to you.
Judge yourself if I deserve such anguish –
Cool my fever,
as I falter outside your door.

(9)

Fortune is severe and coy with us.
What could one short kiss do?
It is like a raindrop, falling
on to a parched, pale desert
that swallows it unrefreshed
and, missing new sustenance,
cracks with renewed heat.

(10)

As I wait, I look at the lovely flower-bed.
It is hedged with purple-black thorn.
Within, flower-cups with speckled spur rise
   up,
inclining ferns, velvety, feathery,
fluffy cluster-heads, watery-green and round;
and in the middle bell-flowers, white and
   mild –
their dewy mouth breathing fragrance
like sweet fruit from the fields of Heaven.

(11)

When, behind the gate overgrown with
   flowers,
we were conscious, at last, only of our own
   breathing –
did we then feel an imagined bliss?

Ich erinnere dass wie schwache rohre
Beide stumm zu beben wir begannen
Wenn wir leis nur an uns rührten
Und dass unsre augen rannen –
So verbliebest du mir lang zu seiten.

I remember that, if we but gently touched
    each other,
we both began to tremble
silently, like feeble reeds,
and tears welled up in our eyes.
Thus for a long time you stayed by my side.

(12)

Wenn sich bei heilger ruh in tiefen matten
Um unsre schläfen unsre hände schmiegen ·
Verehrung lindert unsrer glieder brand:
So denke nicht der ungestalten schatten
Die an der wand sich auf und unter wiegen ·
Der wächter nicht die rasch uns scheiden
    dürfen
Und nicht dass vor der stadt der weisse sand
Bereit ist unser warmes blut zu schlürfen.

(12)

When we take sacred rest in the high mea-
    dows
and our hands nestle against our temples,
when our bodies' ardour is assuaged by
    adoration –
do not then think of the shapeless shadows
that sway up and down the wall,
nor of the guards that may quickly part us,
nor of the white sand before the town
which is ready to drink our warm blood.

(13)

Du lehnest wider eine silberweide
Am ufer · mit des fächers starren spitzen
Umschirmest du das haupt dir wie mit
    blitzen
Und rollst als ob du spieltest dein geschmeide.
Ich bin im boot das laubgewölbe wahren
In das ich dich vergeblich lud zu steigen ·
Die weiden seh ich die sich tiefer neigen
Und blumen die verstreut im wasser fahren.

(13)

You lean against a white willow
at the river bank; with the pointed slats of
    your fan
you shield your head as with flashes of light-
    ning,
and you toy with your trinkets.
Hidden among leaves, I lie in the boat
into which I vainly invited you –
I see the willows bending lower
and scattered flowers floating on the waters.

(14)

Sprich nicht immer
von dem laub ·
Windes raub ·
Vom zerschellen
Reifer quitten ·
Von den tritten
Der vernichter
Spät im jahr ·
Von dem zittern
Der libellen
In gewittern
Und der lichter
Deren flimmer
Wandelbar.

(14)

Do not always speak
of the leaves,
the wind's prey –
of the breaking
of ripe quinces,
of the steps
of destroyers
late in the year;
of dragonflies
trembling
in the storm,
and of lights
that flicker
and change.

(15)
Wir bevölkerten die abend-düstern
Lauben · lichten tempel · pfad und beet
Freudig – sie mit lächeln ich mit flüstern –
Nun ist wahr dass sie für immer geht.
Hohe blumen blassen oder brechen ·
Es erblasst und bricht der weiher glas
Und ich trete fehl im morschen gras ·
Palmen mit den spitzen fingern stechen.
Mürber blätter zischendes gewühl
Jagen ruckweis unsichtbare hände
Draussen um des edens fahle wände.
Die nacht ist überwölkt und schwül.

(15)
We peopled the dusky
arbours, the bright temples, paths, and
    flower-beds,
joyfully. She smiled and I whispered.
Now, it is true, she will leave me for ever.
Tall flowers grow pale or break;
glassy ponds grow pale and break,
and I stumble in the decaying grass;
palms prick with pointed fingers.
The hissing, jerking crowd of dry leaves
is chased by invisible hands
around the pale walls of our paradise.
The night is cloudy and oppressive.

ANTON (VON) WEBERN

Born in Vienna on 3 December 1883. Studied musicology at Vienna University under Guido Adler, receiving a doctorate of music in 1906. While still a student, he met Schoenberg and became his pupil; and it was under Schoenberg's aegis that he first attempted original composition (*Passacaglia for Orchestra*, 1908). From 1908 to 1913 Webern directed orchestras at various provincial theatres and opera houses; in 1917 he accepted a post at the Prague opera house, but returned to Vienna in the following year. Superintended many performances at an 'Association for Private Musical Performances' founded by Schoenberg, and taught composition and harmony. He also worked for a 'Socialist Music Circle' and (from 1927 onwards) for the Austrian radio. After the annexation of Austria by the Germans in 1934 Webern's position became increasingly difficult: his work was proscribed as 'cultural Bolshevism' and he found himself regarded with increasing suspicion because of his friendship with Schoenberg. The Second World War bringing him personal grief (his soldier son was killed just before the truce), he greeted its end with relief, but was shot to death by a soldier of the occupying forces on 15 September 1945. His work includes many vocal compositions (from the choral setting of words by Stefan George, Op. 2, in 1908, to a cantata with words by Hildegard Jone written in 1945), chamber music, and orchestral compositions culminating in the *Orchestral Variations*, Op. 30, of 1943.

Webern's songs and cantatas present formidable difficulties to the singer because of their disconcerting leaps and startling intervals. For the hearer the difficulty lies rather in Webern's extreme concision and economy: nothing is repeated, each effect is made in the shortest possible time. Even the cantata *Das Augenlicht*, for mixed chorus and a complex chamber orchestra, takes less than five minutes to perform. In Webern the single note has often to bear the weight borne by a whole musical phrase or cadence in the nineteenth century *Lied*. From 1924 onwards Webern consistently developed the 'serial' method he had learnt from Schoenberg and had first employed in his *Drei Lieder*, Op. 17. He is now recognized as a master of formal organization; as a master of orchestral coloration (*Klangfarbenmelodie*) in the shortest space and with the most economical means; and as the most powerful innovator since Schoenberg himself. In 1955 Stravinsky acknowledged his influence, and paid tribute to him as a 'great composer' who was at the same time a 'real hero': 'Doomed to failure in a deaf world of ignorance and indifference, he inexorably went on cutting his diamonds, his dazzling diamonds, of whose mines he had such perfect knowledge.'

I OP. 3 [STEFAN GEORGE]

Fünf Lieder aus '*Der siebente Ring*'	Five Songs from '*The Seventh Ring*'
(1)	(1)
Dies ist ein lied	This is a song
Für dich allein:	for you alone:
Von kindischem wähnen	of childish dreams
Von frommen tränen ...	and pious tears ...
Durch morgengärten klingt es	Lightly it wings its way
Ein leichtbeschwingtes.	through morning gardens.
Nur dir allein	Only for you
Möcht es ein lied	it wants to be
Das rühre sein.	a song that stirs the heart.

(2)
Im windes-weben
War meine frage
Nur träumerei.
Nur lächeln war
was du gegeben.
Aus nasser nacht
Ein glanz entfacht –
Nun drängt der mai ·
Nun muss ich gar
Um dein aug und haar
Alle tage
In sehnen leben.

(3)
An baches ranft
Die einzigen frühen
Die hasel blühen.
Ein vogel pfeift
In kühler au.
Ein leuchten streift
Erwärmt uns sanft
Und zuckt und bleicht.
Das feld ist brach ·
Der baum noch grau. . . .
Blumen streut vielleicht
Der lenz uns nach.

(4)
Im morgen-taun
Trittst du hervor
Den kirschenflor
Mit mir zu schaun ·
Duft einzuziehn
Des rasenbeetes.
Fern fliegt der staub. . . .
Durch die natur
Noch nichts gediehn
Von frucht und laub –
Rings blüte nur. . . .
Von süden weht es.

(5)
Kahl reckt der baum
Im winterdunst
Sein frierend leben ·
Lass deinen traum
Auf stiller reise
Vor ihm sich heben!
Er dehnt die arme –
Bedenk ihn oft

(2)
In the murmuring wind
my question
was but a dream.
Only a smile
was what you gave me.
From a damp night
radiance was kindled –
now May wakens desire.
For your eyes and hair
I must now
live in longing
all my days.

(3)
By the edge of the brook,
early, alone,
the hazels bloom.
A bird whistles
in the cool meadow.
Brightness touches us,
warms us gently,
quivers and pales.
The field lies fallow,
the tree is still grey. . . .
Perhaps spring
will strew flowers after us.

(4)
In the morning dew
you come forth
to see the flowering cherry
with me,
to smell the fragrance
of the flower-bed on the lawn.
The dust whirls far off. . . .
Throughout nature
fruit and leaves
are not flourishing yet –
nothing but blossom all around. . . .
The south wind blows.

(5)
The bare tree stretches
his chilled life
through the winter mist.
Let your dream
on its silent journey
rise before him!
He stretches his arms.
Think of him often

Mit dieser gunst   with favour:
Dass er im harme   for in sorrow
Dass er im eise   and in ice
Noch frühling hofft!   he still hopes for spring!

2 OP. 12 FOUR SONGS BY VARIOUS POETS

(1) *Der Tag ist vergangen* (Traditional)

(1) *Day is past*

Der Tag ist vergangen,   Day has passed,
Die Nacht ist schon hier;   night is here;
Gute Nacht, o Maria,   good night, Blessed Virgin,
Bleib ewig bei mir.   stay with me always.

Der Tag ist vergangen,   Day has passed,
Die Nacht kommt herzu;   night is coming;
Gib auch den Verstorbnen   to the dead also
Die ewige Ruh.   give eternal rest.

(2) *Die geheimnisvolle Flöte* (Li-Tai-Po, translated Bethge)

(2) *The Mysterious Flute*

An einem Abend, da die Blumen dufteten
Und alle Blätter an den Bäumen, trug der
    Wind mir
Das Lied einer entfernten Flöte zu. Da
    schnitt
Ich einen Weidenzweig vom Strauche, und
Mein Lied flog, Antwort gebend, durch die
    blühende Nacht.

One evening, when the flowers smelt sweet,
and all the leaves on the trees, the wind bore
    towards me
the sound of a far-off flute. Then I cut
a twig from the willow, and
my song flew, answering, through the blos-
    soming night.

Seit jenem Abend hören, wann die Erde
    schläft,
Die Vögel ein Gespräch in ihrer Sprache.

Since that evening, when the earth is asleep,
the birds hear a colloquy in their own lan-
    guage.

(3) 'Schien mir's, als ich sah die Sonne' (August Strindberg: Gespenstersonate)

(3) 'When I saw the Sun, I seemed . . .' (from Strindberg's Ghost Sonata)

Schien mir's, als ich sah die Sonne,
daß ich schaute den Verborgnen;
jeder Mensch genießt die Werke,
selig, der das Gute übet.
Für die Zornestat, die du verübtest,
büße nicht mit Bosheit;
tröste den, den du betrübtest,

When I saw the sun, I seemed
to see the Hidden One.
Every man enjoys His works,
happy, if he does what is good.
Do not expiate your rash deed
with evil;
comfort him you have saddened,

gütig, und es wird dir frommen.
Der nur fürchtet, der sich hat vergangen:
gut ist schuldlos leben.

be kind, and you will thrive.
Only the wrongdoer lives in fear;
it is good to live free from guilt.

(4) *Gleich und gleich* (Goethe)

Ein Blumenglöckchen
Vom Boden hervor
War früh gesprosset
In lieblichem Flor;
Da kam ein Bienchen
Und naschte fein: –
Die müssen wohl beide
Für einander sein.

(4) *Like to Like*

A little flower-bell
had early sprung
from the ground
in lovely blossom.
A little bee came
and sipped at it gently –
these two must be
made for each other.

3 OP. 17 [TRADITIONAL]

(1)
Armer Sünder, du,
Die Erde ist dein Schuh;
Mark und Blut,
Der Himmel ist dein Hut.
Fleisch und Bein
Sollen von dir gesegnet sein,
Du heilige Dreifaltigkeit
Von nun an bis in Ewigkeit!

(1)
Poor sinner –
the earth is your shoe.
Man of marrow and blood –
heaven guards your head.
O holy Trinity,
bless
flesh and bone
now and in all eternity!

(2)
Liebste Jungfrau, wir sind dein,
Zeig dich, Mutter stets zu sein,
Schreib uns alle deinem Herzen
Unauslöschlich ein.
Groß ist unsrer Feinde Zahl
Hier in diesem Tränental;
Rette, Mutter, deine Kinder
Vor dem Sündenfall.

(2)
Dearest Virgin, we are yours.
Show yourself always our Mother,
Inscribe us all indelibly
Upon your heart.
Our enemies are many
here in this vale of tears.
Mother, save your children
from falling into sin.

(3)
Heiland, unsre Missetaten
Haben dich verkauft, verraten,
Dich gegeißelt, dich gekrönt,
Am dem Kreuze dich verhöhnt.
Laß dein Leiden und Beschwerden,
Jesus, uns zu Nutzen werden,
Laß durch deine Todespein,
Herr, uns nicht verloren sein!

(3)
Saviour, our sins
have sold and betrayed you,
have caused you to be whipped and crowned
    with thorns,
and mocked on the cross.
Jesus, let your sorrow and agony
benefit us,
let your pain and death
be our salvation!

4 OP. 18 [TRADITIONAL]

(1) *Schatzerl klein*

Schatzerl klein,
Mußt nit traurig sein,
Eh das Jahr vergeht,
Bist du mein.
Eh das Jahr vergeht,
Grünt das Rosmarin,
Sagt der Pfarrer laut:
Nehmt's euch hin.
Grünt der Rosmarin,
Grünt der Myrtenstrauß
Und der Nagerlstock
Blüht im Haus.

(1) *Little Sweetheart*

Little sweetheart,
be not sad –
before the year is out
you will be mine.
Before the year is out
rosemary will be green,
and the parson will say:
'Be man and wife!'
Rosemary will be green,
and myrtle too,
and the gillyflower
will blossom in the house.

(2) *Erlösung*

Maria: Mein Kind, sieh an die Brüste mein,
    Kein'n Sünder laß verloren sein.

Christus: Mutter, sieh an die Wunden,
    Die ich für dein Sünd trag alle
    Stunden.
    Vater, laß dir die Wunden mein
    Ein Opfer für die Sünde sein.

Vater: Sohn, lieber Sohn mein,
    Alles, was du begehrst, das soll sein.

(2) *Salvation*

Mary: My son, look on my breasts:
    let no sinner be lost.

Christ: Mother, look on the wounds
    which I ever bear for your sins.
    Father, let my wounds
    atone for sin.

God the Father: My son, my dear son,
    All shall be as you desire.

(3) *Ave, Regina*

Ave, Regina coelorum,
Ave, Domina Angelorum:
Salve radix, salve porta,
Ex qua mundo lux est orta:
Gaude, Virgo gloriosa,
Super omnes speciosa!
Vale, o valde decora,
Et pro nobis Christum exora.

(3) *Hail, Queen of Heaven*

Hail, Queen of Heaven,
Hail, Queen of Angels,
Hail, Spring of Grace, hail, you gate
through which light came to the world.
Rejoice, glorious Virgin,
lovely above all others!
Farewell, most gracious of women,
and intercede for us with Christ.

5 OP. 25 [HILDEGARD JONE]

(1)

Wie bin ich froh!
Noch einmal wird mir alles grün
Und leuchtet so!

(1)

How glad I am!
Once more all grows green before me,
and all is radiant!

Noch überblühn die Blumen mir die Welt!
Noch einmal bin ich ganz ins Werden hinge-
    stellt
Und bin auf Erden.

(2)
Des Herzens Purpurvogel fliegt durch Nacht.
Der Augen Falter, die im Hellen gaukeln,
Sind ihm voraus, wenn sie im Tage schau-
    keln.
Und doch ist er's, der sie ans Ziel gebracht.
Sie ruhen oft, die bald sich neu erheben
Zu neuem Flug. Doch rastet endlich er
Am Ast des Todes, müd und flügelschwer,
Dann müssen sie zum letzten Blick verbeben.

(3)
Sterne, Ihr silbernen Bienen
Der Nacht um die Blume der Liebe!
Wahrlich, der Honig aus ihr
Hängt schimmernd an Euch.
Lasset ihn tropfen ins Herz,
In die goldene Wabe,
Füllet sie an bis zum Rand.
Ach, schon tropfet sie über,
Selig und bis ans Ende mit
Ewiger Süße durchtränkt.

the flowers still bloom about my world!
Once more growth and change enfold me,
once more I am on earth.

(2)
The heart's red bird flies through night.
The eyes' butterflies, fluttering in brightness,
fly before it when they hover in daylight.
Yet it is the heart-bird that led them to their
    goal.
Often they rest, but soon they rise again
to fly once more. But when the heart-bird
    takes its rest at last
tired and heavy-winged, on the branch of
    death,
then they must look their last, tremble, and
    die.

(3)
Stars, night's silvery bees
about the flower of love!
The honey of love
hangs, shimmering, on you.
Let it drop into the heart,
that golden honeycomb,
fill it to the brim.
Already it runs over,
blissful, and filled through and through
with eternal sweetness.

ALBAN (MARIA JOHANNES) BERG

Born in Vienna, 9 February 1885, the son of a German father and an Austrian mother. Although he received little formal musical training in his early years, he soon revealed a talent for composition, attested by some seventy songs composed between the ages of fifteen and twenty; a talent which did not desert him during the years he spent in a local government accounts office (1904–6). It was in this period that he met Schoenberg and became his pupil, absorbing Schoenberg's theories and wedding them to his own more romantic temperament. His early chamber music was first performed at concerts given by and for Schoenberg's pupils and friends; when performed outside (as were the 'Altenberg' songs, Op. 4, first heard in the great hall of the Vienna *Musikverein* in 1913) his music was likely to be greeted with boos and hisses. In May 1914 Berg saw a performance of Georg Büchner's play *Woǫǫek* (or *Woyǫek*), and determined to make it into an opera. Work on this opera was interrupted by service in the Austrian army; but the score was completed in 1920, and the performance of *Woǫǫek* at the Berlin opera in 1925 made Berg famous. Despite its unfamiliar idiom (notably its use of *Sprechgesang*, or free recitative, within a highly differentiated orchestral texture), *Woǫǫek* soon established itself in the repertoire of most of the world's great opera houses. Berg died on Christmas Eve 1935. His works include a 'Lyric Suite' for string quartet written in 1929 (in which Berg for the first time made strict use of the dodecaphonic method), a violin concerto (completed in 1935), a good deal of chamber music, and an unfinished opera, *Lulu*, based on two plays by Frank Wedekind.

As a song-writer Berg began in the Schumann tradition: his choice of texts shows a catholic taste which ranges from Walther von der Vogelweide, Goethe, Heine, and Mörike to Arno Holz, Hofmannsthal, and Rilke. These early songs Berg later disowned; but the *Seven Early Songs* he wrote under Schoenberg's influence (*c.* 1907; orchestrated 1928) still have a Schumannesque flavour, a refreshing emotional directness which never conflicts with formal mastery or progressive vocal techniques. The songs to texts by Peter Altenberg (1912) show a change: an extreme economy rivalling that of Webern (one song is only eleven bars long), with which Berg tries to curb the lyric and dramatic expansiveness natural to him; and reliance on a large symphonic orchestra which is used with Mahlerian skill. The concert aria *Der Wein* (1929) is based on a dodecaphonic 'note-row', but it is remarkable that even here a strong feeling of tonality persists – large sections of the work seem to be in D minor. *Der Wein*, like *Woǫǫek*, is at once romantic and modern; it blends, in an entirely convincing way, the art of Mahler with that of Schoenberg.

I [A POEM BY THEODOR STORM WHICH BERG SET TWICE: IN 1907 AND 1926]

'Schließe mir die Augen beide ...'

Schließe mir die Augen beide
Mit den lieben Händen zu!
Geht doch alles, was ich leide,
Unter deiner Hand zur Ruh.

Und wie leise sich der Schmerz
Well um Weile schlafen leget,
Wie der letzte Schlag sich reget,
Füllest du mein ganzes Herz.

'Close both my eyes ...'

Close both my eyes
with your dear hands!
under your hand
all my sufferings are assuaged.

And as wave after wave of anguish
ebbs away,
as the last pang throbs,
you fill my whole heart.

2 OP. 2 [FRIEDRICH HEBBEL AND ALFRED MOMBERT]

(1) Aus: '*Dem Schmerz sein Recht*' (Hebbel)

Schlafen, Schlafen, nichts als Schlafen!
   Kein Erwachen, keinen Traum!
Jener Wehen, die mich trafen,
   Leisestes Erinnern kaum,
Daß ich, wenn des Lebens Fülle
Niederklingt in meine Ruh,
Nur noch tiefer mich verhülle,
   Fester zu die Augen tu!

(2) Drei Lieder aus: '*Der Glühende*' (Mombert)

i

Schlafend trägt man mich in mein Heimatland.
Ferne komm ich her, über Gipfel, über
   Schlünde,
über ein dunkles Meer in mein Heimatland.

ii

Nun ich der Riesen Stärksten überwand,
mich aus dem dunkelsten Land heimfand
an einer weißen Märchenhand,
hallen schwer die Glocken;
und ich wanke durch die Gassen schlafbe-
   fangen.

iii

Warm die Lüfte, es sprießt Gras auf son-
   nigen Wiesen,
Horch – es flötet die Nachtigall.
Ich will singen:
Droben hoch im düstern Bergforst,
es schmilzt und glitzert kalter Schnee,
ein Mädchen in grauem Kleide lehnt an
   feuchtem Eichstamm,
krank sind ihre zarten Wangen,
die grauen Augen fiebern durch Düster-
   riesenstämme,
'Er kommt noch nicht. Er lässt mich warten.'
Stirb!
Der Eine stirbt, daneben der Andre lebt:
Das macht die Welt so tief-schön.

(1) From: '*Let Anguish Have Its Due*'

To sleep, to sleep, only to sleep!
No awakening, no dream!
Let the pains I had to bear
be hardly remembered –
so that, when the fullness of life
sounds into my sleep
I draw my sheet closer around me
and hold my eyes more tightly shut!

(2) Three Songs from '*Glowing with Ecstasy*'

i

In sleep I am borne to my homeland.
I come from afar, over mountains and
   valleys,
over a dark sea to my homeland.

ii

Now that I have conquered the strongest
   giant
and found my way home from the darkest
   land
led by a white faerie hand,
the bells sound darkly,
and unsteadily, lost in sleep, I walk through
   the streets.

iii

The air is warm, grass grows on sunlit
   meadows.
Listen – the nightingale is singing.
I will sing:
High up in the dark mountain forest,
where cold snow melts and glistens,
a grey-clad girl leans against the wet trunk of
   an oak-tree.
Her tender cheeks show sickness,
her grey eyes look feverishly past dark,
   gigantic tree-trunks.
'Still he does not come. He makes me wait.'
Die!
One dies, while another lives:
This makes the world so lovely and so deep.

3 OP. 4 [PETER ALTENBERG]

Fünf Orchesterlieder nach Ansichts-
kartentexten von Peter Altenberg

Five Songs for Voice and Orchestra, to Picture-Postcard Texts by
Peter Altenberg

(1) *Seele, wie bist du schöner . . .'*

(1) *'O soul, how much lovelier . . .'*

Seele, wie bist du schöner, tiefer, nach
 Schneestürmen.
Auch du hast sie, gleich der Natur.
Und über beiden liegt noch ein trüber
 Hauch, eh das Gewölk sich verzog!

O soul, how much lovelier, how much
 deeper you are after snow-storms.
You have them too, just like nature.
And both are still overcast, before the clouds
 blow away!

(2) *'Sahst du nach dem Gewitterregen . . .'*

(2) *'Did you ever see . . .'*

Sahst du nach dem Gewitterregen den
 Wald?
Alles rastet, blinkt, und ist schöner als zuvor.
Siehe, Fraue, auch du brauchst Gewitter-
 regen!

Did you ever see the wood after the rain-
 storm?
All is at rest, shining and lovelier than
 before.
Lady, you too need such storms!

(3) *Über die Grenzen des All . . .'*

(3) *'Beyond the Bounds of the Universe . . .'*

Über die Grenzen des All blicktest du
 sinnend hinaus;
Hattest nie Sorge um Hof und Haus!
Leben und Traum vom Leben – plötzlich ist
 alles aus.
Über die Grenzen des All blickst du noch
 sinnend hinaus.

You gaze, thoughtfully, beyond the bounds
 of the universe.
You had no care for house or home.
Life and the dream of life – suddenly all is
 over.
Still you gaze, thoughtfully, beyond the
 bounds of the universe.

(4) *'Nichts ist gekommen . . .'*

(4) *'Nothing has come . . .'*

Nichts ist gekommen, nichts wird kommen
 für meine Seele.
Ich habe gewartet, gewartet, oh, gewartet!
Die Tage werden dahinschleichen und
 umsonst wehen meine aschblonden, sei-
 denen Haare um mein bleiches Antlitz!

Nothing has come, nothing will come for my
 soul.
I have waited, waited, oh, waited!
The days will slip by and my ash-blonde,
 silken hair will be blown about my pale
 face in vain.

(5) *'Hier ist Friede . . .'*

Hier ist Friede. Hier weine ich mich aus
  über alles!
Hier löst sich mein unfaßbares, unermeß-
  liches Leid, das mir die Seele verbrennt.
Siehe, hier sind keine Menschen, keine
  Ansiedlungen.
Hier ist Friede! Hier tropft Schnee leise in
  Wasserlachen.

(5) *'Here there is peace . . .'*

Here there is peace, here I weep my fill.
Here dissolves the unfathomable, immeasur-
  able sorrow that burns up my soul.
Look: there are no men here, no dwellings.
Here there is peace. Here the snow drops
  softly into pools of water.

4 OP. [STEFAN GEORGE, AFTER BAUDELAIRE]

Der Wein. Konzertarie mit Orchester

(1) *Die Seele des Weines*

Des weines geist begann im fass zu singen:
Mensch · teurer ausgestossener · dir soll
Durch meinen engen kerker durch erklingen
Ein lied von licht und bruderliebe voll.

Ich weiss: am sengendheissen bergeshange
Bei schweiss und mühe nur gedeih ich recht
Da meine seele ich nur so empfange
Doch bin ich niemals undankbar und
  schlecht.

Und dies bereitet mir die grösste labe
Wenn eines arbeit-matten mund mich hält
Sein heisser schlund wird mir zum süssen
  grabe
Das mehr als kalte keller mir gefällt.

Du hörst den sonntagsang aus frohem
  schwarme?
Nun kehrt die hoffnung prickelnd in mich
  ein:
Du stülpst die ärmel · stützest beide arme
Du wirst mich preisen und zufrieden sein.

Ich mache deines weibes augen heiter
Und deinem sohne leih ich frische kraft
Ich bin für diesen zarten lebensstreiter
Das öl das fechtern die gewandtheit schafft.

Wine. A Concert Aria with Orchestra

(1) *The Wine's Soul*

One evening, the wine's soul began to sing
  in its cask:
Man, dear exile,
a song of light and brotherly love
shall resound for you through my narrow
  prison.

I know: only on burning mountain slopes,
with sweat and toil, do I grow aright;
only thus do I receive my soul.
But I am never ungrateful and wicked.

But this is my greatest joy:
when a toil-wearied man lifts me to his lips.
His parched throat becomes a sweet grave
that I like better than cool cellars.

Do you hear the happy crowd singing on
  Sunday?
Now bubbling hope enters into me.
You turn up your sleeves, put your elbows
  on the table –
you will praise me and be content.

I light up your wife's eyes,
and give new strength to your son –
I am the oil that makes supple the limbs
of this frail athlete of life.

Und du erhältst von diesem pflanzenseime
Das Gott · der ewige sämann niedergiesst
Damit in deiner brust die dichtung keime
Die wie ein seltner baum zum himmel
    spriesst.

And you are given this plant ambrosia,
which God, the eternal sower, pours down,
to make poetry spring up in your heart
and grow to heaven like an exotic tree.

(2) Der Wein der Liebenden

Prächtig ist heute die weite
Stränge und sporen beiseite ·
Reiten wir auf dem wein
In den feenhimmel hinein!

Engel für ewige dauer
Leidend im fieberschauer
Durch des morgens blauen kristall
Fort in das leuchtende all!

Wir lehnen uns weich auf den flügel
Des windes der eilt ohne zügel.
Beide voll gleicher lust

Lass schwester uns brust an brust
Fliehn ohne rast und stand
In meiner träume land!

(2) The Lovers' Wine

The distance looks splendid today.
Let us leave bridles and spurs,
let us ride on wine
into a faerie heaven.

Angels for ever,
racked by fever —
through the blue crystal of morning
into the shining universe!

Softly we lean on the wing
of the hurrying, unbridled wind.
Impelled by the same ardour,

let us fly, sister, breast to breast,
without rest, without stay,
to the land of my dreams.

(3) Der Wein des Einsamen

Der sonderbare blick der leichten frauen
Der auf uns gleitet wie das weisse licht
Des mondes auf bewegter wasserschicht
Will er im bade seine schönheit schauen

Der letzte thaler an dem spielertisch
Ein frecher kuss der hageren Adeline
Erschlaffenden gesang der violine
Der wie der menschheit fernes qualgezisch —

Mehr als dies alles schätz ich · tiefe flasche ·
Den starken balsam den ich aus dir nasche
Und der des frommen dichters müdheit
    bannt.

Du giebst ihm hoffnung liebe jugendkraft
Und stolz · dies erbteil aller bettlerschaft
Der uns zu helden macht und gottverwandt.

(3) The Lonely Man's Wine

The strange glance of light women,
that brushes us like the white light
of the moon on moving waters
when it would see its beauty in the deep;

the last coin at the gaming table,
a bold kiss from lean Adeline,
the enervating song of the violin
hissing like mankind's anguish, far re-
    moved —

more than all these, deep bottle, I cherish
the strong balsam I draw from you,
dispelling a pious poet's weariness.

You give him hope, love, youthful strength,
and pride — that treasure of all paupery
which makes us heroes and akin to gods.

PAUL HINDEMITH

Born at Hanau on 16 November 1895. Studied composition under Arnold Mendelssohn at Darmstadt and Bernhard Sekles at Frankfurt, and became an expert performer on many instruments – notably on the viola (Hindemith was the soloist in the first performance of William Walton's viola concerto in 1929). Achieved prominence as a composer in the 1920s, when he startled and delighted the German bourgeoisie with three one-act 'anti-operas' (*Mörder, Hoffnung der Frauen, Das Nusch-Nuschi, Sancta Susanna*) and a satirical opera *Neues vom Tage* which had much in common with the dramatic satires produced at the same period by Kurt Weill in collaboration with Bertolt Brecht. Hindemith also tried to bridge the gap between musical producers and consumers by writing a good deal of *Gebrauchsmusik* – 'music for use', 'workaday music' – which could be played by amateurs on many kinds of instrument. In 1927 Hindemith became Professor of Composition at the Berlin Conservatoire – but the coming of Hitler brought his work into disrepute as 'degenerate art'. The new régime looked with especial disfavour on Hindemith's masterpiece, the opera *Mathis der Maler* (1934), with its anti-totalitarian tendency. The composer therefore emigrated, teaching at first in Turkey, then in the U.S.A., where he settled in 1939. His work includes many theoretical writings (directed, in later years, more and more openly against what he regarded as the excesses of the Schoenberg school), the full-length operas *Cardillac* and *Die Harmonie der Welt* and the one-act opera *The Long Christmas Dinner*; the oratorio *Das Unaufhörliche*; the Walt Whitman requiem *For Those We Love*; the *Ludus Tonalis* for solo piano; and many orchestral and chamber works. He died on 28 December 1963.

If the songs of Schoenberg and his disciples may be said to continue a line that reaches from Wagner to Mahler, those of Hindemith derive from Brahms via Max Reger. His early work moves gradually away from traditional tonality; yet there is little in the eight songs of Opus 18 or the cycle *Die junge Magd* to offend any but the most hidebound admirer of the romantic *Lied*. The same could not be said of the original version of *Das Marienleben*, first performed in 1923 and presenting, as Paul Stephan has said, 'the whole gamut of possible emotions within the range of Hindemith's musical idiom': for here the music takes too little account of the possibilities of the human voice, placing the tessitura cruelly low for the soprano who has to sing it. This fault Hindemith remedied in his later version of the same cycle (1948); but many will feel that despite its greater singability and formal unity, this second version has suffered from Hindemith's polemic concern to remove all hints of affinity with 'atonal' modes of composition. The song from *Das Marienleben* reprinted on pp. 176–7 is the only one left unchanged in the later version – its cool, polyphonic beauty is entirely characteristic of Hindemith at his best.

I OP. 23/2 [GEORG TRAKL]

Die junge Magd	*The Young Farm Servant*
(1)	(1)
Oft am Brunnen, wenn es dämmert,	Often, in the gloaming, you may see her
Sieht man sie verzaubert stehen,	standing, spellbound, by the well,
Wasser schöpfen, wenn es dämmert.	drawing water as evening falls.
Eimer auf und nieder gehen.	Buckets go up and down.

In den Buchen Dohlen flattern,
Und sie gleichet einem Schatten.
Ihre gelben Haare flattern,
Und im Hofe schrein die Ratten.

Und umschmeichelt von Verfalle,
Senkt sie die entzundenen Lider.
Dürres Gras neigt im Verfalle
Sich zu ihren Füßen nieder.

(2)
Stille schafft sie in der Kammer,
Und der Hof liegt längst verödet.
Im Holunder vor der Kammer
Kläglich eine Amsel flötet.

Silbern schaut ihr Bild im Spiegel
Fremd sie an im Zwielichtscheine
Und verdämmert fahl im Spiegel,
Und ihr graut vor seiner Reine.

Traumhaft singt ein Knecht im Dunkel,
Und sie starrt, von Schmerz geschüttelt.
Röte träufelt durch das Dunkel.
Jäh am Tor der Südwind rüttelt.

(3)
Nächtens über kahlen Anger
Gaukelt sie in Fieberträumen.
Mürrisch greint der Wind im Anger,
Und der Mond lauscht aus den Bäumen.

Balde rings die Sterne bleichen,
Und ermattet von Beschwerde
Wächsern ihre Wangen bleichen.
Fäulnis wittert aus der Erde.

Traurig rauscht das Rohr im Tümpel,
Und sie friert, in sich gekauert.
Fern ein Hahn kräht. Übern Tümpel
Hart und grau der Morgen schauert.

(4)
In der Schmiede dröhnt der Hammer,
Und sie huscht am Tor vorüber.
Glührot schwingt der Knecht den Hammer,
Und sie schaut wie tot hinüber.

Wie im Traum trifft sie ein Lachen;
Und sie taumelt in die Schmiede,
Scheu geduckt vor seinem Lachen,
Wie der Hammer hart und rüde.

Jackdaws flutter in the beech-trees;
she resembles a shadow.
Her yellow hair flutters,
and the rats squeal in the yard.

Wooed by decay
she lowers her inflamed eyelids.
Dry grass, decaying,
sinks down at her feet.

(2)
Silently she works in the room
while the farmyard lies deserted.
In the elder-tree before the room
a blackbird calls sadly.

Her image, silvery in the mirror,
regards her strangely in the twilight
and fades, pale, in the mirror.
She shudders at its purity.

Dream-like, a farm-hand sings in the darkness;
rigid she gazes, shaken by grief.
Redness trickles through the gloom.
The south wind suddenly shakes the gate.

(3)
At night she floats in feverish dreams
over the bare meadow.
The surly wind moans in the meadow,
and the moon listens from the trees.

Soon all around the stars grow pale,
and worn out with sorrow
her cheeks grow pale as wax.
Scents of corruption rise from the earth.

The reeds sough sadly in the pool,
and she huddles in the cold.
A cock crows far off. Over the pool
the morning shudders, hard and grey.

(4)
The hammer rings in the smithy
and she flits by the gate.
The smith swings the glowing-red hammer,
and she looks towards him as though she
were dead.

Laughter strikes her as in a dream;
and she staggers into the smithy,
cowering before his laughter
that is hard and rude like his hammer.

Hell versprühn im Raum die Funken,
Und mit hilfloser Gebärde
Hascht sie nach den wilden Funken,
Und sie stürzt betäubt zur Erde.

(5)
Schmächtig hingestreckt im Bette,
Wacht sie auf voll süßem Bangen,
Und sie sieht ihr schmutzig Bette
Ganz von goldnem Licht verhangen,

Die Reseden dort am Fenster
Und den bläulich hellen Himmel.
Manchmal trägt der Wind ans Fenster
Einer Glocke zag Gebimmel.

Schatten gleiten übers Kissen,
Langsam schlägt die Mittagsstunde,
Und sie atmet schwer im Kissen,
Und ihr Mund gleicht einer Wunde.

(6)
Abends schweben blutige Linnen,
Wolken über stummen Wäldern,
Die gehüllt in schwarze Linnen.
Spatzen lärmen auf den Feldern.

Und sie liegt ganz weiß im Dunkel.
Unterm Dach verhaucht ein Girren.
Wie ein Aas in Busch und Dunkel
Fliegen ihren Mund umschwirren.

Traumhaft klingt im braunen Weiler
Nach ein Klang von Tanz und Geigen,
Schwebt ihr Antlitz durch den Weiler,
Weht ihr Haar in kahlen Zweigen.

The sparks fly brightly about the smithy,
and with a helpless gesture
she catches at the wild sparks
and falls – stunned – to the ground.

(5)
Slenderly stretched in her bed
she wakes full of sweet trepidation,
and sees her soiled bed
overhung with golden light,

sees the mignonettes at her window,
and the bright, bluish sky.
Sometimes the wind bears to the window
the shy tinkling of a bell.

Shadows flit across her pillow,
a bell slowly announces noon.
On her pillow she breathes heavily,
her mouth gaping like a wound.

(6)
As bloody strips of linen, clouds hover
in the evening over silent woods
which are wrapt in black linen.
Sparrows twitter in the fields.

All white, she lies in the darkness.
The cooing fades under the roof.
Flies flit about her mouth
as about carrion in the dark bush.

As in a dream the sound of dancing and
    fiddling
trembles through the brown village;
her face floats through the village,
her hair waves in bare branches.

2 OP. 27 [RAINER MARIA RILKE]

From: *Das Marienleben*

Stillung Mariä mit dem Auferstandenen

Was sie damals empfanden: ist es nicht
vor allen Geheimnissen süß
und immer noch irdisch:
da er, ein wenig blaß noch vom Grab,
erleichtert zu ihr trat:
an allen Stellen erstanden.

The Life of the Virgin Mary

Consolation of Mary with the Risen Christ

What they felt at that time: is it not
sweet above all mysteries
and yet of this earth?
When he, still a little pale from the grave,
came to her, disburdened –
resurrected in every place.

O zu ihr zuerst. Wie waren sie da
unaussprechlich in Heilung.
Ja sie heilten, das wars. Sie hatten nicht
    nötig,
sich stark zu berühren.
Er legte ihr eine Sekunde
kaum seine nächstens
ewige Hand an die frauliche Schulter.
Und sie begannen
still wie die Bäume im Frühling,
unendlich zugleich,
diese Jahreszeit
ihres äußersten Umgangs.

Oh, to her he came first. How inexpressibly
they were then healed.
Yes, that was it – they were healed. They did
    not need
to touch each other firmly.
For hardly a second he laid
his hand, that was soon to be eternal,
on her woman's shoulder.
And they began –
still as the trees in spring,
and eternal together –
the season
of their uttermost communing.

NOTES ON THE POETS

(Numbers indicate the pages of this book on which examples of their work may be found.)

HERMANN LUDWIG ALLMERS (born Rechtenfleth an der Weser 11 February 1821, died there, 9 March 1902). Hoped to become a traveller and geographer, but was forced to take over his father's farm. He wrote descriptions of his native landscape (*Marschenbuch*, 1858) and travel books (*Römische Schlendertage*, 1869) in his spare time. His lyric poetry (*Dichtungen*, 1860) enjoyed an ephemeral fame, but now only 'Feldeinsamkeit' is remembered, and that because Brahms chose to set it. Allmers himself was dissatisfied with Brahms's setting and strongly preferred one by Gerhard Focken. [99]

PETER ALTENBERG (pseudonym of Richard Engländer, born Vienna 9 March 1862, died there 8 January 1919). A true bohemian, who sought to preserve the most fleeting impressions in tiny prose-poems. He became known to a wider public primarily through the impassioned advocacy of the great Viennese satirist Karl Kraus. His works, which include some autobiographical studies (*Vita ipsa*, 1918, *Mein Lebensabend*, 1919), were long out of print, but are now being made available by Kösel Verlag of Munich. [171–2]

ARNIM: see *Knaben Wunderhorn, Des.*

CHARLES PIERRE BAUDELAIRE (1821–67). The great French poet enters the history of the German *Lied* at one remove: Alban Berg's *Der Wein* is based on Stefan George's version of three of his poems. [172–3]

BETHGE: see *Chinesische Flöte, Die.*

OTTO JULIUS BIERBAUM (born Grünberg/Silesia 28 June 1865, died Dresden 1 February 1910). The son of a well-to-do innkeeper, Bierbaum studied law and oriental languages in order to enter the German consular service. His father's bankruptcy forced him to abandon this plan – he became a successful journalist, and soon graduated to the writing of novels and short stories (*Stilpe*, 1897; *Prinz Kuckuck*, 1906–7) which retain a sociological interest today. His poetry (*Irrgarten der Liebe*, 1901; *Die schönsten Früchte vom Bierbaum*) is no longer read. Bierbaum deserves to be remembered as founder and patron of the intellectual cabaret movement in Germany, which influenced such notable writers as Frank Wedekind and Bertold Brecht. [153]

BRENTANO: see *Knaben Wunderhorn, Des*

JOACHIM HEINRICH CAMPE (born Deensen 29 June 1746, died Braunschweig 22 October 1818). Studied theology and became a notable educationist in Prussia (Tegel and Potsdam) and in Hamburg. Influenced by Rousseau, he wrote voluminously on educational problems and was the first German author to write books specifically for children (*Robinson der Jüngere*, 1779). He also compiled dictionaries (1807–12) and a treatise – ridiculed by Goethe and Schiller – on the pollution of the German language through foreign influences. His poems (one of which was set by Mozart) may still occasionally be heard in German nurseries. [21]

ADALBERT VON CHAMISSO (Louis Charles Adelaide Chamisso de Boncourt, born Castle Boncourt, Champagne 31 January 1781, died Berlin 21 August 1838). Member of a family of French nobles driven out by the Revolution of 1789. Became a page at the court of Prussia and later entered the Prussian army. Chamisso hated military life and felt out of place, torn between allegiance to France and to Prussia; this conflict is embodied in his greatest work (*Peter Schlehmihls wundersame Geschichte*, 1814). He was a notable lyric poet, though the work by which Schumann has made him remembered (*Frauen-Liebe und -Leben*) is embarrassingly sentimental. Chamisso was also a noted botanist, travelled round the world as member of a scientific expedition (1815–18) and ended his life as curator of the botanical gardens in Berlin. [77–80]

CHINESISCHE FLÖTE, DIE. A collection of poems by Li-Tai-Po and others, translated from the Chinese by Hans *Bethge* (born Dessau 9 January 1876, died Göppingen 1 February 1946), published by the Insel Verlag in 1907 and used by Mahler as a source of texts for *Das Lied von der Erde*. [146–50, 165]

MATTHIAS CLAUDIUS (born Reinfeld, Holstein 15 August 1740, died Hamburg 21 January 1815). Descended from a long line of Lutheran country pastors, Claudius studied theology and law and became editor, in 1771, of a country newspaper to which he gave the name *Der Wandsbecker Bote*. Here he wrote a number of prose-reflections, stories, and poems in the popular German 'calendar' style which made his name (and his paper) famous throughout Germany. The simplicity of his style conceals great complexity and maturity of feeling, and his work is as fresh today as it was when his first collection (*Asmus omnia sua secum portans*, 1775) drew the attention of the discerning. 'Der Tod und das Mädchen' is an excellent example of his manner and a worthy match for Schubert's music. [38]

MATTHÄUS KASIMIR VON COLLIN (born Vienna 3 March 1779, died there 23 November 1824). Trained as a lawyer, Collin obtained a university Chair of Aesthetics and Philosophy at Vienna in 1812. He was also an industrious journalist (editor of the *Allgemeine Literaturzeitung*), acted as private tutor to the son of the Austrian emperor and the Duke of Reichstadt, and wrote many (now forgotten) libretti, historical plays, and poems. Schubert knew him personally and dedicated one of his *Liederhefte* to him. His brother Heinrich wrote the play *Coriolan* for which Beethoven composed his overture. [42]

HUGO CONRAT, named as the translator of Brahms's *Zigeunerlieder*, was translator only at second hand: he turned into verse a prose-version of Hungarian folk-poems by a Fräulein Witzl who is not otherwise known to history. Brahms, who was on friendly terms with Conrat, selected eleven of the twenty-five songs in Conrat's collection for his Op. 103. [103–5]

JAKOB NIKOLAUS CRAIGHER DE JACHELUTTA (born Ligosullo, Venetia 1797, died Cormons 1855). Came to Vienna from Italy in 1820, settled there as an accountant and cultivated the friendship of Friedrich Schlegel and other important figures in Viennese intellectual life. His poems are collected in *Poetische Betrachtungen in freien Stunden*, (1828), a book which includes two of the three poems set by Schubert. He was also an assiduous translator and travelled widely. [41]

GEORG FRIEDRICH DAUMER (born Nuremberg 5 March 1800, died Würzburg 13 December 1875). The son of an artisan, Daumer studied theology and classical philology at various universities and made his name with a number of important theological works; but his leaning towards eastern religions increasingly earned him hostility and ridicule. His greatest contributions to German literature were his translations from oriental and classical originals (*Hafis*, 1846 and 1852; *Polydora, ein weltpoetisches Liederbuch*, 1855). Brahms, who admired him greatly, set some sixty of his poems. [95–6, 98]

RICHARD DEHMEL (born Wendisch-Hermsdorf, Brandenburg 18 November 1863, died Blankenese, Hamburg 8 February 1920). Son of a forester, studied natural sciences and philosophy, and became editor of a provincial newspaper. From 1887 to 1895 he was secretary of the Union of German Fire Insurance Companies; after 1895 he lived purely by his pen. Dehmel was one of the founders of the influential journal *Pan*, which introduced a new style in literature and the arts ('Jugendstil'). He served in the First World War, and published a journal of his experiences (*Zwischen Volk und Menschheit*) in 1919. He wrote some of the truest and most deeply felt love-poetry in modern German literature, as well as powerful poems of social revolt. His best poems are accessible in a collected edition (ten volumes) published 1906–9. [154]

JOSEF KARL BENEDIKT VON EICHENDORFF (born Castle Lubowitz, Silesia 10 March 1788, died Neisse, Silesia 27 February 1857). During his student days at Halle and Heidelberg, Eichendorff came into personal contact with many of the most eminent leaders of the German Romantic movement and he began to publish poems and short stories after his return to Silesia in 1808. He fought under both Prussian and Austrian commands during the 'Wars of Liberation' (1810–15) and entered the Prussian civil service after Napoleon's defeat. Many of his finest poems (*Gedichte*, 1837) were written out of longing for the countryside during his period as a civil servant in Breslau and Berlin. The 'good-for-nothing' hero of his best-known short story (*Aus dem Leben eines Taugenichts*, 1826) is clearly an anti-self: the wishful dream of a conscientious government official. [72–6, 112–13, 157]

FERDINAND FREILIGRATH (born Detmold 17 June 1810, died Kannstadt 18 March 1876). The son of a schoolmaster, Freiligrath became a merchant, but soon devoted all his time to poetry. In the 1840s, Freiligrath lived (for political reasons) in Switzerland and England; he returned to Germany in 1848 and became one of the principal contributors to the *Neue Rheinische Zeitung* edited by Karl Marx. In 1851, political persecution drove Freiligrath once again to London, but he returned to Germany in 1868 and stayed there for the last few years of his life. He is best known for the exotic 'desert and lion poetry' of his *Gedichte* of 1839 and for the poems of social revolt collected in such volumes as *Ça ira!* (1846). [31]

EMANUEL GEIBEL (born Lübeck 17 October 1815, died there 6 April 1884). One of the most popular poets of the nineteenth century, his work lives today by virtue of a handful of nostalgic songs in the folk-song manner (like 'Der Mai ist gekommen') which have been set to simple tunes. In his own day, he was highly honoured as a conservative poet, a pillar of throne and altar – he received a pension from the king of Prussia in the 1840s and was called to Munich as Professor of Aesthetics in 1852. Of his many collections of verse, the most notable are *Zeitstimmen* (1841) and *Neue Gedichte* (1856); his translations from the Spanish (*Spanisches Liederbuch*, 1852, with Paul Heyse) have been immortalized by Hugo Wolf. [119–20]

CHRISTIAN FÜRCHTEGOTT GELLERT (born Hainichen 4 July 1715, died Leipzig 13 December 1791). Professor of Moral Philosophy and Rhetoric at Leipzig. His fame rests chiefly on a collection of moral tales in verse (*Fabeln und Erzählungen*, 1746 and 1748), and on a volume of devotional poems (*Geistliche Oden und Lieder*, 1737), which express the 'rational piety' of the Enlightenment and which provided Beethoven with the text of six of his songs. Gellert also wrote a novel, and a number of plays. Frederick the Great called him '*le plus raisonnable de tous les savants allemands*'. [24]

JOHANN WILHELM LUDWIG GLEIM (born Ermsleben 2 April 1719, died Halberstadt 18 February 1803). Secretary of the Prussian general Dessauer, whom he accompanied in the Second Silesian War. In 1747 he was made secretary to the Cathedral chapter at Halberstadt; a comfortable situation which enabled him to devote himself to writing harmless 'anacreontic' verses in praise of wine, love, and life (first attempted in *Versuch in scherzhaften Liedern*, 1744) and to help needy poets. He became a beloved paternal figure ('Vater Gleim'). [18]

STEFAN GEORGE (born Büdesheim 12 July 1868, died Locarno 4 December 1933). The son of a wine-merchant, George studied at Paris (where he came under the influence of the French Symbolists), Berlin and Munich, and lived in great seclusion in various German towns, mainly in Berlin, Munich, and Bingen. He inspired fierce loyalty in a circle of disciples, which included poets, philosophers, and literary critics. His poetry is distinguished by great strictness of form and by peculiarities of orthography. George is known also as editor of the journal *Blätter für die Kunst*, and as translator of Dante,

Shakespeare, Baudelaire, and Verlaine. His works are conveniently available in *Werke in zwei Bänden*, Verlag Helmut Küpper (formerly Georg Bondi), Düsseldorf and Munich. [158–62, 163–5, 172–3]

JOHANN WOLFGANG VON GOETHE (born Frankfurt-am-Main 28 August 1749, died Weimar, 22 March 1832). Germany's greatest poet, who enriched the German novel with such works as *Die Leiden des jungen Werthers* (1774) and *Wilhelm Meisters Lehrjahre* (1795–6), the German stage with *Faust* (1775–1832) and *Iphigenie auf Tauris* (1787). The son of a Frankfurt patrician, he studied law and entered the service of Duke Karl August of Sachsen-Weimar first as companion, then as councillor of state. He made distinguished contributions to science as well as literature, and helped, in successive posts, to administer nearly all the departments of the state of Weimar. His earlier lyrics have a pristine freshness and natural singing quality which inspired composers to match them with music – the German *Lied* is in no small measure the result of his liberation of poetry from *Aufklärung* fetters. Goethe continued to write lyric poetry throughout his long life; its wealth of human experience constitutes a quarry that German composers have even now not managed to exhaust. [20, 24, 25, 33–6, 39, 113–18, 166]

KLAUS JOHANN GROTH (born Heide, Dithmarschen 24 April 1819, died Kiel 1 June 1899). Born in the North German township from which the Brahms family also stemmed, Groth spent most of his life as a schoolteacher in his native region. He was one of the few German poets who wrote in the Low German Dialect (*Quickborn*, 1853 and 1871; *Vertelln*, 1856–60). He also wrote lyrics in the standard High German (*Hundert Blätter*, 1854); and it is these that Brahms chose to set. In 1866 he became a professor at Kiel University, and also administered the local museum of antiquities. He visited England in 1872 and lectured at Oxford. [98–9]

PAUL GRAF VON HAUGWITZ (born Reichenbach 22 January 1791, died Dresden 8 September 1856). Son of a Prussian minister for foreign affairs. Studied in Vienna and Heidelberg; took part in the 'Wars of Liberation' against Napoleon as adjutant to various Prussian generals, then retired to his estates in Silesia. Many of his poems were published in the *Frauentaschenbuch* (edited by de la Motte Fouqué) between 1816 and 1821. He also published translations from the English, including poems by Byron and Thomas Moore. [25]

CHRISTIAN FRIEDRICH HEBBEL (born Wesselburen, Holstein 18 March 1813, died Vienna, 13 December 1863). The son of a bricklayer, Hebbel experienced bitterest poverty and humiliation in his youth, until the editor of a fashionable Hamburg journal made it possible for him to study: first at Hamburg, later at the university of Munich. In these late student-years, Hebbel began writing tragedies which were to place him in the forefront of German dramatists. On a travelling scholarship from the king of Denmark, Hebbel visited France and Italy; in later life he settled in Vienna, where he married a leading actress of the *Burgtheater*. His plays include *Judith* (1841), *Herodes und Mariamne* (1850), and the trilogy *Die Nibelungen* (1862); his poems are collected in *Gedichte* (1842) and *Neue Gedichte* (1848). [170]

HEINRICH HEINE (born Düsseldorf 13 December 1797, died Paris 17 February 1856). Studied law at Bonn and then moved to Berlin and Göttingen, where he abandoned, for reasons of expediency, the Jewish faith into which he had been born without, however, obtaining the state-employment he had hoped for. A collection of poems (*Gedichte*, 1822, later incorporated in *Buch der Lieder*, 1827) and a brilliant volume of journalistic prose (*Reisebilder*, 1826) made Heine famous. After the 1830 revolution he left Germany and settled in Paris, where the bulk of his work was to be written. In the last eight years of his life he was confined to a 'mattress grave' by a painful paralytic illness, which could not, however, impair his wit and mental alertness. His last poems are collected in *Romanzero*

(1851) and the posthumous *Letzte Gedichte und Gedanken*. The concentration and suggestive power of his lyrics have made them the favourite texts of German *Lied*-composers from Schubert's late works to those of Richard Strauss. [64–6, 67–8, 70–71, 81–5, 86–7, 100, 155]

KARL HENCKELL (born Hanover 17 April 1864, died Lindau 13 July 1929). A fervent socialist and leader of the Naturalist revolt in German literature – he was one of the editors of *Moderne Dichtercharaktere* (1885) which sought to proclaim a new spirit in the German lyric without breaking with the old rhythms and themes. In 1894, disgusted by German politics, he emigrated to Zürich, where he became a publisher. His verse is embodied in a collected edition of his works (second edition 1923) which runs to five volumes. [152]

HERMANN HESSE (born Calw 2 July 1877, died Montagnola, 9 August 1962). He was destined by his father for a career in the Church; but he escaped from the theological seminary to which he was sent and made his living as a bookseller. He soon attracted attention with novels and short stories that analyse, with subtle psychological perception, the social and personal dilemmas of modern man. His finest work is the novel *Der Steppenwolf* (1927); but European readers know him best as the author of the symbolic *Das Glasperlenspiel* (1943). He was awarded the Nobel Prize for Literature in 1946. His lyric poetry continues the strain of German Romantic poetry and has been notably influenced by the work of Hesse's fellow-Swabian Eduard Mörike. It is conveniently collected in Volume V of Hesse's *Gesammelte Dichtungen* published by the Suhrkamp Verlag. [156–7]

PAUL VON HEYSE (born Berlin 15 March 1830, died Munich 2 April 1914). A voluminous writer of lyric poems, novels, and short stories, whom King Maximilian II called to Munich in 1854 to form (with Emanuel Geibel) the centre of a Bavarian literary circle. He published his collected *Gedichte* in 1871, 1897, and 1910; they were preceded by his excellent translations from the Spanish (*Spanisches Liederbuch*, 1852, with Geibel) and the Italian (*Italienisches Liederbuch*, 1860). He is now best remembered for the translations set by Wolf and for a somewhat sentimental short story called *L'Arrabbiata*. [119–32]

LUDWIG CHRISTOPH HEINRICH HÖLTY (born Mariensee, Hanover 21 December 1748, died Hanover 1 September 1776). Studied at Göttingen, where he was one of the members of a group known as the 'Göttinger Hain', vowed to a cult of friendship, sensibility, and poetry. His uneventful life was early wasted by consumption, and he died at the age of 28. His poetry was collected by two friends and published in a posthumous volume of *Gedichte* (1783) which exerted its influence far into the nineteenth century, attracting poets like Mörike and composers like Schubert and Brahms by the sweetness and truth of its sentiments and the musical purity of its form. [97]

ANNE HUNTER (1742–1821) was the wife of the eminent surgeon John Hunter. Her parties in London were famous, her poems rather less so. Haydn met her during his stay in England, and set several of her verses (including 'My Mother bids me bind my Hair'). 'O tuneful Voice' was written by Mrs Hunter as a farewell to Haydn himself when he prepared to leave England at the end of his second visit (1794). [19]

ALOYS ISIDOR JEITTELES (or Jeiteles; born Prague September 1764, died Vienna 16 April 1858). A Jewish doctor, who also wrote poems and parodies (*Schicksalsstrumpf*, 1818). He acquired fame through his devotion to his patients, shown particularly during a plague epidemic at Brünn. Beethoven was attracted by the man as well as the poet when he decided to set six of his early lyrics in *An die ferne Geliebte*. [25–8]

HILDEGARD JONE-HUMPLIK (born Sarajevo 1 June 1891). A poet and painter, who married the sculptor Josef Humplik (1888–1958). She published several volumes of poetry (*Selige Augen*, 1938; *Anima*, 1948) and individual lyrics in such journals as the Austrian *Der Brenner* and the German *Die Schildgenossen*. Met Anton Webern in 1926; a firm friendship soon developed, and Webern set many of her poems, notably in the cantatas Op. 26 (*Das Augenlicht*), 29, and 31. [167–8]

JUSTINUS KERNER (born Ludwigsburg 18 September 1786, died Weinsberg 21 February 1862). Studied medicine at the University of Tübingen, where he came into contact with the best-known Swabian poets (notably Ludwig Uhland), who inspired in him a love of literature that was never to leave him. He became a general practitioner, but failing sight forced him to retire from practice in 1851. Famous as an alienist, he became more and more interested in the occult sciences and chronicled the visions of mesmerized and hysterical subjects (*Geschichte zweier Somnambulen*, 1824; *Die Seherin von Prevorst*, 1929). As a poet (*Gedichte*, 1826) he was deeply influenced by folk-song; many of his verses breathe a gloom that was not habitual with him. Schumann admired him greatly and set several of his poems. [70]

KNABEN WUNDERHORN, DES. A collection of (largely reworked and rewritten) German folk-poems published in 1806–8 by Achim von Arnim (1781–1831) and Clemens Brentano (1778–1842). The *Wunderhorn*, together with the folk-tales of the brothers Grimm, has proved the most enduring and perennially popular monument of German Romanticism. Only the Bible and Goethe's poems have had a comparable influence on the themes and the style of German poets. The title means 'The boy's magic horn', and is taken from one of the poems in the collection. [134–5, 137–40, 144–5, 153]

EMIL KUH (born Vienna 13 December 1828, died Meran 30 December 1876). The son of a well-to-do merchant, he tried his hand at a business career (in his father's firm), and administration (in the new German railways), but felt ever more strongly drawn to literature and journalism. He became a close friend of the dramatist Friedrich Hebbel, whose works he edited and interpreted to the contemporary public. From 1861 onwards he earned his living entirely by his pen; he became a professor of German literature in 1864, and was created an 'Imperial Councillor' for his services to letters. [88]

NIKOLAUS LENAU (Nikolaus Niembsch von Strehlenau; born Csatád, Hungary 3 August 1802, died Oberdöbling, Vienna 22 August 1850). The most consistently melancholy poet in the German language. Embittered by the social and political conditions of Austria and Germany, Lenau emigrated to America and tried to become a farmer. The experiment failed disastrously; he returned to Germany and settled in Swabia. In 1844 his mind became deranged and he spent the rest of his life in various institutions. Lenau published several epics on such themes as the Albigensian crusade, the life of Savonarola, and the Faust legend, but is best remembered by his lyric poems (*Gedichte* 1832, 1838, and 1844). [87, 93]

GOTTHOLD EPHRAIM LESSING (born Kamenz 22 January 1729, died Braunschweig 15 February 1781). A dramatist and critic, one of the most acute and independent minds of Germany, who embodies all that is best in the Enlightenment (*Aufklärung*) of the eighteenth century. Like that movement as a whole, Lessing did not, however, make a great contribution to lyric poetry, and among the great composers only Haydn was tempted to set one of his poems. Lessing's greatest plays are *Minna von Barnhelm* (1763), *Emilia Galotti* (1772), and *Nathan der Weise* (1779); his best-known critical works *Laocoon* (1766) and *Hamburgische Dramaturgie* (1767–9). [19]

DETLEV VON LILIENCRON (born Kiel 3 June 1844, died Alt-Rahlstedt, Hamburg 22 July 1909). A soldier and administrator who served with distinction in the Austro-Prussian and Franco-Prussian wars and then entered the German civil service. Despite his bullet-headed, bull-necked, and fiercely moustachioed exterior and despite the glorification, in many of his poems, of unreflective action and enjoyment of life, he was a highly sensitive man and poet who had much in common with other (more obviously introverted) North German artists – with Klaus Groth, for instance, or with Brahms (who set some of his best lyrics). He was also highly musical, and was one of the first to recognize the genius of Hugo Wolf. The four volumes of his *Gesammelte Gedichte* appeared between 1897 and 1903. [101]

HERMAN VON LINGG (born Lindau 22 January 1820, died München 18 June 1905). One of the poets called to Munich by King Maximilian II of Bavaria (cf. *Heyse* and *Geibel*). Wrote stillborn dramas, monstrously long epics, short stories with cultural–historical backgrounds, patriotic ballads, and plangent poems (*Gedichte*, 1854 ff.) in an outworn romantic tradition. His conventional and self-indulgent poem 'Immer leiser wird mein Schlummer' is kept alive by Brahms's splendid setting. [100]

JOHN HENRY MACKAY (born Greenock, Scotland 6 February 1864, died Charlottenburg 21 May 1933). A Scotsman brought up in Germany who rose to prominence during the Naturalist revolt in literature with his novels *Die Anarchisten* (1891), *Albert Schnells Untergang* (1895), and *Der Schwimmer* (1901). A rugged individualist and born rebel, he was greatly attracted by the individualist philosophy of Max Stirner, to whom he devoted a biographical and critical study in 1914. He has left an autobiography thinly disguised as fiction (*Der Freiheitssucher*) which is reprinted, together with some of his poems, in *Werke in einem Band* (1928). [152]

FRIEDRICH VON MATTHISSON (born Hohendodeleben, Magdeburg 23 January 1761, died Wörlitz 12 March 1831). The son of a Lutheran country pastor, he studied theology and philosophy at the University of Halle and in 1781 became a teacher at the famous *Philantropinum* – a school in Dessau, established by the pioneer educationalist Basedow. In the same year he published his first volume of poems (*Lieder von Friedrich Matthisson*). He attracted the attention of many of Germany's leading writers, notably Schiller, who published a laudatory critical essay of his work; and his verses (including *Adelaide*, first printed in 1790) provided *Lied*-texts for many composers from Reichardt to Beethoven and the young Schubert. He became chief librarian of the king of Württemberg in 1794. His fame as a poet was soon overshadowed by the advent of greater men; today he is more often sung than read. [23]

JOHANN MAYRHOFER (born Steyr 3 November 1787, died Vienna 7 February 1836). Began as a student of theology; soon found, however, that this was not his real vocation and turned to the study of law. He was a gifted poet; and when he met Schubert in 1814 and struck up a close friendship with him, there began a fruitful collaboration which was to give the world such songs as *Memnon*, *Erlafsee*, *Am Strome*, *Der Fischer*, *Abendstern*, *Nachtviolen*, and over a hundred others. Poet and composer even shared lodgings from 1819 until 1821. Mayrhofer tried, for a time, to make a living by his pen; later, however, he entered the Austrian civil service and found himself assigned to the hated censorship office. Tendencies towards melancholia, of which his poems show clear signs, became more and more marked in him; he committed suicide in 1836. His poems are collected in *Gedichte* (1824) and the posthumous *Gedichte: Neue Sammlung* (1843). [39]

CONRAD FERDINAND MEYER (born Zürich 11 October 1825, died Kilchberg, Zürich 28 November 1898). The last (and physically degenerate) son of a patrician family, he studied law, but his studies were interrupted by signs of insanity. Lived at Lausanne and Zürich, and first came before the public as a translator of French historical works. His first collections of poetry went unnoticed. In 1871 he experienced his 'Indian summer', both as a man and as poet. He discovered his genius for the historical novel and *nouvelle*; and a distinguished volume of *Gedichte* appeared in 1882. These lyric poems Meyer constantly polished and rewrote, even after publication; a revised edition was published in 1892. His Indian summer ended in that same year, and he spent the last six years of his life in mental darkness. [155]

MICHELANGELO BUONAROTTI (born Caprese, Casentino 6 March 1475, died Rome

18 February 1564). The great painter and sculptor had occasionally written poetry in his youth, but it was not until the sonnets to Tornasso Cavaliere (1533-4) and the poems to Vittoria Colonna (1537-47) that he found his real voice: a voice stern and powerful even in tenderness. Hugo Wolf set three of his poems in Walter Robert-Tornow's German translation, while Benjamin Britten's *Seven Sonnets of Michelangelo* keep to the original Italian. A fourth Michelangelo-setting by Hugo Wolf was never published because the composer was not satisfied with it. [133]

ALFRED MOMBERT (born Karlsruhe 6 February 1872, died Winterthur 8 April 1942). Studied law at Heidelberg, Leipzig, Munich, and Berlin, and practised as a solicitor at Heidelberg from 1900 to 1906. Travelled widely, and devoted his life to literature after 1906. His ecstatic, cosmic poetry is collected in such volumes as *Der Glühende* (1896), *Aeon* (1907), and *Der himmlische Zecher* (1909). In 1940 Mombert was arrested by the Gestapo and sent to a concentration camp in southern France; Swiss friends managed to secure his release but he died soon afterwards in Switzerland. All rights in his work are now reserved by the Kösel Verlag, Munich. [170]

EDUARD MÖRIKE (born Ludwigsburg 8 September 1804, died Stuttgart 4 June 1875). Studied theology at Tübingen and became, after long and often unhappy years as curate in various Swabian villages, pastor of Cleversulzbach; an office he administered more to the satisfaction of his tiny congregation (to whom he could seldom, however, be induced to preach) than that of his ecclesiastical superiors. He retired in 1843 and moved to Mergentheim; taught literature at a young ladies' academy in Stuttgart, married, and for all his delight in his children found himself forced, by temperamental incompatibility, to separate from his wife in 1873. His first volume of *Gedichte* appeared in 1838, the last augmented edition in 1867. After a period of comparative neglect, he is now recognized as one of the greatest German poets – thanks in no small measure to the influence of Wolf's *Mörike-Liederbuch*. He also wrote a masterly short story: *Mozart auf der Reise nach Prag* (1856). [71-2, 93-4, 108-12]

JULIUS MOSEN (born Marieney, Saxony 8 July 1803, died Oldenburg 10 October 1867). A lawyer and dramatist whose house near Dresden became a meeting-place of the German poets of the mid nineteenth century. In the same way his plays, verse epics, short stories, and lyrics were a meeting-place of 'influences' that ensured their popularity in his day but have effectively killed interest in them today. He issued his collected works (eight volumes) in his own lifetime; an attempt to revive interest in him through a judicious selection (*Das Julius-Mosen-Buch*, 1925) has not, however, had any success. [69]

WILHELM MÜLLER (born Dessau 7 October 1794, died there 30 September 1827). The son of a shoemaker, who became a grammar-school teacher of classical languages and librarian, he was a gifted poet in the German Romantic manner who carried on worthily the tradition Arnim and Brentano had begun with *Des Knaben Wunderhorn* (q.v.). Schubert set forty-five of his poems: his quarry were the *Gedichte aus den hinterlassenen Papieren eines reisenden Waldhornisten* published in 1821 and 1824. In his own day, Müller was best known for his enthusiastic support of the Greek struggle against Turkish domination – his *Lieder der Griechen* (1821-6) earned him the sobriquet 'Greek Müller'. His son was the Oxford philologist F. Max Müller. [42-63]

CHRISTIAN ADOLF OVERBECK (born Lübeck 21 August 1755, died there 9 March 1821). An educationist, lawyer, and senator, who also achieved a modest fame as composer and poet. His most popular collection of poems was a volume in which he tried to speak with the very voice of a child: *Fritzchens Lieder* (1781). He also published more 'adult' poems (*Vermischte Gedichte*, 1794) and a number of translations from the Greek. [21]

HEINRICH FRIEDRICH LUDWIG RELLSTAB (born Berlin 13 April 1799, died there 27 November 1860). After receiving a thorough musical training in early youth, he became an officer in the Prussian army and teacher of mathematics at an army training college. He soon abandoned the army, however, in order to devote himself to the study of literature and the composition of poems, novels, and opera libretti. In 1826 he became editor of the influential *Vossische Zeitung*; from 1830 to 1841 he edited a journal of his own (*Iris*) in which he proved himself an able music critic. His many works of fiction are now forgotten; but his autobiography (*Aus meinem Leben*, 1861) still repays its readers with glimpses of many notable contemporaries (among them Beethoven and Goethe) with whom Rellstab had come into contact in the course of his extensive travels, and with a vivid picture of life in nineteenth-century Germany and Austria. [64]

RAINER MARIA RILKE (born Prague 4 December 1875, died Muzot 29 December 1926). Intended by his parents for a military career, he entered the officers' academy at St Pölten, but soon left it in 1890. Journeyed through Russia, then returned to Berlin and lived at Westerwede. As a poet, Rilke found his real voice with *Das Stundenbuch* (1905), which has remained his most popular collection. From 1902 until 1904 he lived in Paris, where he worked for a time with the sculptor Auguste Rodin, on whom he wrote a monograph. *Neue Gedichte* appeared in 1907 and 1908 and Rilke's chief prose work, the autobiographical *Aufzeichnungen des Malte Laurids Brigge*, in 1910. *Das Marienleben*, on which Hindemith based his song-cycle, was first published in 1913; it was followed by a long period of inactivity, which led into Rilke's greatest creative period: that in which the *Duineser Elegien* and *Sonette an Orpheus* (1923) were produced. The first full edition of Rilke's works is now being brought out by the Insel Verlag of Wiesbaden. [176-7]

JOHANN MICHAEL FRIEDRICH RÜCKERT (born Schweinfurth 16 May 1788, died Neuess, Koburg 31 January 1866). The son of a lawyer, he studied law and classical philology; a stay in Vienna (1818) brought him into contact with a noted orientalist, Joseph von Hammer-Purgstall, who inspired him with a lasting love of oriental poetry. He became professor of oriental languages at Erlangen (1826) and Berlin (1841-8). His best-known poems, often distinguished by complexity of form, are contained in *Liebesfrühling* (1823), *Die Weisheit des Brahmanen* (1836-9), and *Haus- und Jahreslieder* (1838). The *Kindertotenlieder*, published posthumously in 1872, were written in memory of his two children Ernst and Luise, who died of scarlet fever in December 1833 and January 1834. [40, 140-44]

ADOLF FRIEDRICH VON SCHACK (born Brüsewitz, Mecklenburg 2 August 1815, died Rome 14 April 1894). An art-collector, traveller, diplomat, and distinguished linguist, who from 1855 onwards made his home in Munich, Schack's translations from the Persian are classics of their kind (*Epische Dichtungen . . . des Firdusi*, 1853). His dramas and lyric poems – though they were once thought 'advanced' even by the leaders of the Naturalist revolt in German literature – have not stood the test of time. [151-2]

JOHANN CHRISTOPH FRIEDRICH VON SCHILLER (born Marbach 10 November 1759, died Weimar 9 May 1805). The son of an army officer who had risen from the ranks, Schiller was forced to abandon his plan of studying theology and to enter instead a newly founded military academy, in order to become an army surgeon. There he wrote his first play, *Die Räuber*, successfully performed at Mannheim in 1782. He fled from his native Württemberg that same year, and found at Leipzig and Dresden friends who helped him morally, socially, and financially. In these years he wrote his best-known poem – 'An die Freude' (1785), used by Beethoven in the finale of his last symphony. In 1787 he moved to Weimar and became, in 1789, professor of history at Jena. The 1790s saw the appearance of a number of reflective and philosophical poems and also of his most important essays on ethics, aesthetics, and education. From 1794 dates his close friendship and collaboration with Goethe; and the last years of his life saw the appearance of that great series of blank-verse plays (from *Wallenstein*, 1798–9, to *Wilhelm Tell*, 1804) which made Schiller Germany's national dramatist. [38]

HANS SCHMIDT was a tutor in the house of the violinist Josef Joachim (1831–1907). He studied music at Vienna in the 1880s and later worked at Riga as composer, teacher, and critic. His poems were collected in *Gedichte und Übersetzungen* (Offenbach, Main, n.d.): he sent a copy of this volume to Brahms (to whom Joachim had introduced him) and Brahms selected from it the text for one of his best-loved songs: 'Sapphische Ode' (Op. 94). [100]

GEORG PHILIPP SCHMIDT VON LÜBECK (born Lübeck 1 January 1766, died Ottensen, Hamburg 28 October 1849). A patrician who studied medicine but abandoned his practice in order to enter Danish service as director of a state bank (1806). As a poet he had early come under the influence of Hölty (q.v.) and Stolberg (q.v.) – an influence still perceptible in his volume of *Lieder* (first published 1821) of which the most memorable is that set by the young Schubert under the title *Der Wanderer* (Op. 4). He also published a number of historical studies. [36]

FRANZ VON SCHOBER (born Torub Castle, Malmö, 1796, died Dresden 1882). Came to Vienna as a law student in 1815 and soon met Schubert, who became one of his closest friends. He also became a dominant figure in Schubert's circle, on which he is said to have exerted an occasionally baneful influence. Twelve of his (intrinsically not very interesting) verses – later collected in the *Gedichte* of 1842 – were set by Schubert. It was at Schober's house that Schubert first heard poems of Heine read aloud. Schober later opened a lithographic establishment, which closed in 1829; accompanied the young Liszt on several journeys; and married the poetess Thekla von Gumpert in 1856 (marriage dissolved in 1864), subsequently living the life of a literary and artistic dilettante at his home in Dresden. [37]

CHRISTIAN FRIEDRICH DANIEL SCHUBART (born Obersontheim, Württemberg 24 March 1739, died Stuttgart 10 October 1791). A musically and poetically gifted man whose outspoken comments on public affairs drew down on him the wrath of Duke Karl Eugen of Württemberg. He was dismissed from his post of court organist, and imprisoned for ten years (1777–87). After his release he again became director of music at court and edited the journal *Vaterlandschronik*. His *Gesammelte Gedichte* appeared while their author was still languishing in prison (1785–6). [37]

FRIEDRICH LEOPOLD VON STOLBERG (born Bramstedt 7 November 1750, died Sondermühlen, Osnabrück 5 December 1819). Stolberg studied at Göttingen in the 1770s, where he came under the influence of the poet Klopstock and where, with his brother Christian and his friend Hölty (q.v.), he founded the literary group known as the 'Göttinger Hain'. After the revolutionary ardour of his youth, he veered more and more towards religious orthodoxy and political conformism. He became a Roman Catholic in 1800. He was also a successful diplomat. His works, which include translations from the Greek and travel accounts, were published together with those of his brother in 1820–25. [40]

THEODOR WOLDSEN STORM (born Husum, Schleswig 14 September 1817, died Hademarschen, Holstein 4 July 1888). Studied law and settled in Husum, where he married in 1846. In 1853 he left Husum in protest against Danish policy in Schleswig–Holstein. Settled in Prussia and became a county-court judge at Heiligenstadt. In 1864 Storm returned to Husum and rose high in the legal hierarchy there, retiring from office in 1880. Known chiefly as a writer of short stories (*Immensee*, 1850; *Der Schimmelreiter*, 1888), he published a slender volume of *Gedichte* in 1852 which reappeared in a revised and augmented form in 1885. [169]

AUGUST STRINDBERG (born Stockholm 22 January 1849, died there 14 May 1912). Sweden's greatest poet–dramatist enters the history of the German *Lied* only because Anton Webern chose to set some lines from his *Ghost Sonata* in his Opus 12. [165–6]

GEORG TRAKL (born Salzburg 3 February 1887, died Cracow 4 November 1914). Trakl studied at Vienna and then moved to Innsbruck, where he came to know the editor and publisher Ludwig Ficker, who encouraged him and published his early work in the journal *Der Brenner*. He worked as a chemist, and in that capacity he was attached to the Austrian army medical corps at the beginning of the First World War. Overwhelmed by the sufferings of the wounded he had to tend, he committed suicide. Trakl's sad, mysterious poems, which wring beauty from consciousness of decay and death, were first collected in *Gedichte*, 1913, and *Die Dichtungen*, 1917; they are now conveniently available in the complete edition of his works published by the Otto Müller Verlag of his native Salzburg. [174–6]

JOHANN LUDWIG TIECK (born Berlin 31 May 1773, died there 28 April 1853). The son of a Prussian ropemaker, Tieck studied at various German universities and devoted himself from the first to literature and the theatre. His writings include dramatic satires (*Der gestiefelte Kater*; *Die verkehrte Welt*) and many variations on fairy-tale and folk motifs (*Der blonde Eckbert*, *Genoveva*). *Die Schöne Magelone*, a retelling of a favourite chapbook tale with many incidental poems, served Brahms as a repository of texts for his songcycle of the same name. Tieck collaborated with A. W. Schlegel in producing a magnificent translation of Shakespeare's plays, from which he used to read aloud, with great success, before a distinguished public. His poems are remarkable more for melodiousness than for precision of meaning. [96]

JOSEF WENZIG (born Prague 18 January 1807, died Turnau, Bohemia 28 August 1876). Equally at home in both languages, Wenzig translated and adapted many Czech works into German – notably Czech folk-songs (*Slavische Volkslieder*, 1830) and folk-tales (*Westslavischer Märchenschatz*, 1857). As a teacher, and as director of various schools, he fought hard to establish Czech rather than German as the official language of instruction in the Austrian Bohemia of his day. [96–7]

MATHILDE WESENDONK (born Elberfeld 23 December 1828, died Traunblick 31 August 1902). Mathilde Luckemeyer of Elberfeld married a wealthy fellow townsman, the merchant Otto Wesendonk, and moved with him to Zürich in 1851. In Zürich the Wesendonks became patrons of Richard Wagner, who fell in love with Mathilde and set five of her poems in 1857–8, and whose *Tristan und Isolde* too shows the profound influence of the 'Mathilde' experience. She moved to Dresden in 1871 and to Berlin in 1882. Her occasional writings (poems, short stories, and plays) found no echo outside her own immediate circle. [89–92]

SELECT BIBLIOGRAPHY OF BOOKS
IN ENGLISH

General Works

Grove's Dictionary of Music and Musicians (5th edn, ed. Eric Blom), London, 1954, and supplementary volume 1961. (For articles on 'Song' and individual composers)

Harman, A., and Mellers, W., *Man and his Music. The Story of Musical Experience in the West*, London, 1962

Plunket Greene, H., *Interpretation in Song*, London, 1911

Moore, Gerald, *Singer and Accompanist. The Performance of Fifty Songs*, London, 1953

Schumann, Elisabeth, *German Song*, London, 1948

Stevens, Denis (ed.), *A History of Song*, London, 1961

Young, P. M., *The Story of Song*, London, 1956

For the lives of individual song-composers, see

Bacharach, A. L. (ed.), *The Music Masters* (new edn), Penguin Books, 1957–8

Haydn

Geiringer, K., *Haydn – A Creative Life in Music*, London, 1947

Hadden, J. C., *Haydn* (rev. edn), London, 1932

Hughes, R., *Haydn*, London, 1950 and 1956

Mozart

Blom, E., *Mozart* (rev. edn), London, 1952

Einstein, A., *Mozart. His Character, his Work*, London, 1947 and 1956

Hussey, D., *Mozart*, London, 1928

Hyatt King, A., *Mozart in Retrospect*, London, 1955

Landon, H. C. R., and Mitchell, D. C., *The Mozart Companion*, London, 1956

Turner, W. J., *Mozart. The Man and his Works*, London, 1938

Beethoven

Dickinson, A. F., *Beethoven*, London, 1941

Grove, George, *Beethoven–Schubert–Mendelssohn*, London, 1951

Riezler, W., *Beethoven*, London, 1935–44

Scott, M. M., *Beethoven*, London, 1934

Sullivan, J. W. N., *Beethoven*, New York, 1956

Tovey, D. F., *Beethoven*, Oxford, 1944

Loewe

Bach, A. B., *The Art Ballad*, Edinburgh, 1890

Schubert

Abraham, G. (ed.), *Schubert. A Symposium*, London, 1947

Barne, M. C., *Introducing Schubert*, London, 1957

Brown, M. J. E., *Schubert. A Critical Biography*, London, 1958

Capell, R., *Schubert's Songs*, London, 1928 and 1957

Deutsch, O. E., *Schubert. A Documentary Biography*, London, 1946

Grove, George, *Beethoven–Schubert–Mendelssohn*, London, 1951

Hutchings, A. J. B., *Schubert* (3rd edn), London, 1956

Porter, E. G., *Schubert's Song Technique*, London, 1961

Tovey, D. F., 'Franz Schubert' in *The Heritage of Music*, Vol. I (ed. H. J. Foss), Oxford, 1927

Mendelssohn

Foss, H. J., 'Felix Mendelssohn-Bartholdy' in *The Heritage of Music*, Vol. II, Oxford, 1934

Grove, George, *Beethoven–Schubert–Mendelssohn*, London, 1951

Jacob, H. E., *Felix Mendelssohn and his Times*, London, 1963

Radcliff, P., *Mendelssohn*, London, 1954

Werner, Eric, *Felix Mendelssohn: A New Image of the Composer and his Age*, New York, 1963

Young, P. M., *Introduction of the Music of Mendelssohn*, London, 1949

Schumann

Abraham, G. (ed.), *Schumann. A Symposium*, Oxford, 1952

Chisell, Joan, *Schumann*, London, 1948

Hadow, W. H., *Studies in Modern Music*, Vol. I, London, 1926

Peyer, H. F., *Robert Schumann. Tone-Poet, Prophet and Critic*, New York, 1948

Schauffler, R. H., *Florestan. The Life and Work of Robert Schumann*, New York, 1945

Young, P. M., *The Tragic Muse. The Life and Works of Robert Schumann*, London, 1957

Liszt

Beckett, W., *Liszt*, London, 1956

Hill, R., *Liszt*, London, 1936

Newman, Ernest, *The Man Liszt*, London, 1934

Searle, H., *The Music of Liszt*, London, 1954

Sitwell, Sacheverell, *Liszt* (rev. edn), London, 1955

Wagner

Capell, R., 'Richard Wagner' in *The Heritage of Music*, Vol. I, Oxford, 1927; *The Life of Richard Wagner*, London, 1933–47

Hight, G. A., *Richard Wagner. A Critical Biography*, London, 1925

Newman, E., *Wagner as Man and Artist* (2nd ed), New York, 1925

Stein, J. M., *Richard Wagner and the Synthesis of the Arts*, Detroit, 1960

Viereck, P., *Metapolitics: From the Romantics to Wagner*, New York, 1941

Brahms

Abell, A. M., *Talks with Great Composers*, London, 1956

Colles, H. C., *Brahms*, London, 1920

Friedländer, Max, *Brahms's Lieder*, Oxford, 1929

Geiringer, K., *Brahms. His Life and Work* (2nd edn), London, 1948

Latham, P., *Brahms*, London, 1948

Niemann, W., *Brahms*, London, 1929

Specht, R., *Brahms*, London, 1930

Wolf

Newman, Ernest, *Hugo Wolf*, London, 1907

Walker, Frank, *Hugo Wolf. A Biography*, London, 1951

Sams, E., *The Songs of Hugo Wolf*, London, 1961

Mahler

Cardus, Neville, 'Mahler' in *Ten Composers*, London, 1945

Carner, Mosco, *Of Men and Music*, London, 1944

Mahler, Alma, *Gustav Mahler. Memories and Letters*, London, 1946

Mellers, W., *Studies in Contemporary Music*, London, 1947

Mitchell, D. C., *Gustav Mahler. The Early Years*, London, 1958

Newlin, Dika, *Bruckner–Mahler–Schönberg*, New York and London, 1947

Redlich, H. J., *Bruckner and Mahler*, London, 1955

Stefan, P., *Gustav Mahler. A Study of his Personality and Work*, New York, 1913

Walter, Bruno, *Gustav Mahler* (new edn), London, 1958

Strauss

Abell, A. M., *Talks with Great Composers*, London, 1956

Cardus, N., 'Strauss' in *Ten Composers*, London, 1945

Del Mar, N., *Richard Strauss. A Critical Commentary on his Life and Works*, London, 1963

Gray, C., 'Richard Strauss' in *A Survey of Contemporary Music*, Oxford, 1924

Huneker, J., 'Richard Strauss' in *Overtones*, New York, 1928

Newman, Ernest, *Richard Strauss*, London, 1908

Schoenberg

Goehr, W., and A., 'Arnold Schoenberg's Development toward the Twelve-Note System' in *European Music in the Twentieth Century* (ed. H. Hartog), rev. edn, Pelican Books, 1961

Gray, C., 'Arnold Schoenberg' in *A Survey of Contemporary Music*, Oxford, 1924

Krenek, E., *Music Here and Now*, New York, 1939

Leibowitz, R., *Schoenberg and His School*, New York and London, 1949

Mellers, W., *Studies in Contemporary Music*, London, 1947

Newlin, D., *Bruckner, Mahler, Schoenberg*, New York, 1948

Rufer, J., *The Works of Arnold Schoenberg*, London, 1963

Schoenberg, Arnold, *Style and Idea*, New York, 1950

Stefan, P., 'Arnold Schoenberg' in *The Book of Modern Composers* (ed E. Ewen), New York, 1942

Wellesz, E., *Arnold Schoenberg*, London, 1925

Webern

Die Reihe, 2: *Anton Webern*, ed. H. Eimert and K. H. Stockhausen (English edn), London, 1958

Demuth, N., *Musical Trends in the Twentieth Century*, London, 1952

Hamilton, I., 'Alban Berg and Anton Webern' in *European Music in the Twentieth Century*, Pelican Books, 1961

Berg

Hamilton, I., 'Alban Berg and Anton Webern' in *European Music in the Twentieth Century*, Pelican Books, 1961

Pisk, P. A., 'Alban Berg' in *The Book of Modern Composers*, New York, 1942

Redlich, H. F., *Alban Berg. The Man and His Music*, London, 1957

Hindemith

Del Mar, N., 'Paul Hindemith' in *European Music in the Twentieth Century*, Pelican Books, 1961

Hindemith, Paul, *A Composer's World. Horizons and Limitations*, London, 1952

Pannain, G., 'Paul Hindemith' in *Modern Composers*, London, 1932

Rosenfeld, P., 'Paul Hindemith' in *The Book of Modern Composers*, New York, 1942

The Literary Background

Closs, A., *The Genius of the German Lyric* (rev. edn), London, 1961

Prawer, S. S., *German Lyric Poetry*, London, 1952

Robertson, J. G., *A History of German Literature* (rev. and enlarged edn, ed. E. Purdie), Edinburgh and London, 1962

INDEX OF TITLES AND FIRST LINES

PELICAN BOOKS

Introducing Music

Ottó Károlyi

Some acquaintance with the grammar and vocabulary of music –
enough to understand the language without speaking it – greatly
broadens the pleasure of hearing it.

Introducing Music makes the attempt to convey the elements of
the art to music-lovers with no technical knowledge. Setting out
from the relatively open ground of tones, pitches, timbres, sharps,
flats, bars and keys, Ottó Károlyi is able to conduct the reader out
into the more exciting territory of dominant sevenths and symphonic
structure. His text is clearly signposted by musical examples and
illustrations of instruments described, and no intelligent reader
should have any difficulty in following the path. On arrival at the
end, in place of being confused by the technicalities of a programme
note, he should be within reach of following the music in a score.

'Here is one of those rare things – an instruction book that seems
to succeed completely in what it sets out to do. . . . The author
develops the reader's knowledge of the language and sense of music
to the stage where he can both follow, though not necessarily read
from scratch, a full score, and even make sense of some of the
exceedingly complex programme-notes' – *Recorder*

'He has presented the grammar of music with great clarity' –
The Times Educational Supplement

'A great deal of information is packed into the 174 pages' –
Music in Education

'The book is well organized in the way one subject leads
progressively to the next, terms are crisply defined and
explanations ate lucid' – *The Times Literary Supplement*

The Pelican History of Music

I: ANCIENT FORMS TO POLYPHONY

Edited by Alec Robertson and Denis Stevens

The '1066' of our music lies somewhere in the Middle Ages, when the Western tradition seemed to spring, fully armed with tonality, harmony, and rhythm, from the head of medieval man. It is easy to forget that musical languages had been evolving, both in the East and the West, for at least five thousand years before music in Europe began to assume the laws we are tempted to regard as perfect and unalterable. This first volume in the Pelican History of Music traces the story of music from the earliest known forms as far as the beginnings of the polyphonic period in the first half of the fifteenth century. A full section on non-Western music indicates how our tradition is linked with or has evolved from the forms of music prevailing in other parts of the world.

II: RENAISSANCE AND BAROQUE

Edited by Alec Robertson and Denis Stevens

This second volume of the Pelican History of Music is particularly concerned with the social and artistic environment during the two centuries associated with Renaissance and Baroque music. By the mid fifteenth century the Church's monopoly of influence was gone; alongside its rites a wealth of courtly and civil occasions demanded music and opened the way to every kind of experiment.

Europe knew no musical frontiers and it is possible to trace a whole pattern of influence and counter-influence: the motet, the chanson, and early opera are much alike in their regional forms and adaptations.

Towards the end of the period the musician, like the artist, has become emancipated. Composers such as Monteverdi, Vivaldi, Purcell, and the Bachs are as individually distinct as the works that make them famous.

The Pelican History of Music

III: CLASSICAL AND ROMANTIC

Edited by Alec Robertson and Denis Stevens

The third volume of the Pelican History of Music is mainly concerned with the eighteenth and nineteenth centuries, but works by Mahler, Bloch, Bax and others are discussed in a coda.

Even in the age of enlightenment a patron's 'good taste' was something that composers had to contend with and the so-called *style galant* forms the background to the achievement of C. P. E. Bach, Mozart and Haydn. But Beethoven scorned conventional taste, and the great classical works of later eighteenth-century composers owe their boldness to the *style bourgeois*.

Nineteenth-century romantic composers, such as Wagner and Verdi, were aware of the enormous material expansion and adventure of their age. And unlike previous composers they were conscious of their kinship with writers and painters; some of their greatest musical triumphs are to be found in opera.

A New Dictionary of Music

Arthur Jacobs

A basic reference book for all who are interested in music, containing entries for composers (with biographies and details of compositions); musical works well known by their titles; orchestras, performers and conductors of importance today; musical instruments; and technical terms.

This new edition incorporates hundreds of changes bringing the dictionary even more up to date – new composers and performers, titles of new works and technical terms in newer use are all to be found.

Penguin Songbooks

THE PENGUIN BOOK OF ENGLISH FOLK SONGS

A classic collection of the rarer songs recovered from the counties of England by enthusiasts during this century and presented here by Dr Ralph Vaughan Williams and A. L. Lloyd with melodies and notes on their origins.

THE PENGUIN BOOK OF ENGLISH MADRIGALS

FOR FOUR VOICES

In compiling this collection Denis Stevens has adopted an entirely new style of presentation. Each madrigal is prefaced by a fully edited version of the poem, with notes on features of special interest in lyric or music. The music has also been set out in a new way, to help singers achieve a finer balance and more perfect ensemble in this most subtle of musical styles.